Good
Housekeeping
ONE-
DISH
DINNERS

Good
Housekeeping

ONE-DISH DINNERS

Good Housekeeping Books

New York

GOOD HOUSEKEEPING BOOKS

Editor MINA WHITE MULVEY
Art Director WILLIAM LEFT
Senior Editor JOHN WALSH
Copy Editor JUANITA G. CHAUDHRY
Assistant to Art Director LYNN THOMPSON

FOOD PUBLICATIONS DIVISION

Director HEDDA SCHLOSBERG
Consultant DOROTHY B. MARSH
Associate Food Editors MARJORIE GRIFFITHS
           JEANNE CAMPBELL
Assistant Food Editors EILEEN RUNYAN
           PATRICIA ASHCROFT

FOR GOOD HOUSEKEEPING MAGAZINE

Editor WADE H. NICHOLS
Executive Editor JOHN B. DANBY
Managing Editor BENSON SRERE
Art Director BERNARD SPRINGSTEEL
Director, The Institute WILLIE MAE ROGERS

All photographs by James Viles except pictures on pages 33, 58-59, 133 and 160, courtesy The National Magazine Company, Ltd.

Drawings by Maggie MacGowan

CONTENTS

BEFORE YOU BEGIN
Ground rules for one-dish dinners that save time while they step up flavor

Hard-cooked eggs and cooked chicken and seafood are often called for in one-dish dinner recipes. Prepare them our easy way.

HARD-COOKED EGGS

To cook: Place eggs in a saucepan (not aluminum). Cover with cold water; bring to boiling. Remove from heat and cover tightly. Let stand 15 minutes. Drain; cover with cold water to chill.

To shell: Crack entire surface, then roll egg between palms to loosen shell. Peel under cold water, starting at large end.

BASIC SIMMERED CHICKEN

For about 4 cups diced chicken, simmer 2 broiler-fryers or one stewing chicken.

To cook: Place chicken(s), quartered, in Dutch oven; add 3 cups water, 1 teaspoon monosodium glutamate, 2½ teaspoons salt, 2 whole allspice, 3 peppercorns, 1 bay leaf, 1 lemon slice, 1 sliced onion, 2 celery stalks. Bring to boiling. Cover; reduce heat. Simmer 1 to 2 hours, or until fork-tender. Remove from heat; strain broth.

BASIC SIMMERED SHRIMP

For about 1½ cups shrimp, cook one pound fresh or frozen shrimp purchased in shell, or ¾ pound frozen and shelled. Canned shrimp may be used for cooked: one 5-ounce can holds about 1 cup.

To remove shell: With scissors, slit underside of shell between feelers. Holding tail end, pull meat out of shell.

To devein: With sharp knife, cut along outside curve; lift out vein; rinse well.

To cook: Drop shrimp into 1 quart boiling water; add 1 tablespoon salt, 4 peppercorns, 1 lemon slice. Cover and simmer 2 to 5 minutes, or until pink and tender. Drain well; refrigerate.

LOBSTER

For approximately ½ pound or 1¼ cups of lobster meat, cook two 1-pound lobsters or 1 pound frozen rock-lobster tails. Frozen canned lobster meat can be used in recipes calling for cooked lobster: one 14-ounce can holds about 1¾ cups.

BOILED LIVE LOBSTER

To cook: In deep saucepan, bring 3 quarts water to boiling; add two 1-pound lobsters, 3 tablespoons salt, 3 peppercorns, 1 bay leaf and 1 lemon slice. Cover; bring to boiling. Reduce heat; simmer 10 minutes. Drain; cover with cold water.

To remove meat: Twist off claws as close to body as possible; crack claws with nutcracker or hammer; pick the meat out. With sharp knife or scissors, split the thin undershell of body from head to tail; spread open and remove dark vein. Gently pull tail meat from shell. Cut tail shell from body shell; pull body out, leaving small sac just below the head in shell. Discard sac and grayish lungs covering sides of body. Break body in pieces; pick out meat from cartilage. Cover; refrigerate.

BOILED ROCK-LOBSTER TAILS

To cook: Cover 1 pound solidly frozen lobster tails with boiling salted water (1 teaspoon salt per quart of water). Bring to boiling; reduce heat and simmer 3 minutes longer than ounce weight of tails. Drain; rinse in cold water. Cut away thin underside membrane. Grasp tail meat between thumb and forefinger; gently remove from shell. Cover and refrigerate.

One of the most useful ingredients for one-dish dinners is a really good tomato sauce. Here is one that can be made in quantity and kept frozen until needed.

DO-AHEAD TOMATO SAUCE
pictured on page 34

Time in Kitchen: 20 minutes
Free Time: 2 hours 20 minutes
Yield: 1 gallon or 8 pints

3 tablespoons salad oil
4 medium onions, chopped
3 small garlic cloves
4 29-ounce cans tomatoes
4 6-ounce cans tomato paste
1 pound mushrooms, sliced
1 cup chopped parsley
3 tablespoons granulated sugar
3 tablespoons salt
4 teaspoons oregano leaves
2 bay leaves

Up to 3 months ahead: In large kettle over medium heat, in hot salad oil, cook onions and garlic until onions are limp; discard garlic. Add remaining ingredients. Reduce heat to low and simmer, covered, for 2 hours. Discard bay leaves.

To freeze: Ladle sauce into eight or nine 1-pint freezer containers, leaving at least 1 inch head space for expansion. Refrigerate until chilled; cover; freeze.

To thaw: Let container sit overnight in refrigerator, or in container of hot water for 2½ to 3 hours.

For meat pies and other main dishes that require a crust, there are many good pastry mixes on the market. But cooks who like to make their own will find this recipe produces a beautifully light, flaky version.

STANDARD FLAKY PASTRY

9- to 10-inch one-crust pie

1½ cups sifted all-purpose flour
½ teaspoon salt
½ cup shortening
3 tablespoons cold water

8- to 9-inch two-crust pie

2½ cups sifted all-purpose flour
1 teaspoon salt
¾ cup plus 2 tablespoons shortening
⅓ cup cold water

In bowl, mix flour and salt. With pastry blender or two knives used scissor-fashion, cut in shortening until mixture resembles coarse cornmeal.

Sprinkle in water, one tablespoon at a time, tossing quickly with fork until particles cling together and dough almost cleans side of bowl.

Gather dough into ball; shape into flattened round on lightly floured surface. (For two-crust pie, divide in half; shape into two rounds.) Roll out with floured or stockinette-covered rolling pin into circle about 1½ inches wider in diameter than pan. Gently ease pastry into pan.

For one-crust pie: Trim overhanging edge of pastry 1 inch from rim of pan. Fold pastry under, even with pan. Fill; bake, following recipe directions.

For baked pie shell: Prick bottom and sides thoroughly with fork. Bake in 450°F. preheated oven 10 to 15 minutes.

For two-crust pie: Fill unbaked shell; cover with top crust. Cut slits in top so steam can escape. Fold top edge over and under bottom edge; press edges to seal; flute and bake as directed.

The basic formula for a casserole is meat + extender + topping. In many casseroles, the extender consists of pasta and/or rice. Here's what you should know about these ingredients.

PASTA

Spaghetti, lasagna, noodles, shells— the shapes and names may be different, but they're all pasta. Noodles have an added ingredient—egg solids, weighing a minimum 5½ per cent (required by law).

Spaghetti. Solid rods, either oval or round. Come in 16 diameters, ranging from the smallest (fidellini), to the largest (spagettoni).

Noodles. Flat ribbonlike lengths, in fine, medium and broad widths. (One shape, Fettucine, means "ribbons" in Italian.) They may be curly on one or both sides; the largest of this group is lasagna.

Hollow Tubes. Here the variety is almost endless. The tubes may be smooth or ridged, and they may be cut into any length from thin to thicker slices. Elbow macaroni belongs in this category.

Specialty Products—Sea shells, snails, nut shells, alphabet noodles, round and square wheels, many twisted types, curls, and so on. Different types may be used interchangeably in a recipe; substitute weight for weight.

HOW MUCH TO COOK

Macaroni and spaghetti almost double in volume after cooking, while noodles stay about the same. Eight ounces will usually provide 4 servings.

	Uncooked	*Cooked*
Macaroni	2 cups (8 ounces)	4½ cups
Spaghetti	8 ounces	5 cups
Noodles	4 cups (8 ounces)	4 cups

HOW TO COOK

The following directions are for cooking 8 ounces. When cooking larger quantities, use 4 to 6 quarts of water and 2 tablespoons salt for each pound of macaroni.

1. In large saucepan, bring 3 quarts water to boiling. Add 1 tablespoon salt.
2. Gradually stir in macaroni, being sure water continues to boil. For spaghetti, take a handful and place one end of strands in boiling water; as strands soften, gently push under water.
3. Cook, uncovered, stirring occasionally until tender. Cooking time will vary with size and type; follow label directions. If pasta is to be used in a dish that needs further cooking (or if it's to be frozen), cut recommended cooking time by one third.
4. Immediately drain in colander. Do not rinse unless pasta is to be used in a cold salad; then use cold water.

SUGGESTIONS FOR USING

Elbows, shells, corkscrew macaroni, bows and other shapes about the same size: Casseroles (meat, fish, cheese, poultry and vegetable), salads, soups and stews.
• Spaghetti of all sizes: With sauces (tomato, clam, meat), as a simple side dish with butter, oil, herbs or grated cheese.
• Noodles—fine, medium, wide: Casseroles, with sauces, as a simple side dish, in soups, or in noodle pudding.

• Leftover pasta: Add to soup during the last 5 minutes of cooking. For salad, combine leftover pasta, leftover meat, fish, poultry or vegetables with salad dressing or mayonnaise; season to taste. Or add to scrambled eggs or to an omelet (½ cup leftover pasta to 1 egg).

• Pasta storage: Store cooked pasta products in a covered container in refrigerator no longer than one week. If you have leftover sauce as well as pasta, mix them together. Spoon into individual foil containers. Wrap and freeze. To serve, thaw, then bake, uncovered, in a 375° F. oven for 20 to 25 minutes or until heated through.

RICE

Rice is one of the original convenience foods; no peeling, scraping, washing or waste. It goes from package to pan to plate in less than half an hour. Brown rice takes longer, but only minutes.

There are over 7,000 varieties of rice, but we are concerned with only four kinds, regular white, regular brown, processed and precooked. Wild rice is not rice at all, but the seed of a wild grass found in the Great Lakes region.

KINDS OF RICE

Regular white rice—available in long, medium and short grain. All the outer bran coating has been removed; may be enriched and polished or unpolished.

Long Grain is nice to serve as a side dish; grains are fluffy, separate and distinct when cooked.

Medium Grain requires a shorter growing period; can be less expensive and is ideal for puddings and croquettes, or in any dish where creaminess is more important than texture.

Short grain is least expensive. Can be used interchangeably with medium grain.

Processed (*also known as parboiled*) rice is long grain rice which has been processed to retain the natural vitamins and minerals.

Precooked enriched white rice (*quick cooking*) is completely cooked long grain rice which has been dehydrated.

Brown rice is whole, unpolished rice with only the outer hull removed. It requires more cooking time than white rice, but it has a delightful, nutlike flavor and chewy texture.

HOW TO COOK

Steamed white rice: Measure 1 cup regular white rice, 2 cups water and 1 teaspoon salt into saucepan with a tight fitting lid. Bring to boiling; stir once or twice, then cover. Turn heat as low as possible; cook 14 minutes without peeking. Turn heat off, remove lid and fluff grains gently with fork. Yields 3 cups.

For parboiled or brown rice, use 2½ cups water. Cook brown rice 45 minutes; parboiled, 25 minutes. Yields 3 to 4 cups.

Oven-baked white rice: Measure 1 cup regular white rice into 1½-quart baking dish which has cover (or use foil). Bring 2 cups water and 1 teaspoon salt to boiling (2½ cups water for parboiled or brown). Pour over rice; stir once.

Continued on page 14

SPICE CHART

SPICE	USE
ALLSPICE A delicately fragrant spice which tastes like a blend of cinnamon, nutmeg and cloves	*Whole* Vegetable soups, stews, boiled fish, pot roast. *Ground* Squash, sweet potatoes, carrots, turnips.
CAYENNE The most pungent spice; a blend of chili peppers. Hot	*Crushed* Hot sauces, pickles, highly spiced meat dishes. *Ground* Meats, sauces, fish and egg dishes, curries.
CINNAMON Spicy bark of the cinnamon tree grown in India; light brown color, sweet flavor	*Whole* Pickles, preserves. *Ground* Mashed sweet potatoes, cinnamon toast, hot breads, beef stew, sauerbraten.
CLOVES Flower bud of the clove tree. Spicy, almost hot	*Whole* Pickled fruit, garnishing ham and pork. *Ground* Stews, spiced fruit, tomato sauces.
GINGER Tuberous root. Warm spicy-sweet taste	*Cracked* Chutney, pickles, stewed dried fruit, applesauce. *Ground* Gingerbread, pot roast, Oriental meat dishes.
MACE Fragrant, orange-red dried covering of nutmeg seed with similar, but stronger flavor	*Whole* Fish sauces, pickles and preserves. *Ground* Chicken fricassee, stew, yeast breads.
MUSTARD A small seed. Ground, it is classified as a spice	*Ground* Cheese dishes, deviled sandwich spreads, meat loaf, salad dressing, ham and other meat and egg salads. *Prepared* Hot dogs and ham sandwiches.
NUTMEG Dried seed of nutmeg tree; very spicy, almost bitter	*Whole* Nutmeg grater. *Ground* Sweet yeast breads, spinach.
PAPRIKA Ground sweet peppers; mild, slightly aromatic	*Ground* Vegetables, goulash, fish, salads, beef, veal or chicken paprikash.
PEPPER World's most popular spice. Dried fruit of East Indian vine; outer covering is rubbed off to obtain white pepper	*Whole* Pickling, soups, pepper grinders. *Cracked or Ground* Eggs, gravy, soup, salad, stew, vegetables—in fact, in most foods except delicate desserts. (Wherever black specks would be undesirable, as in white sauce or pale cream soups, use white pepper.)
SAFFRON Most expensive spice; adds golden color, subtle flavor	*Whole* Soups, sauces, court bouillon, chicken stew. *Crushed* Breads, curries, rice, bouillabaisse.
TURMERIC Bright yellow color, mild ginger-pepper flavor	*Ground* Mustards, curries, pickling mixtures, deviled eggs, pilafs, potato and chicken salads.

HERB CHART

HERB	USE
BASIL Aromatic annual of the mint family; tastes a little like licorice and cloves	Spaghetti sauce, tomato dishes, scrambled eggs, fish. Add a pinch to pea and bean soup, chowder. Sprinkle on pizza pie, sliced tomatoes, roasts, fried chicken.
BAY LEAVES Leaves of the laurel tree	Beef, lamb and veal stews and pot roasts; tomato sauce and aspic, poached fish, pickled fish. (Use sparingly.)
CHERVIL Resembles parsley; slightly peppery taste	Cottage and cream cheeses; egg, fish, tomato and poultry dishes; cream-of-potato and spinach soup.
MARJORAM Perennial of mint family; distinctively aromatic	Roast lamb, meat pies, poultry stuffing, peas, lima beans, spinach, cheese and egg dishes. (Use sparingly.)
MINT Widely used, easy to grow; fresh clean minty smell	Boiled new potatoes, peas, lamb; in mint sauce and jelly. Also use as garnish.
OREGANO Called "wild marjoram" in Italy; lustier and stronger than marjoram	Pork, mushroom and tomato dishes, stuffing for fish, pizza pie, omelets, stew, spaghetti sauce, chili con carne. (Use sparingly.)
PARSLEY Easy to grow; too often used only as garnish; fresh sweet spicy taste	Salads, soups, stews, all vegetables; finely chopped for "aux fines herbes" or with other herbs in "bouquet garni." Also use as garnish.
ROSEMARY Fragrant as a flower; used sparingly, one of the most pleasing herbs	Lamb, chicken, green beans, asparagus, mashed potatoes, zucchini, tomatoes, sauces for meat and fish, tossed in fruit or vegetable salads.
SAGE Hardy perennial; easy to grow; strong and fragrant	Pork dishes of all kinds, poultry seasoning, in stuffing for seafood and cheese dishes, yeast bread, sausage, salad greens. (Use sparingly.)
SAVORY Two kinds: summer, most common variety, mild; winter, more potent	Green or dried beans, poultry seasoning, meats, chicken soup, scrambled eggs, salads, sauces, and potato, tomato and rice dishes.
TARRAGON Flavor and fragrance like anise; best fresh; grow from root or cutting, not seed	Green salad, mayonnaise, fish sauce, béarnaise sauce, "fines herbes" mixtures, tomato dishes. (Use sparingly.)
THYME Widely used, easy to grow; delightfully fragrant; many varieties; not too potent	Clam chowder, poultry seasoning, cheese dishes, stuffing for fish, oyster stew, Creole seafood, and with peas, eggplant and carrots.

Cover tightly; bake in 350°F. preheated oven 30 minutes (45 to 50 for parboiled and 60 to 65 minutes for brown) or until rice is tender and liquid absorbed. Rice is done when grain, pressed with spoon, is soft throughout. Yield is same as for steamed rice.

Packaged precooked rice: Cook, following label instructions. One cup of uncooked precooked rice yields 1 to 2 cups cooked.

DO'S AND DON'TS

• *Don't* wash rice before cooking or rinse after it is cooked.
• *Do* measure water carefully, following label instructions. Too much water makes rice soggy; too little makes it hard and dry.
• *Don't* peek while cooking. Steam will escape and temperature will be lowered.
• *Do* serve rice as soon as it's cooked. To hold, place in covered serving dish in warm oven. Or place rice in colander or large strainer; cover with foil; place over gently boiling water.

SPICES AND HERBS

A different combination of seasonings can give new taste to a familiar dish. Experiment with the many herbs and spices available, using the charts on pages 12 and 13 as a guide.

Another mainstay of the one-dish dinner is cheese. For the best results, follow these tips.

CHEESE

Cheese is a nearly perfect food. Made from milk, it has essentially the same food elements, plus the high-quality protein found in meat. For taste-tempting, well-balanced meals, use cheese in cooking. You'll get more than your money's worth in flavor and nutrition.

The varieties of cheese are endless. The recipes given here call for only about a dozen different kinds. These are cooking cheeses, as opposed to nibbling or dessert cheese. Some recipes call for process cheese and some for natural cheese, but you may substitute one for the other.

KINDS TO BUY

Natural cheese is made directly from rich whole milk. Milk is heated with an enzyme which separates the milk into solid curds and liquid whey. Most cheeses are made from the curds; ricotta is made from the whey. Some are ripened or aged to develop their characteristic flavor and texture; some aren't. Some, such as Cheddar, are labeled mild, medium or sharp, depending on how long they've been aged. There are robust ones like Roquefort. Textures vary, too, from the smooth creaminess of cream cheese to the firm elasticity of Swiss.

Process cheese is a blend of two or more natural cheeses that are melted together, pasteurized and mixed with emulsifiers to give a smooth, soft, even texture. These cheeses are convenient to use in cooking because they slice easily, melt quickly, blend well and have no waste.

STORING

All cheese keeps best when refrigerated. How long it keeps depends on the variety and how well it's protected. Unripened cheeses such as cottage or ricotta are very perishable and should be used within 3 to 5 days. Cream cheese and Neufchâtel will keep for 2 weeks if tightly covered. Hard cheeses such as Swiss and Cheddar will keep several months, Parmesan and Romano even longer; cut edges may be coated with butter or melted paraffin to keep them from drying out. Process cheese will keep unopened on the shelf for about a year. Once it's opened, refrigerate.

All cheeses should be stored in their original wrappings if possible; or wrapped tightly in foil or plastic wrap. If mold should develop on a hard natural cheese, scrape it off, it's not harmful.

Freezing is not recommended for most cheeses; they get crumbly and mealy. Blue and Roquefort may be frozen for later use in salads and salad dressings where a crumbly texture is not objectionable. Small pieces of natural Cheddar, Swiss, provolone and mozzarella may be frozen if tightly wrapped and kept for no more than 6 months. Process, cottage and cream cheeses tend to become watery when thawed.

HOW TO COOK

Cheese is best cooked briefly at a low temperature. You'll find process cheeses melt more easily than natural ones and make a smoother sauce. Shred cheese first on a coarse grater or dice (one-half pound cheese yields 2 cups shredded). If you're cooking on top of the range, use a double boiler. Bake casserole dishes containing cheese in a slow to moderate oven; if cheese is used as topping, add it 5 to 10 minutes before dish is done.

Don't discard that dried out bit of hard cheese; grate it and use in soup or spaghetti sauce. It won't melt unless you add some moisture.

The time- and work-saving advantages of the one-dish dinner can be increased still further by proper use of your freezer. Here's how.

DINNER FROM THE FREEZER

Meal planning can be easy with a well stocked freezer, and you can have a well stocked freezer with a little planning. The next time you plan a casserole, stew, soup or sauce, make twice as much as you need and freeze half for another day. In no time, you'll have a variety of dishes in the freezer to choose from.

COOKING FOR THE FREEZER

• Cook food to be frozen until barely tender; remember it will get more cooking when you reheat it for serving.
• Some things don't freeze well; cheese (see at left), potatoes in soup or stew, hard-cooked egg whites, gelatin salads, mayonnaise and stuffing in raw or cooked poultry. Both flavor and texture change.
• Seasonings may increase in strength when frozen, so use sparingly. You can always add more when the dish is reheated.
• Fat and flour used to thicken gravies and sauces should be thoroughly blended and cooked to keep them from separating in freezing. If separation does occur, stir well while reheating.
• Skim excess fat from meat or chicken stock before freezing.
• Add crisp toppings such as bread crumbs, cheese or potato chips when casserole goes into the oven for reheating, not before freezing.

PACKAGING DO'S AND DON'TS

• *Do* chill food quickly in refrigerator or over ice water before freezing.
• *Don't* use waxed paper, lightweight foil or plastic wrap, or cartons made to hold cottage cheese or ice cream, for holding frozen food longer than a few

days. Use heavy-duty foil, freezer-weight plastic, or plastic bags alone or as liners for cardboard freezer boxes.
• *Do* use polyethylene containers and glass freezer jars that can be washed and used over and over. Shortening and coffee cans with snap on lids also work well if lids are sealed on with freezer tape.
• *Don't* put all your casserole dishes in the freezer. Line casserole with heavy-duty foil, extended above the rim. Fill with cooked food; freeze. Remove food in foil from dish; wrap and return to freezer. To serve, remove foil, slip frozen food into original dish and bake until done.
• *Do* freeze foods in meal-size portions. Choose containers that stack well and go directly from freezer to preheated oven.
• *Don't* forget to label everything: date, number of servings and contents. You think you'll remember, but you may not.
• *Do* freeze liquids in straight-sided, wide mouth glass, plastic or metal containers. Allow 1½ inches for expansion.

FREEZING TIPS

Don't try to freeze too many things at one time; do only the amount that will freeze within twenty-four hours. Place food to be frozen in quick-freeze part of upright or chest model, or touching the walls in refrigerator-freezer; have temperature controls on lowest setting; containers should not touch each other so air can circulate around them freely.

HOW TO REHEAT

When reheating cooked foods that are completely thawed, simply heat to serving temperature in double boiler or oven, stirring as little as possible. Bake at original oven temperature.

For quick thawing, water-tight containers may be immersed in warm water. Foods frozen in china, earthenware and pottery must be defrosted be-fore the dish goes into the oven. Keep refrigerated during and especially after thawing.

GLOSSARY OF TERMS

À la king: Meat, fish or poultry served in a cream sauce usually with pimiento, green pepper and mushrooms.

Au gratin: Food in sauce, covered on top with buttered bread crumbs and cheese, then baked or broiled until browned.

Bake: To cook in oven by dry heat.

Baste: To spoon liquid over food as it cooks; keeps food moist, adds flavor.

Blanch: To plunge food quickly into boiling water to loosen outer skin, or precook.

Boil: To cook in bubbling liquid at 212°F.

Bouillon: Broth or stock made by cooking meat, fish or vegetables in liquid.

Bouillon cube: Concentrated chicken, meat or vegetable stock.

Bouquet garni: A small bundle of herbs, such as parsley, thyme and bay leaf, tied together and used for seasoning.

Braise: To cook slowly with a small amount of liquid, covered tightly.

Broil: To cook over or under direct heat.

Broth: The liquid food has been cooked in.

Brown: To cook quickly, until a brown color, in oven, broiler or pan on top of range.

Casserole: A heavy ovenproof dish in which food can be roasted, browned, stewed or baked; food cooked in a "casserole."

Chill: To place in refrigerator or over ice until cold but not frozen.

Chop: To cut into small pieces with knife or food chopper.

Coat: To cover food with a thin film of either a dry or liquid substance.

Consommé: Seasoned clear soup that jells when it's chilled.

Cool: To let stand at room temperature until no longer warm to touch.

Crouton: Tiny squares of bread sautéed in oil or toasted in the oven.

Cube: To cut into small or ½-inch squares.

Dice: To cut into very small "cubes."

Dissolve: To mix dry substance with liquid to make a solution; heat until melted.

Dot: To scatter small pieces of butter, margarine, etc., over top of food.

Drain: To remove liquid, usually by letting food stand in colander or strainer.

Dredge: To coat heavily with a dry mixture.

Dutch oven: Large, covered, heavy pot for top of range or oven cooking; usually of heavy gauge aluminum or cast iron.

Fold: To combine two mixtures with an up-over-and-down gentle motion, using a rubber spatula or wire whisk until the ingredients are blended.

Fork-tender: Easily pierced with a fork.

Fricassee: To stew chicken; braise meat.

Fry: To cook in ⅛ inch hot oil or fat.

Goulash: A thick Hungarian stew; usually flavored with paprika.

Grate: To cut into fine, medium, or coarse shreds, using a grater.

Grease: To rub with butter, shortening, etc.

Gumbo: Thick soup of seafood or poultry thickened with okra or "file" powder.

Julienne: To cut food such as carrots or ham into thin match-like strips.

Marinate: To let stand in seasoned liquid so as to add flavor and/or tenderize.

Mash: To break up and make smooth with a masher, fork or the back of a spoon.

Meat tenderizer: An enzyme sprinkled on meat to make it tender.

Mince: To cut or chop into fine pieces.

Monosodium glutamate: White crystals which enhance the natural flavor of food.

Parboil: To partially cook in boiling liquid; complete cooking by another method.

Pare: To remove outer covering, as of apples, with a knife or other paring tool.

Peel: To pull off outer covering, as of bananas, with the fingers.

Pilaf: Rice or cracked wheat, sautéed in fat, then cooked in seasoned liquid.

Poach: To cook, immersed in liquid that is barely simmering.

Preheat: To bring oven or broiler up to desired temperature before using.

Pressure cooker: Pan which cooks quickly using superheated steam under pressure.

Puree: To press food through sieve or food mill.

Roast: To cook with dry heat in oven.

Sauté: To fry in small amount of fat or oil.

Score: To make shallow cuts in surface of meat to decorate or prevent curling.

Season: To add salt, spices, etc. for flavor.

Simmer: To cook barely below boiling point.

Skillet or frying pan: Shallow round pan used to sauté, brown or fry.

Skim: To remove fat or grease from surface.

Slice: To cut in thin, flat pieces.

Stew: To cook slowly in liquid on low heat.

Stir: To mix with spoon in circular motion.

Thicken: To add flour, cornstarch, eggs, to liquids to get a heavier consistency.

Toss: To mix lightly with two forks, or with a spoon and fork.

Tortilla: Thin pancake-like Mexican bread made with cornmeal.

Unmold gelatin: Dip knife blade in warm water; use to loosen gelatin around edge of mold. Quickly dip mold, just to rim, in warm water. Remove; shake to loosen gelatin. Moisten plate; place over mold. Invert mold and plate; lift off mold.

Yogurt: Milk to which a bacterial starter has been added; creamy, smooth, tangy.

HELPFUL HINTS

• In a recipe calling for grated citrus peel as well as juice, always grate before you squeeze. Place the grater over waxed paper; you'll catch all the precious oils as well as the peel and save dish washing.

• If canned anchovies are too salty for your taste, soak them in milk, then rinse well in cold water before using.

• To keep sliced apples, bananas and pears picture pretty, dip the slices in lemon juice; they won't turn brown.

• Use sprigs of parsley for garnish, but save the stems for the soup or stew pot. They're loaded with flavor.

• The next time you cook bacon, save the drippings to use in browning meat for stew. Saves a penny or two and adds extra flavor. Wonderful for home-fried potatoes too.

• For a super glossy, smooth sauce, save a tablespoon of the butter or margarine called for in the recipe to beat in at the last minute with a wire whisk or wooden spoon. If calories are no problem, just add an extra spoonful.

• Buttered bread crumbs are called for in so many recipes, make a large batch while you're at it. Use one tablespoon of melted butter or margarine to each half cup of bread crumbs. Store what you don't need in the refrigerator in a plastic bag. If you run out of bread crumbs, try cornflakes, crisp rye cereal or wheat germ.

• Too much salt in the stew, sauce or soup? Add a peeled raw potato to absorb some of the salt, but don't forget to take it out before serving.

• A meat thermometer takes the guesswork out of roasting meat. Insert the thermometer in the thickest part of the meat, being careful not to touch bone or fat.

• Time Savers: A chopping board on the countertop; favorite cooking spoons in a jar; waxed paper to hold sifted dry ingredients; an egg slicer for quick, uniform slices of cooked beets and mushrooms as well as eggs; an ice cream scoop for serving mashed potatoes, rice, cottage cheese, mashed turnips; a timer to eliminate clock watching.

• Take a short cut to sauce and gravy making with a "roux" done ahead and kept in the refrigerator. This is simply a mixture of equal parts of butter or margarine and flour blended to a smooth paste. Instead of melting butter and blending in flour, then stirring in the hot mixture, stir three tablespoons of roux into one cup of the hot mixture and stir until smooth and thickened.

A NOTE ON THE RECIPES

A special feature of this book is a recipe format that tells you at a glance how much time you must spend in the kitchen and how much free time you have while the dish is cooking, cooling, or whatever. Headlined too are the number of servings and, when appropriate, the fact that the recipe is for a dish you can make way ahead and finish at the last minute.

For extra convenience, the Index groups recipes under cooking method: Broiler Meals, Oven Dishes and so on. These heads are italicized for easy reference.

SELF-SUFFICIENT SOUPS
Whether simmered for hours or assembled in minutes, these are hearty enough to be the mainstay of any meal

BEEF-VEGETABLE SOUP
pictured on page 36

Do-Ahead Dish*
Time in Kitchen: 15 minutes
Free Time: 2½ hours
Servings: 14

6 to 8 pounds crosscut beef shanks
salt
3 stalks celery, diced
3 large carrots, diced
2 medium onions, diced
1 28-ounce can tomatoes
½ cup chopped parsley
½ teaspoon basil
½ teaspoon thyme leaves
½ teaspoon pepper
1 10-ounce package each: frozen lima
   beans, corn and peas

About 2 hours and 45 minutes before dinner: In very large kettle (about 2 gallons), bring 10 cups water to boiling; add beef shanks, 2 tablespoons salt and next 8 ingredients. Cover; simmer 2 hours.

Stir in frozen vegetables and 2 teaspoons salt; continue cooking about ½ hour or until meat and vegetables are fork-tender. Makes about 26 cups.

*To Freeze: Ladle soup into 1-quart freezer containers, leaving at least 1½ inches head space for expansion. (Remove meat from bones, if desired.) Cover; refrigerate until chilled; freeze up to 3 months.

About ½ hour before dinner: Remove frozen soup from container. In medium saucepan over medium heat, bring to boiling.

Serve with: Corn bread • Compote of canned apricots, pears and cherries

DINNER-IN-A-SOUP

Do-Ahead Dish
Time in Kitchen: 45 minutes
Free Time: 3½ hours
Servings: 12

2 pounds shin beef, plus split large
   soup bone
1 tablespoon salt
½ medium cabbage, sliced
2 medium onions, chopped
6 carrots, cut into 3-inch pieces
2 celery stalks, cut in chunks
¼ medium green pepper, diced
1 28-ounce can tomatoes (3½ cups)
½ 9-ounce package frozen cut green
   beans
½ 10-ounce package frozen limas
½ 10-ounce package frozen peas
1 12-ounce can vacuum-packed
   whole-kernel corn
1 potato, cubed
2 tablespoons chopped parsley
¾ cup catchup
½ teaspoon ground cloves
1 teaspoon granulated sugar
1 teaspoon salt
¼ teaspoon pepper

Day before or early in day: In large kettle, place meat, bone, 4 quarts water, salt. Bring to boiling; skim. Add cabbage, onions, carrots, celery, green pepper, tomatoes. Cover, cook ½ hour. Add green beans and rest of ingredients; cover; simmer 3½ hours. Taste; season if needed.

Remove meat and bone from soup. Cut up meat; return to soup. Cool; refrigerate.

About ½ hour before dinner: Skim any fat from soup. Heat soup to boiling.

Serve with: Crisp crackers • Apple pie à la mode • Coffee

BEEF SOUP WITH DUMPLINGS

Time in Kitchen: 1½ hours
Free Time: 1 hour
Servings: 6

---

3 tablespoons butter or margarine
2 cups chopped onions
1½ tablespoons paprika
1 pound boned beef chuck, cut into 1-inch cubes
2 garlic cloves, minced
salt
1 tablespoon caraway seed
1 green pepper, coarsely chopped
1 tomato, cut in chunks
3 cups diced potatoes
½ cup plus 2 tablespoons all-purpose flour
1 egg

About 2½ hours before dinner: In Dutch oven, in butter, sauté onions until tender; stir in paprika and chuck; brown chuck well; add garlic, 1 tablespoon salt, caraway seed, green pepper and tomato. Let meat simmer in its juices a few minutes, stirring occasionally. Add 7 cups water; simmer, covered, 1 hour. Add potatoes and continue cooking, covered, 1 hour.

About 45 minutes before dinner: In small bowl, blend flour with egg and ¼ teaspoon salt until firm dough forms. With fingers, tear off small pieces of this dough and drop into simmering soup. Continue simmering, covered, until meat and potatoes are fork-tender. If soup becomes thicker than you like, add a little hot water.

Serve with: Canned purple plums, with sour cream • Toasted pound cake

WINTER BORSCHT

Do-Ahead Dish
Time in Kitchen: 1 hour
Free Time: 2 hours
Servings: 6

2½ pounds short ribs, cut up
2 medium onions, sliced
3 stalks celery, cut into 1-inch lengths
4 large beets, sliced
4 carrots, sliced
1 bay leaf
salt
1 cup coarsely grated beets
1 6-ounce can tomato paste
2 tablespoons vinegar
1 tablespoon granulated sugar
1 head green cabbage

Day before or early in day: In large kettle, place 6 cups water, short ribs, onions, celery, sliced beets, carrots, bay leaf and 1 tablespoon salt. Simmer, covered, 2 hours. Add grated beets, tomato paste, vinegar, sugar and 1 tablespoon salt. Cover; simmer 20 minutes; cool; refrigerate.

About ½ hour before dinner: Remove fat from surface of borscht; remove bones from meat. Bring borscht to boiling; lower heat; add cabbage, cut in 8 wedges; cover; simmer 20 minutes or until cabbage is fork-tender.

Serve with: Cottage-cheese salad • Basket of rye or pumpernickel bread and butter

MINESTRONE

Do-Ahead Dish
Time in Kitchen: ½ hour
Free Time: 3 hours
Servings: 8

1 pound shin beef with bone
3 tablespoons salt
1 cup dried red kidney beans
2 tablespoons salad or olive oil
2 garlic cloves
1 medium onion, minced
½ cup chopped parsley
½ pound beef chuck, ground
¼ teaspoon pepper
1 cup diced celery
2 cups finely shredded cabbage
1½ cups diced carrots
1 28-ounce can tomatoes (3½ cups)
1½ cups broken-up spaghetti
1 cup thinly sliced zucchini
1 10-ounce package frozen peas
grated Parmesan or Romano cheese

Day before or early in day: In large kettle, place shin beef with bone, 5 quarts water, salt, beans. Bring to boiling; skim. Cover; simmer 3 hours.

In skillet, in oil, sauté garlic, onion, parsley, chuck and pepper until onion is tender; discard garlic.

Remove bone from soup; cut off meat. Add meat to soup, along with onion mixture, celery, cabbage, carrots, tomatoes. Cover; simmer 20 minutes or until vegetables are fork-tender. Cool; refrigerate.

About ½ hour before dinner: Skim fat from soup. Bring soup slowly to boiling; add spaghetti, zucchini, peas; cover; cook about 10 minutes. Add salt, pepper to taste. Top with cheese.

Serve with: Fresh fruit such as apples, pears and grapes

HAMBURGER-VEGETABLE SOUP

pictured on page 35

Do-Ahead Dish*
Time in Kitchen: 25 minutes
Free Time: 20 minutes
Servings: 6

6 beef-bouillon cubes
1 16-ounce can tomatoes
1 large onion, diced
¾ cup diced celery
1 medium carrot, diced
1 garlic clove, crushed
1 bay leaf
½ teaspoon salt
⅛ teaspoon pepper
½ pound beef round steak, ground
1 10-ounce package frozen peas
3 tablespoons chopped parsley for garnish

About 45 minutes before dinner: In large saucepan, heat 5 cups water to boiling; add bouillon cubes and stir until dissolved. Add tomatoes and next 7 ingredients; cover; simmer 20 minutes.

Meanwhile, in small skillet, cook meat, stirring constantly, until it loses its bright red color. Add meat and peas to soup; cook 10 minutes or until peas are fork-tender; discard bay leaf. Stir in parsley just before serving.

*To Freeze: Up to 2 months before serving, prepare a double batch of the recipe but do not stir in parsley. Divide soup into portions and freeze. Add parsley at end of reheating.

Serve with: Poppy Seed Rolls, page 215 • Raspberries and peaches topped with baked meringue

MEATBALL-VEGETABLE SOUP

Do-Ahead Dish
Time in Kitchen: 1 hour
Free Time: ½ hour
Servings: 4

salt
½ cup diced celery
½ cup chopped celery leaves
1 large onion, minced
2 medium carrots, sliced
1 cup cubed potatoes
1 19-ounce can tomatoes (2½ cups)
¼ cup minced onion
2 tablespoons salad oil
½ cup fresh bread crumbs
¼ cup milk
½ pound beef chuck, ground
1 egg
shredded process sharp cheese
chopped parsley

1. *About 1½ hours before dinner:* In large kettle, combine 2 cups water, 1½ teaspoons salt, celery and next 5 ingredients; cover; bring to boiling; cook ½ hour.
2. Meanwhile, in small skillet, sauté ¼ cup minced onion in salad oil until golden. Soften bread in milk; add to chuck with onion, egg and ½ teaspoon salt. Shape into 12 meatballs. Chill ½ hour.
3. Drop chilled meatballs into boiling soup. Cover; simmer 10 minutes. Serve soup topped with cheese and parsley.
   To make soup ahead: Complete steps 1 and 2; refrigerate soup and meatballs. To serve, bring soup to boiling; add meatballs; complete step 3.

Serve with: Tossed fruit salad • Brown-and-serve rolls • Tapioca pudding layered with butterscotch sauce

OXJOINT-VEGETABLE SOUP

Do-Ahead Dish
Time in Kitchen: 1 hour
Free Time: 2 hours 45 minutes
Servings: 8

½ cup all-purpose flour
1 teaspoon seasoned salt
2½ pounds oxjoints, cut into 2-inch lengths
3 tablespoons salad oil
½ cup minced onions
1 tablespoon salt
⅛ teaspoon black pepper
3 bay leaves
4 or 5 parsley sprigs
1 29-ounce can tomatoes
12 3-inch bias-cut celery slices
½ cup diced celery
12 3-inch yellow-turnip sticks
½ cup diced yellow turnips
12 3-inch bias-cut carrot slices
½ cup diced carrots
few drops hot pepper sauce

Day before or early in day: In small bowl, combine flour and seasoned salt; dredge each piece of oxjoint.
   In large Dutch oven, in hot oil, brown oxjoint pieces well; remove; brown onion. Return oxjoint pieces to Dutch oven; add salt, pepper, bay leaves, parsley, tomatoes, and 1½ quarts water. Cover; simmer 2 hours or until fork-tender. Cool; chill.
   About 1 hour before dinner: Skim fat from soup; bring soup to boiling. Add celery and rest of vegetables; cover; simmer 45 minutes or until vegetables are fork-tender. Add hot pepper sauce.

Serve with: Toasted cheese sandwiches, cut into fingers • Broiled grapefruit halves with brown sugar • Coffee

LEMONY LAMB SOUP

Do-Ahead Dish
Time in Kitchen: 1 hour
Free Time: 2 hours
Servings: 8

3 pounds lamb shanks, cracked
1 onion, quartered
1 carrot, coarsely shredded
1 tablespoon salt
butter or margarine
⅓ cup all-purpose flour
2 egg yolks
2 to 3 tablespoons lemon juice
1 tablespoon paprika
dash cayenne

1. *Day before or early in day:* In large kettle, combine lamb shanks with onion, carrot, salt and 2 quarts water; bring to boiling. Skim; cover; simmer 2 hours or until meat is tender. Cool; cover; refrigerate overnight.
2. *About 1 hour before dinner:* Skim any fat from soup; heat soup until it is liquified; remove meat from bones; dice meat; remove bones and onion.
3. In small skillet, melt ¼ cup butter; add flour; stir until smooth and light brown; carefully stir into soup with diced meat. Bring to boiling; simmer 15 minutes, stirring occasionally.
4. Meanwhile, beat egg yolks with lemon juice; beat in about 1 cup of hot soup, then carefully stir this mixture into soup. Do not boil. Melt about ¼ cup butter with paprika and cayenne and use as topping for soup.

Serve with: Green salad with tomatoes, cucumbers and ripe olives • Fresh fruit • Coffee

LENTIL-BURGER SOUP

Do-Ahead Dish
Time in Kitchen: 45 minutes
Free Time: 1 hour
Servings: 6

1 pound lentils
salt
¼ teaspoon pepper
½ cup butter or margarine
1 20-ounce can tomatoes
1 large onion, minced
2 tablespoons chopped fresh dill
3 or 4 garlic cloves, minced
2 bay leaves
1 pound lamb, ground
¼ teaspoon pepper
1 egg, slightly beaten
all-purpose flour
1 tablespoon salad oil
¼ cup elbow macaroni

Day before or early in day: Wash lentils; place in large kettle. Add 2½ quarts water, 2 tablespoons salt, ¼ teaspoon pepper, butter, tomatoes, onion, dill, garlic, bay leaves. Cover; cook over low heat 1 hour and 45 minutes or until lentils are soft.

Meanwhile, combine ground lamb with 1½ teaspoons salt, ¼ teaspoon pepper and egg; shape into 24 balls. Roll balls in flour. In skillet, in hot salad oil, brown meatballs; add, with macaroni, to soup; cook 20 minutes more. Cool; refrigerate.

About ½ hour before dinner: Heat soup to boiling; cover; simmer 10 minutes.

Serve with: Cabbage slaw • Hot corn sticks • Frozen mixed fruit, partially thawed

PEA SOUP PLUS

pictured on page 40

Time in Kitchen: 2 hours 10 minutes
Servings: 8

1 3-pound smoked pork butt
2 cups quick-cooking split peas
1½ cups thinly sliced carrots
1 small onion, chopped
1½ cups thinly sliced celery
½ teaspoon peppercorns
½ teaspoon whole allspice
1 bay leaf
salt

About 2 hours and 10 minutes before dinner: In Dutch oven, in 2 quarts boiling water, cook pork and next 4 ingredients. Tie peppercorns, allspice and bay leaf in cheesecloth bag; add to soup. Cover; simmer 1 hour and 45 minutes or until meat is tender; stir frequently. Discard bag. Add salt to taste. Remove pork; let stand 10 minutes; slice; serve with soup.

Serve with: Waldorf salad • Club rolls • Coffee

PANTRY-SHELF PEA SOUP

Time in Kitchen: 20 minutes
Servings: 4

½ pound link sausages
1 onion, thinly sliced
1 11¼-ounce can condensed green-pea soup
1 10¾-ounce can condensed vegetable soup
sliced ripe olives, for garnish

About 20 minutes before dinner: In saucepan, brown sausages and onion. Drain fat. Set onion aside. Cut sausages into ½-inch slices; blend in undiluted soups and 1 soup-can water. Simmer a few minutes. Garnish with onion rings and olive slices.

Serve with: Hot Biscuits, page 217 • Cucumber salad • Apple strudel

BOSTON CLAM CHOWDER

Time in Kitchen: 35 minutes
Servings: 8

3 dozen shucked raw soft-shell clams, with strained liquid
¼ pound salt pork, diced
2 medium onions, sliced
2 tablespoons flour
¼ teaspoon celery salt
¼ teaspoon pepper
salt
3 cups diced potatoes
3 cups milk, scalded
1 tablespoon butter or margarine

About 35 minutes before dinner: Snip off necks of clams; with scissors, finely cut necks; leave soft parts whole; place all in saucepan with their liquid. Add 2 cups water; bring to boiling. Drain, reserving liquid and clams.

In large kettle, sauté salt pork until golden. Add onions; cook until tender. Into onions, stir flour, celery salt, pepper, clam liquid, 2 teaspoons salt, potatoes. Cover; cook 8 minutes or until potatoes are fork-tender. Add milk, clams, 1½ teaspoons salt, butter; heat.

Serve with: Spinach salad • Danish pastries • Coffee

BOUILLABAISSE, AMERICAN STYLE

pictured on page 38

Time in Kitchen: 1 hour
Servings: 8 to 10

2 tablespoons salad oil
1 cup chopped onions
½ cup chopped celery
2 16-ounce cans whole tomatoes
1 garlic clove, minced
1 tablespoon chopped parsley
1½ teaspoons seasoned salt
¼ teaspoon thyme leaves
1 teaspoon monosodium glutamate
2½ pounds striped or sea bass fillets, cut into large pieces (or 2½ pounds halibut steak, cut into chunks)
1½ dozen clams (little neck) in shell
1 tablespoon cornstarch
1 pound fresh or frozen shrimp, peeled and deveined

About 1 hour before dinner: In Dutch oven, in oil, sauté onions and celery 5 minutes. Stir in tomatoes and next 5 ingredients. Cover; simmer 10 minutes. Add bass; cook until almost tender, 10 minutes.

Meanwhile, scrub clams under running water; place in small kettle with ½ inch boiling water. Cover and steam until shells just open, about 5 minutes. Strain hot broth through cheesecloth; reserve 1 cup. Keep clams warm.

Blend cornstarch with clam juice; stir into tomato mixture; bring to boiling. Add shrimp; simmer 5 minutes or until shrimp are pink and tender. Add clams.

Serve with: French bread slices, rubbed with garlic and browned in olive oil • Fruit and cheese

OYSTER-CORN CHOWDER

Time in Kitchen: 40 minutes
Servings: 4

1 medium onion, thinly sliced
½ cup chopped celery
½ teaspoon salt
dash each: garlic salt, black pepper, nutmeg
1 16-ounce can cream-style corn
1 10½-ounce can condensed chicken broth
1 soup-can liquid from oysters
2 hard-cooked eggs, thinly sliced
2 dozen shucked oysters

About 40 minutes before dinner: In large saucepan, simmer onion and next 8 ingredients 20 minutes. Add eggs and oysters; simmer 3 minutes or until oysters curl.

SCALLOP STEW

Time in Kitchen: ½ hour
Servings: 4

¼ cup butter or margarine
1 pound sea scallops, halved across grain
1 quart milk
1 tablespoon Worcestershire
2 teaspoons monosodium glutamate
2 teaspoons salt
dash pepper
4 ounces process cheese spread
oyster crackers

About ½ hour before dinner: In large skillet, in butter, sauté scallops until golden, about 7 minutes. Add milk and seasonings; simmer until bubbly. Add cheese; stir until melted. Top with crackers.

SHRIMP GUMBO

Do-Ahead Dish*
Time in Kitchen: ½ hour
Free Time: 45 minutes
Servings: 8

¼ cup butter or margarine
2 tablespoons all-purpose flour
2 garlic cloves, minced
2 onions, sliced
½ green pepper, thinly sliced
1 19-ounce can tomatoes (2½ cups)
1 15½-ounce can okra, drained or 1
    10-ounce package frozen okra
1 6-ounce can tomato paste
3 beef-bouillon cubes
4 teaspoons Worcestershire
⅛ teaspoon ground cloves
½ teaspoon chili powder
pinch basil
1 bay leaf
1½ tablespoons salt
¼ teaspoon pepper
1½ pounds raw shrimp, shelled and
    deveined
rice to make 3 cups cooked, page 11
¼ cup chopped parsley

Early in day: In Dutch oven or heavy kettle, melt butter. Stir in flour; cook over low heat until browned. Add garlic, onions, green pepper; cook slowly until tender. Add 3 cups water, tomatoes, okra, tomato paste, bouillon cubes, Worcestershire, cloves, chili powder, basil, bay leaf, salt and pepper. Simmer, uncovered, 45 minutes. Cool; refrigerate.

About 15 minutes before dinner: Heat tomato mixture over medium heat just to boiling; add shrimp; cover; simmer about 5 minutes or until shrimp are pink and tender. Meanwhile, cook rice as label directs. Combine rice with parsley. Serve gumbo in shallow plates; add "island" of parsley and rice at side.

To Freeze: Make tomato mixture in advance; freeze. Before serving, bring to boiling; add shrimp.

Serve with: Assorted-cracker basket • Lettuce wedges • Lemon pudding

SPICY TUNA CHOWDER

Time in Kitchen: 25 minutes
Free Time: 35 minutes
Servings: 4

1 12½-ounce can tuna
1 medium onion, sliced
1 medium potato, cubed (about 1 cup)
2 carrots, diced
¼ cup diced celery
2 16-ounce cans tomatoes
1 teaspoon salt
½ teaspoon thyme leaves
¼ teaspoon pepper
chopped parsley for garnish

About 1 hour before dinner: Drain oil from tuna into large saucepan. In hot oil, sauté onion until golden; stir in potato, carrot, celery, tomatoes, 1½ cups water, salt, thyme and pepper. Simmer, covered, 35 minutes or until vegetables are tender. Add tuna; heat. Sprinkle with parsley.

Serve with: Brown-and-serve rolls • Sliced avocado and greens with lime dressing • Fruit-filled pineapple halves

COTTAGE-SALMON BISQUE

Time in Kitchen: 20 minutes
Servings: 6

1 tablespoon butter or margarine
1 medium onion, chopped
2 tablespoons all-purpose flour
2 cups milk
2 cups cottage cheese
1 7¾-ounce can salmon, drained
½ teaspoon salt
dash pepper
dash hot pepper sauce

About 20 minutes before dinner: In large saucepan, in hot butter, sauté onion until tender; blend in flour. Gradually stir in milk. Cook over moderate heat, stirring constantly, until thickened. Stir in cheese, salmon, salt, pepper, hot pepper sauce. Heat.

POACHED EGGS IN TOMATOES
pictured on page 39

Time in Kitchen: ½ hour
Servings: 4

2 tablespoons butter or margarine
1 large green pepper, cut in thin strips
1 28-ounce can tomatoes
salt and pepper
8 eggs

About ½ hour before dinner: In large skillet, in hot butter, sauté green pepper 5 minutes. Add tomatoes, 1½ teaspoons salt and ⅛ teaspoon pepper. Cook 5 more minutes.

Into simmering mixture, carefully drop eggs, one at a time. Cover and cook gently about 10 minutes or until eggs are just firm. Spoon vegetable mixture over eggs.

Serve with: Toasted Poppy Seed Bread, page 218 • Chocolate brownies

MANHATTAN CLAM CHOWDER

Time in Kitchen: 1 hour 50 minutes
Free Time: 40 minutes
Servings: 8

5 bacon slices, diced
2½ cups diced onions
1½ cups diced carrots
1 cup diced celery
2 tablespoons chopped parsley
1 29-ounce can whole tomatoes
3 dozen hard-shell clams, shucked, in their liquid
1½ teaspoons salt
¼ teaspoon pepper
1 bay leaf
1 teaspoon thyme leaves
2 cups chopped potatoes

1. *About 2½ hours before dinner:* In large kettle, sauté bacon until almost crisp; add onions; cook until tender; add carrots, celery, parsley; cook 5 minutes.
2. Drain tomatoes, putting liquid into measuring cup; add tomato pulp to kettle.
3. Drain clams. Add liquid to tomato liquid; add enough water to make 7 cups; add to kettle with salt, pepper, bay leaf and thyme; simmer, covered, 40 minutes.
4. Add potatoes; cook 20 minutes or until almost tender.
5. Meanwhile, chop clams; add to chowder; simmer 10 minutes.

PENNSYLVANIA DUTCH CHICKEN-CORN CHOWDER

Do-Ahead Dish
Time in Kitchen: 1 hour
Free Time: 2 hours
Servings: 12

2 3- to 4-pound stewing chickens
3 medium onions, minced
1 cup chopped celery
2½ tablespoons salt
¼ teaspoon pepper
1¼ teaspoons nutmeg
10 ears fresh corn
1 egg
½ cup milk
1 cup sifted all-purpose flour
2 hard-cooked eggs, chopped
chopped parsley, for garnish

1. *Day before or early in day:* In Dutch oven, place chickens, 3 quarts water, onions, celery, salt, pepper, nutmeg. Simmer, covered, 2 hours or until tender; add water if needed.
2. Remove chickens from broth; refrigerate separately until fat solidifies on broth. Cut off kernels from corn; refrigerate.
3. *About 45 minutes before dinner:* Remove fat from broth. If necessary, add water to broth to make 10 cups; add corn; simmer, covered, until tender.
4. Meanwhile, remove chicken from bones; cut into 1½-inch chunks; add to broth. In small bowl, beat 1 egg until light in color; add milk; beat in flour until mixture is smooth.
5. Bring broth to simmering. Drop batter into broth from large serving spoon. Make each "rivel" (drop) the size of a cherry pit by using a knife to stop the flow of batter. Simmer 2 to 3 minutes or until rivels are cooked.
6. Stir in eggs; top with parsley.

LOBSTER STEW

Time in Kitchen: 20 minutes
Servings: 6

3 tablespoons butter or margarine
2 cups cooked lobster meat, page 8
1 quart milk
1½ teaspoons salt
1 teaspoon paprika
⅛ teaspoon pepper
dash cayenne

About 20 minutes before dinner: In small skillet, melt butter; sauté lobster meat about 5 minutes.

Meanwhile, scald milk; season with salt, paprika, pepper and cayenne. Add lobster; simmer gently 5 minutes. Let stand for a while to improve flavor.

Serve with: Sesame-seed crackers • Tossed green salad • Cherry pie

DELMARVA CHICKEN SPECIAL

Do-Ahead Dish
Time in Kitchen: 45 minutes
Free Time: 1½ hours
Servings: 8

1 3-pound broiler-fryer
1 tablespoon salt
½ teaspoon monosodium glutamate
2 tablespoons butter or margarine
¾ cup packaged precooked rice
2 eggs
¼ cup lemon juice
½ lemon, sliced, for garnish
2 tablespoons chopped parsley
   for garnish

Day before or early in day: In large kettle, place chicken, 2½ quarts water, salt, monosodium glutamate and butter; simmer, covered, about 1½ hours or until chicken is tender. Remove chicken from soup. Cut meat into serving-size pieces; return to soup. Chill.

About ½ hour before dinner: Bring chicken mixture to boiling; add rice; simmer 10 minutes or until rice is tender; remove from heat. Beat eggs well; slowly stir in lemon juice; gradually stir in 2 cups broth only; stir mixture back into soup. Garnish with lemon slices, parsley.

Serve with: Bread with apple butter • Radish coleslaw • Cherry gelatin

CREAMED TURKEY SOUP
pictured on page 37

Time in Kitchen: 1 hour
Servings: 6

2 tablespoons butter or margarine
1 large onion, minced
2 13¾-ounce cans chicken broth
3 cups diced potatoes
2 cups cubed, cooked turkey
1 10-ounce package frozen peas and
   carrots
2 teaspoons salt
½ teaspoon pepper
⅛ teaspoon rubbed sage
1 cup light cream
1 cup milk

About 1 hour before dinner: In large Dutch oven, in butter, sauté onion until tender. Add broth and potatoes; cook 20 minutes. Stir in turkey, peas and carrots, salt, pepper and sage; cook 10 minutes or until vegetables are done. Stir in cream and milk; heat.

Serve with: Citrus-avocado salad • Chocolate pudding

SOUPE À L'OEUF
pictured on page 37

Time in Kitchen: 1 hour
Servings: 6

¼ cup butter or margarine
3 stalks celery, diced
2 carrots, diced
2 leeks, diced
1 large onion, diced
1 turnip, diced
1 teaspoon granulated sugar
½ teaspoon salt
3 13¾-ounce cans chicken broth
1 10-ounce package frozen peas
6 eggs
¼ teaspoon chervil (optional)

About 1 hour before dinner: In Dutch oven or kettle, place butter, celery, carrots, leeks, onions, turnip, sugar and salt. Cover; cook over medium heat, stirring occasionally, for 20 minutes or until vegetables are fork-tender. Add chicken broth and peas; cover; cook 15 minutes or until peas are tender.

Break one egg into saucer; lower saucer close to soup surface and quickly slip egg into soup. Repeat, using all eggs. Cover pan and continue simmering until eggs are of desired doneness. Serve soup in deep soup plates with an egg for each serving; sprinkle chervil on each.

Serve with: Oven-fresh Bran Muffins, page 215 • Baked apples with cream

SWEDISH CABBAGE SOUP

Do-Ahead Dish
Time in Kitchen: ½ hour
Free Time: 2 hours
Servings: 6

1 tablespoon whole allspice
2 lamb shanks (3 pounds)
2 beef-bouillon cubes
½ teaspoon pepper
2 tablespoons salt
1 cup chopped leeks or onions
½ cup diced, pared parsnips
1 cup sliced carrots
¼ cup chopped parsley
½ cup sliced celery
2 quarts medium shredded cabbage
2 cups diced potatoes

Day before or early in day: Tie allspice in cheesecloth; place in large kettle with shanks, bouillon cubes, pepper, salt, 2 quarts water. Simmer, covered, 2 hours. Cool; chill.

About 45 minutes before dinner. Skim fat from soup. Remove meat; cube. Bring broth to boiling; remove allspice; add leeks and next 4 ingredients. Cover; simmer 10 minutes. Add cabbage, potatoes, meat; cook, covered, 20 minutes.

Serve with: Corn bread • Tomato aspic

AMERICAN POTAGE

Time in Kitchen: 15 minutes
Free Time: 15 minutes
Servings: 4

¼ cup salad oil
½ pound beef chuck, ground
¼ cup cubed carrot
1 cup diced potatoes
1 10½-ounce can condensed onion soup, undiluted
grated Parmesan cheese

About ½ hour before dinner: In saucepan, in oil, brown beef. Add carrot, potatoes, soup, 1 soup-can water. Simmer, covered, 15 minutes or until vegetables are tender. Top with cheese.

DEVILED CORN CHOWDER

Time in Kitchen: 15 minutes
Servings: 4

¼ cup butter or margarine
1 medium onion, sliced
2 10½-ounce cans condensed cream-of-chicken soup
3 2¼-ounce cans deviled ham
1 16-ounce can cream-style corn
1 12-ounce can whole-kernel corn
dash nutmeg
½ teaspoon paprika
Melba toast rounds

About 15 minutes before dinner: In saucepan, in butter, sauté onion 5 minutes. Stir in undiluted soup, 1 can of ham, 1 soup-can water, corn, nutmeg and paprika. Bring to boiling. Spread toast with rest of ham; float on soup.

Serve with: Biscuits • Green salad • Pecan pie

CHICKEN BORSCHT

Time in Kitchen: 20 minutes
Servings: 4

1 16-ounce can julienne beets, undrained
2 10½-ounce cans condensed beef broth
1 tablespoon all-purpose flour
¼ teaspoon pepper
1 cup cut-up cooked or canned chicken
⅓ cup lemon juice

About 20 minutes before dinner: In large saucepan, combine beets, broth and 1½ cups water. Stir a little of this liquid into flour to form paste; stir back into remaining liquid; add pepper. Simmer, covered, about 10 minutes. Remove from heat; stir in chicken, lemon juice.

Serve with: Buttered pumpernickel-bread fingers • Strawberry-topped angel-food cake

CREAMY POTATO SOUP

Time in Kitchen: ½ hour
Servings: 4

6 bacon slices
1 cup chopped onions
2 cups cubed potatoes
2 10½-ounce cans condensed cream-of-chicken soup
milk
1 teaspoon salt

About ½ hour before dinner: In saucepan, cook bacon until crisp; set aside. Pour off all but 3 tablespoons drippings; add onions; brown. Add potatoes and 1 cup water. Cook, covered, until potatoes are tender, about 15 minutes. Stir in undiluted soup, 2 soupcans milk, salt; heat, do not boil. Garnish with bacon.

Serve with: Molded fruit salad • Rolls • Tea

GERMAN LENTIL SOUP

Time in Kitchen: ½ hour
Free Time: 3 hours
Servings: 8

1 16-ounce package lentils
¼ pound bacon, diced
2 medium onions, sliced
2 medium carrots, diced
1 cup sliced celery
2½ to 3 teaspoons salt
½ teaspoon pepper
½ teaspoon thyme leaves
2 bay leaves
1 large potato
1 ham bone (left from cooked shank)
2 tablespoons lemon juice

1. *Night before:* Wash lentils. Soak overnight in cold water to cover.
2. *About 4 hours before serving:* Drain lentils. In Dutch oven, sauté bacon until golden. Add onions, carrots and sauté until onions are golden. Add lentils, 2 quarts water, celery, salt, pepper, thyme, bay leaves.
3. With medium grater, grate potato into lentil mixture; add ham bone. Cover; simmer 3 hours (lentils should be tender). Remove bay leaves.
4. Remove ham bone; cut away meat and return to soup; Add lemon juice.

Serve with: Buttered toast • Chilled grapefruit halves

*From top: Spaghetti and Fettuccine, Folded
Fine Egg Noodles. Between Strips of La-
sagna: Wagon Wheels, Rigatoni Shells.
Long-grained Rice and Brown Rice*

Do-Ahead Tomato Sauce, page 9

Hamburger-Vegetable Soup, page 22
Poppy-Seed Rolls, page 215

Beef-Vegetable Soup, page 20

Top: Soupe à l'Oeuf, page 30
Bran Muffins, page 215
Bottom: Creamed Turkey Soup, page 30

Bouillabaisse, American Style, page 26

Poached Eggs in Tomatoes, page 28
Toasted Poppy-Seed Bread, page 218

Pea Soup Plus, page 25

FAMILY
DINNERS Among their other virtues, which

include great taste, one-dish meals are a

boon for the budget

BEEF-AND-VEGETABLE CASSEROLE
pictured on page 62

Time in Kitchen: 1 hour
Free Time: 2 hours
Servings: 6

1½ pounds boneless beef chuck
unseasoned meat tenderizer
salad oil
1 pound onions, thinly sliced
5 medium tomatoes
seasoned salt
seasoned pepper
½ pound green beans, cut up
2 carrots, sliced
1½ cups seeded diced green peppers
1½ cups pared, cubed eggplant
½ cup regular white rice

Day before: Sprinkle chuck with tenderizer as label directs; cut into 1-inch cubes. In skillet, in ¼ cup salad oil, sauté onions until tender; remove onions. In same skillet, brown chuck; add ¼ cup water; cover; simmer ½ hour; refrigerate with onions.

About 2 hours and 15 minutes before dinner: Preheat oven to 375°F. Lightly grease a 12″ by 8″ baking dish; on bottom of it, arrange half of onions and 3 tomatoes cut in ½-inch slices. Sprinkle with ½ teaspoon seasoned salt, ⅛ teaspoon seasoned pepper; cover with half of beans, carrots, green peppers and eggplant. Top with rice, 1 teaspoon seasoned salt, dash seasoned pepper, chuck and its juices.

Top chuck with rest of vegetables, ½ teaspoon seasoned salt. Over all, pour ⅔ cup water. Down top center, arrange remaining sliced tomatoes; sprinkle with ½ teaspoon seasoned salt. Cover with foil; bake 2 hours or until all are tender.

SWISS STEAK
pictured on page 59

Time in Kitchen: 45 minutes
Free Time: 1 hour 45 minutes
Servings: 4

1½ pounds beef round steak, ¾ inch thick
2 tablespoons all-purpose flour
1 teaspoon salt
⅛ teaspoon pepper
2 tablespoons salad oil
1 16-ounce can whole tomatoes
1 8-ounce can tomato sauce
1½ cups minced onions
1 bay leaf
¼ cup minced parsley

About 2½ hours before dinner: Trim excess fat from meat and cut into 2-inch-square pieces. Combine flour, salt, pepper; using mallet, edge of plate or dull edge of French knife, pound seasoned flour into meat until all flour is used.

In heavy skillet, in hot oil, brown meat well on both sides, about 15 minutes. Place meat in 2½-quart greased baking dish.

Meanwhile, preheat oven to 350°F. Drain juice from tomatoes into meat juices in skillet. Stir to remove any browned bits; pour over meat; add tomato sauce, onion, bay leaf and parsley.

Cover; bake 1½ hours or until fork-tender. Add drained tomatoes; cover and bake 15 minutes more. Remove bay leaf before serving.

Serve with: Jellied apricot salad • Hot rolls • Chocolate pudding with cream

BEEF-AND-ONION STEW

pictured on page 60

Do-Ahead Dish
Time in Kitchen: ½ hour
Free Time: 2 hours 10 minutes
Servings: 10

3 pounds beef stew meat, cut in 1½-inch cubes
¼ cup all-purpose flour
1½ teaspoons salt
⅛ teaspoon pepper
¼ cup salad oil
1 10½-ounce can condensed beef consommé
½ teaspoon thyme leaves
1½ pounds tiny white onions (about 20)
¼ cup chopped parsley
1 cup small pimiento-stuffed olives

Early in day: Preheat oven to 350°F. In large bowl, toss meat with flour, salt and pepper. In Dutch oven over medium heat, in hot salad oil, brown meat. Stir in undiluted consommé and thyme. Bring to boiling; bake in oven, covered, 1½ hours, stirring occasionally. Add onions and 1 cup more water, if necessary; continue baking 40 minutes. Remove from oven; refrigerate.

About 20 minutes before dinner: Sprinkle with parsley; top with olives. Cook over medium heat, covered, until bubbling hot, about 15 minutes.

Serve with: Tomato juice • Green salad • Fruit • Coffee

BROWN BEEF STEW

Do-Ahead Dish
Time in Kitchen: 45 minutes
Free Time: 2 hours
Servings: 6

⅓ cup all-purpose flour
¼ teaspoon pepper
½ teaspoon celery salt
2 pounds boned beef chuck, cut into 2-inch pieces
¼ cup salad oil
¼ cup minced onion
1 garlic clove, minced
3 beef-bouillon cubes
½ teaspoon salt
½ teaspoon Worcestershire
16 small white onions
8 small carrots, halved crosswise
1 pound fresh mushrooms, sliced
chopped parsley

1. *Day before or early in day:* In bowl, combine flour, pepper, celery salt. Coat meat, a few pieces at a time. Reserve leftover flour.
2. In Dutch oven, in hot oil, brown meat, a few pieces at a time; set aside.
3. To drippings in Dutch oven, add onion, garlic; sauté until just tender. Stir in reserved flour until blended.
4. Slowly stir in 3 cups hot water, bouillon cubes, salt, Worcestershire; add meat; cover; simmer over low heat about 2 hours or until meat is tender.
5. Add whole onions, carrots; cover; simmer 20 minutes. Add mushrooms; cover; simmer 10 minutes or until vegetables are tender. Cool. Refrigerate.
6. *About ½ hour before dinner:* Reheat stew; sprinkle with parsley.

Serve with: Brown-and-serve rolls • Pickled cucumbers • Chocolate ice-cream roll

BEEF RAGOÛT

Time in Kitchen: ½ hour
Free Time: 1 hour
Servings: 6

2 teaspoons butter or margarine
1 pound boned beef chuck, in 1-inch cubes
1 teaspoon salt
1 beef-bouillon cube
6 small carrots, cut into ½-inch chunks
4 medium tomatoes, peeled, quartered
12 small white onions
1 cup sliced mushrooms
4 stalks celery, sliced
2 tablespoons chopped parsley

About 1½ hours before dinner: In large skillet, in hot butter, brown meat about 5 minutes. Add boiling water to cover, salt, bouillon cube; cover; simmer ½ hour or until meat is almost tender. Skim off fat. Add carrots and next 4 ingredients. Cover; cook ½ hour or until vegetables are fork-tender.

Ladle into soup plates; sprinkle with parsley.

BARBECUED POT ROAST

Time in Kitchen: ½ hour
Free Time: 2½ hours
Servings: 6

1 4-pound beef chuck steak, 1½ inches thick
salt and pepper
2 tablespoons salad oil
1 18-ounce bottle onion-flavored barbecue sauce
2 16-ounce cans cut green beans
2 16-ounce cans whole white potatoes

About 3 hours before dinner: Sprinkle meat with 1 teaspoon salt, ¼ teaspoon pepper. In Dutch oven, in hot oil, brown meat well.

Meanwhile, preheat oven to 350°F. When meat is browned, add barbecue sauce; cover; bake 2 hours.

Spoon surface fat from liquid; add drained beans and potatoes. Cover; bake ½ hour or until meat is fork-tender and vegetables are hot.

Serve with: Hearts of lettuce with chiffonade dressing • Vanilla ice cream

MEXICAN BEEF-RICE

Time in Kitchen: 25 minutes
Free Time: 25 minutes
Servings: 6

3 tablespoons shortening
½ cup regular white rice
1 large onion, thinly sliced
1 small garlic clove, minced
1 pound beef chuck, ground
2 teaspoons salt
2 to 3 teaspoons chili powder
⅓ cup catchup
1 19-ounce can tomatoes (2½ cups)
¾ cup dark seedless raisins

About 50 minutes before dinner: In skillet, in hot shortening, cook rice, stirring frequently, until lightly browned. Add onion, garlic and ground chuck; cook, stirring, until meat is browned; stir in salt, chili powder, catchup, tomatoes, 1 cup water and raisins. Cover; simmer, stirring occasionally, 25 minutes or until rice is tender.

Serve with: Coleslaw • Bananas with strawberries • Cookies

STUFFED TORTILLA BAKE

Time in Kitchen: 45 minutes
Free Time: 15 minutes
Servings: 4

1½ pounds beef round, ground
2 tablespoons minced onion
2 teaspoons instant coffee
1¼ teaspoons chili powder
1¼ teaspoons salt
1 teaspoon granulated sugar
¼ teaspoon pepper
¼ cup chopped green pepper
1 6-ounce can tomato paste
1 8-ounce can tomato sauce
1 11-ounce can condensed hot-dog-bean soup
¼ cup salad oil
10 canned tortillas
1 3-ounce package cream cheese
¼ cup catchup

About 1 hour before dinner: In large skillet, sauté meat and onion until meat loses its pink color and onion is tender. Add coffee, chili powder, salt, sugar, pepper, green pepper, tomato paste, tomato sauce and undiluted soup. Simmer over low heat 5 minutes, stirring often.

Preheat oven to 350°F. In small skillet, in hot salad oil, fry tortillas one at a time, on both sides, for just an instant. Spread center of each tortilla with some cream cheese; top with 1 heaping tablespoon of the meat mixture, then fold in half. Repeat, until all the tortillas have been prepared.

Arrange tortillas, open side up and overlapping, lengthwise down center of 12″ by 8″ baking dish. Around tortillas spoon remaining meat mixture. Spoon catchup down center top of tortillas. Bake 15 minutes or until hot.

Serve with: Caramel custard • Coffee

CASSEROLE TWINS

Do-Ahead Dish*
Time in Kitchen: ½ hour
Free Time: ½ hour
Servings: 8

1 pound beef chuck, ground
½ cup chopped onions
¾ cup milk
1 8-ounce package cream cheese
1 12-ounce can whole-kernel corn, Mexican style
¼ cup diced canned pimientos
1 10½-ounce can condensed cream-of-mushroom soup
1½ teaspoons salt
¼ teaspoon pepper
1 8-ounce package medium noodles, cooked
¼ cup grated Parmesan cheese

About 1 hour before dinner: In large skillet, brown chuck; add onion and sauté until tender. Stir in milk and cream cheese until smooth; transfer to large bowl. Mix in corn, pimiento, undiluted mushroom soup, salt, pepper and cooked noodles.

Divide meat mixture between two 1½-quart casseroles; sprinkle top of each with 2 tablespoons Parmesan cheese.

Bake casseroles at 350°F. ½ hour. Run under broiler to brown top, just before serving, if desired.

To Freeze: Freezer-wrap unbaked casseroles; freeze for another day.

About 2 hours before dinner: Unwrap casseroles; bake at 350°F. 1 hour and 45 minutes or until bubbly. Brown under broiler, if desired.

Serve with: Marinated cold vegetables on romaine leaves • Angel-food cake

LASAGNA

Time in Kitchen: ½ hour
Free Time: ½ hour
Servings: 6

1 pound beef chuck, ground
2 pints Do-Ahead Tomato Sauce, thawed, page 9
9 lasagna noodles
1 16-ounce container ricotta cheese (2 cups)
1 pound mozzarella cheese, thinly sliced

About 1 hour before dinner: In medium skillet over medium heat, brown beef well. Pour off drippings. Add tomato sauce and bring to boiling. Preheat oven to 350°F.

Meanwhile, cook lasagna noodles as label directs; drain well; return to pan with a little cold water to prevent sticking.

In 13″ by 9″ baking pan, spread 1 cup sauce; lay 3 noodles lengthwise in pan; spread with 1 cup sauce, then half of ricotta cheese; arrange fourth of cheese slices evenly on top. Repeat layers; top with remaining 3 noodles, sauce and mozzarella cheese. Bake for ½ hour. Let stand 10 minutes for easier serving.

Serve with: Antipasto: pickled artichokes and peppers, stuffed eggs, celery hearts, green onions • Fruit basket • Coffee

BURGER STROGANOFF

Time in Kitchen: ½ hour
Servings: 4

¼ cup butter or margarine
½ cup minced onions
1 pound beef chuck, ground
2 tablespoons all-purpose flour
2 teaspoons salt
¼ teaspoon monosodium glutamate
¼ teaspoon each: pepper and paprika
1 pound fresh mushrooms, sliced
1 10½-ounce can condensed cream-of-chicken soup
1 cup sour cream
chopped parsley, chives

About ½ hour before dinner: In skillet, in hot butter, sauté onion until golden. Add chuck and next 6 ingredients. Sauté 5 minutes. Add undiluted soup; simmer, uncovered, 10 minutes. Remove from heat; stir in cream. Sprinkle with parsley or chives.

BEEF CASSEROLE

Do-Ahead Dish
Time in Kitchen: ½ hour
Free Time: 1 hour 10 minutes
Servings: 6

2 tablespoons butter or margarine
1½ pounds beef chuck, ground
1 large onion, chopped
1 teaspoon each: chili powder and salt
¼ teaspoon pepper
1½ cups uncooked elbow macaroni
1 17-ounce can red kidney beans
1 16-ounce can tomatoes
1 10¾-ounce can condensed tomato soup

Day before: In large skillet, in hot butter, sauté ground beef with onion, chili powder, salt and pepper until beef loses its red color. Meanwhile, cook macaroni as label directs; drain.

In 3-quart casserole, place beef mixture, macaroni; stir in undrained kidney beans, tomatoes and undiluted tomato soup. Cover; refrigerate.

About 1 hour and 15 minutes before dinner: Preheat oven to 400°F. Bake casserole, covered, 1 hour or until hot and bubbly. Remove from oven; let stand 10 minutes before serving.

Serve with: Beet-and-onion salad with French dressing • Nectarines

BEANS AND BURGERS

Time in Kitchen: 35 minutes
Servings: 6

1½ pounds beef chuck, ground
1 small onion, minced
1 tablespoon bottled thick meat sauce
1 tablespoon chopped parsley
½ teaspoon oregano leaves
½ teaspoon rosemary
dash paprika
salt
¼ teaspoon pepper
¼ cup packaged dried bread crumbs
2 tablespoons salad oil
1 8-ounce can tomato sauce
⅓ cup catchup
½ cup sour cream
1 16-ounce can red kidney beans, well drained

About 35 minutes before dinner: In large bowl, thoroughly mix chuck, onion, meat sauce, parsley, oregano, rosemary, paprika, 1½ teaspoons salt and pepper.

Shape meat into 10 or 12 meatballs; roll in bread crumbs. In large skillet, in hot oil, sauté until browned.

Meanwhile, stir together tomato sauce, catchup, sour cream and ¾ teaspoon salt; add with kidney beans to meatballs in skillet; stir gently. Simmer, uncovered, 10 minutes or until meat is done.

Serve with: Cauliflower-greens salad • Rice pudding

BEEF-NOODLE DINNER

Time in Kitchen: 25 minutes
Free Time: 20 minutes
Servings: 4

2 tablespoons salad oil
1 pound beef chuck, ground
1 large onion, sliced
½ diced green pepper
1 cup diced celery
4 ounces medium noodles
1 16-ounce can red kidney beans, undrained
1 28-ounce can tomatoes
1 3-ounce can whole mushrooms, undrained
1 teaspoon salt
2 teaspoons seasoned salt
1- to 1¼-teaspoons chili powder
⅛ teaspoon black pepper

About 45 minutes before dinner: In large skillet, in hot oil, sauté chuck, onion, green pepper and celery until meat is browned. Stir in noodles, kidney beans with liquid, tomatoes, mushrooms with liquid, salt, seasoned salt, chili powder and pepper.

Cover; simmer 20 minutes. If mixture seems thin, cook, uncovered, a few minutes.

MANICOTTI
pictured on page 83

Do-Ahead Dish*
Time in Kitchen: 1½ hours
Free Time: ½ hour
Servings: 8

1 pound Italian sweet-sausage links
1 pound beef chuck, ground
1 medium onion, chopped
2 16-ounce cans tomato puree
1 6-ounce can tomato paste
basil
salt
1 teaspoon granulated sugar
½ teaspoon pepper
1 8-ounce package manicotti shells
2 15- or 16-ounce containers ricotta or
    cottage cheese (4 cups)
1 8-ounce package mozzarella cheese,
    diced
2 tablespoons chopped parsley
grated Parmesan cheese

1. *About 2 hours before dinner:* In covered Dutch oven, cook sausage links in
¼ cup water 5 minutes. Uncover;
brown well; drain on paper towels.
2. Pour fat from Dutch oven; in same
Dutch oven, brown beef and onion well;
stir in tomato puree, tomato paste, 1
teaspoon basil, 1 teaspoon salt, sugar,
pepper and 1 cup water; simmer, covered, 45 minutes. Cut sausage into
bite-size pieces; add to mixture; cook
15 minutes; stir frequently.
3. Meanwhile, cook manicotti shells as
label directs; drain.

4. Preheat oven to 375°F. In large
bowl, combine ricotta and mozzarella
cheeses, parsley, ¾ teaspoon basil, ½
teaspoon salt; stuff into cooked shells.
5. Spoon half of meat sauce into one
13″ by 9″ or two 9″ by 9″ baking
dishes. Arrange half of stuffed shells
over sauce in one layer. Spoon remaining sauce, except ¾ cup, over shells.
Top with remaining shells and reserved
sauce. Sprinkle with Parmesan cheese.
Bake ½ hour or until hot.

   To Freeze: Use freezerproof-and-
ovenproof baking dish or dishes; prepare steps 1 through 5. Cool; wrap;
freeze. To serve, preheat oven to
375°F. Bake manicotti, covered, for 1
hour; uncover; bake 15 minutes.

Serve with: Green salad with red-
onion rings • Pound cake

HAMBURGER CASSEROLE

Time in Kitchen: ½ hour
Free Time: 1 hour 45 minutes
Servings: 6

1 8-ounce package fine noodles
6 bacon slices, diced
1 large onion, chopped
1 pound beef chuck, ground
1 3-ounce bottle stuffed olives, sliced
1½ 10¼-ounce cans condensed
    tomato soup
1 10½-ounce can condensed
    consommé
½ teaspoon salt
⅛ teaspoon pepper
½ teaspoon granulated sugar
1½ teaspoons bottled thick meat
    sauce
½ teaspoon oregano leaves
½ teaspoon thyme leaves
1 cup shredded Cheddar cheese

About 2 hours and 15 minutes before dinner: Preheat oven to 300°F. Cook noodles as label directs; drain. Meanwhile, in skillet, cook bacon until crisp; remove.

In bacon fat, brown onion; add chuck; quickly brown. Stir in olives, undiluted tomato soup, ½ soup-can water, undiluted consommé, salt, pepper, sugar, meat sauce, oregano and thyme; heat.

Arrange noodles in greased 2½-quart casserole. Pour on sauce; add bacon; toss well; sprinkle with cheese. Bake, covered, 1 hour, then uncovered, ½ hour. Remove from oven; let set 15 minutes; serve.

Serve with: Tossed salad with mushrooms • Melon wedges • Coffee

---

ZESTY SPAGHETTI CASSEROLE

Time in Kitchen: 20 minutes
Free Time: 40 minutes
Servings: 6

1 8-ounce package spaghettini, broken
2 teaspoons shortening
1 pound beef chuck, ground
¼ cup finely chopped onion
2 teaspoons chili powder
½ teaspoon salt
⅛ teaspoon pepper
1 16-ounce can tomatoes
¼ cup grated Parmesan cheese
1 12-ounce can whole-kernel corn with sweet peppers
1 tablespoon butter or margarine

About 1 hour before dinner: Preheat oven to 350°F. Cook spaghettini as label directs; drain. In large skillet, in hot shortening, brown meat; reduce heat and add onion; cook about 5 minutes. Drain off any excess fat. Add seasonings and tomatoes; simmer 5 minutes, stirring occasionally.

In greased 2½-quart casserole, combine spaghettini with cheese. Add meat in a layer; top with corn. Dot with butter. Cover; bake 40 minutes.

Serve with: Sautéed zucchini • Apples and pears with crackers • Cheese

---

CHILI BEANS AND MEATBALLS
pictured on page 61

Do-Ahead Dish*
Time in Kitchen: 1½ hours
Free Time: 45 minutes
Servings: 8

1½ pounds beef round steak, ground
1 egg
¼ cup packaged dried bread crumbs
2 tablespoons minced onion
salt
⅛ teaspoon pepper
3 tablespoons salad oil
3 15-ounce cans red kidney beans, drained
1 28-ounce can tomatoes
1 6-ounce can tomato paste
1 garlic clove, crushed
2½ tablespoons chili powder
½ head lettuce, finely shredded
1 green pepper, diced
1 medium red onion, thinly sliced
1½ cups shredded natural Cheddar cheese

1. *Day before:* Prepare chili beans and meatballs. In large bowl, mix meat, egg, crumbs, onion, 1 teaspoon salt and pepper. Using about a tablespoon for each, shape mixture into meatballs.

2. In large skillet, in hot salad oil, brown meatballs, shaking skillet often to keep them from sticking.

3. Meanwhile, in Dutch oven or large saucepan, combine kidney beans, tomatoes, tomato paste, garlic, chili powder and 1 teaspoon salt. Add meatballs; cook over low heat, covered, for 45 minutes, stirring occasionally; refrigerate.

4. *About ½ hour before dinner:* In large saucepan, heat beans and meatballs; stir often; serve in warm dish.

5. Arrange small bowls of lettuce, green pepper, onion and cheese around main dish. Guests help themselves first to lettuce, green-pepper and onions then top with Chili Beans and Meatballs, then cheese.

   *To Freeze: At end of step 3, place in covered freezerproof container, leaving 1½ inches head room; freeze. Thaw overnight in refrigerator. Reheat as in step 4.

BEEF AND SPAGHETTI

Time in Kitchen: ½ hour
Servings: 4

1 tablespoon salad oil
1 small onion, minced
½ pound beef chuck, ground
½ teaspoon salt
1 15¼-ounce can spaghetti in tomato
   sauce with cheese

About ½ hour before dinner: In skillet, in salad oil, sauté onion until tender; brown chuck; add salt, spaghetti; heat through.

Serve with: Green salad • Pie

FROMAGE-BURGER PIE

Time in Kitchen: 45 minutes
Servings: 6

1½ pounds beef chuck, ground
¾ cup uncooked oatmeal
1 cup canned tomato juice
1 small onion, minced
2 teaspoons salt
¼ teaspoon pepper
dash hot pepper sauce
1 egg, beaten
¼ cup chopped parsley
2 10-ounce packages frozen green
   peas and pearl onions
4 ounces shredded Cheddar cheese
   (1 cup)

About 45 minutes before dinner: Preheat oven to 350°F. In bowl, combine chuck, oatmeal, tomato juice, onion, salt, pepper, hot pepper sauce, egg and parsley. Press mixture evenly over bottom and up sides of 9-inch pie plate, making a high stand-up edge. Bake 25 minutes; drain off any liquid.

   Meanwhile, cook frozen peas and onions as label directs; fill drained burger shell. Sprinkle cheese over top; bake 5 minutes more or until cheese melts.

Serve with: Carrot coleslaw • Chocolate whipped dessert

BEEF LIVER AND RICE

Time in Kitchen: 45 minutes
Servings: 4

3 tablespoons butter or margarine
1 pound beef liver, cut in small cubes
salad oil
¼ pound mushrooms, sliced
¼ cup port wine
1 medium eggplant, peeled and sliced
1 small zucchini, sliced
1 tomato, chopped
1 cup regular white rice
1¼ cups chicken broth
1½ teaspoons salt
½ teaspoon pepper

About 45 minutes before dinner: In large skillet, in hot butter, brown liver on all sides. With slotted spoon, remove liver to warm bowl. In same skillet over medium heat, in 1 tablespoon salad oil, cook mushrooms until tender, about 3 minutes; add to liver. Add wine to skillet and over high heat, cook 2 minutes; pour over liver and mushrooms.

In same skillet, in ¼ cup salad oil, fry eggplant, zucchini and tomato for 5 minutes. Stir in rice and cook until rice is translucent. Add chicken broth; cover and cook over low heat 15 minutes.

Lightly mix liver and mushroom mixture, salt and pepper into vegetables. Cover; cook over low heat 5 minutes or until rice is tender.

Serve with: Sliced cucumbers in sour cream • Hot hero rolls • Sliced cantaloupe with lemon wedge • Iced tea

SPANISH BEANS WITH LIVER

Time in Kitchen: ½ hour
Free Time: 2 hours
Servings: 4

1 12-ounce package dried red kidney beans (1¾ cups)
1 cup canned tomatoes
2½ teaspoons salt
¼ teaspoon pepper
1 bay leaf
¼ teaspoon thyme leaves
¼ cup salad oil
2 medium onions, sliced
1 garlic clove, minced
½ pound beef liver, thinly sliced
1 tablespoon all-purpose flour

1. *Day before:* Wash beans; pick over; soak in cold water overnight.
2. *About 2½ hours before dinner:* Drain beans; measure liquid and add enough water to make 3 cups. In Dutch oven, combine bean liquid, beans, tomatoes, salt, pepper, bay leaf and thyme.
3. In skillet, in salad oil, sauté onions and garlic until golden; remove onions; add onions to beans.
4. Cover; bring to boiling; simmer 2 hours or until beans are tender. Dredge liver with flour and sauté in reserved oil in skillet until lightly browned on both sides. Cut liver into pieces; fold into beans.

Serve with: Jellied consommé • Hearts of lettuce with French dressing • Cake • Tea

INDIVIDUAL LAMB ROASTS

Time in Kitchen: ½ hour
Free Time: 2 hours
Servings: 4

1 garlic clove, quartered
4 lamb shanks, well trimmed
¼ cup all-purpose flour
salt
1 teaspoon paprika
2 tablespoons salad oil
¼ cup lemon juice
2 bay leaves
4 peppercorns
2 large yams, pared, quartered
1 9-ounce package frozen
   cut green beans, thawed enough
   to separate

About 2½ hours before dinner: Insert piece of garlic into each lamb shank. Combine flour, 2 teaspoons salt, paprika; use mixture to coat lamb shanks.

In skillet, in hot oil, brown shanks on all sides; place in 3-quart casserole. Add lemon juice to oil in skillet; stir to loosen browned bits; pour over shanks; add bay leaves and peppercorns. Preheat oven to 350°F.

Bake shanks, covered, 1 hour. Top with yams and thawed green beans; sprinkle with 1 teaspoon salt; cover; bake 1 hour longer or until meat is tender.

Serve with: Red-and-green-cabbage slaw • Warm rye bread • Fresh pineapple chunks with scoop of raspberry sherbet

LAMB STEW WITH CORNMEAL DUMPLINGS

Time in Kitchen: 45 minutes
Free Time: 1 hour
Servings: 6 to 8

2 pounds lamb stew meat, cut in 2-inch
   chunks
all-purpose flour
salad oil
1 onion, quartered
2 teaspoons salt
1 teaspoon basil
¼ teaspoon pepper
2 cups diced celery
4 whole carrots, diced
10 small white onions
Cornmeal Dumplings (below)

About 1 hour and 45 minutes before dinner: Coat lamb with ¼ cup flour. In large Dutch oven, in 2 tablespoons hot salad oil, brown lamb. Add 1 quart water, onion, salt, basil and pepper; cover; simmer over medium heat 1 hour. Then add celery, carrots and onions; over high heat, bring stew to boiling.

Meanwhile, prepare Cornmeal Dumplings (below). Drop dough by spoonfuls into *boiling* stew. Cook uncovered, over low heat 10 minutes; cover and cook 10 minutes more over low heat.

Cornmeal Dumplings: In medium bowl, with fork, lightly mix 1½ cups buttermilk-biscuit mix, ½ cup yellow cornmeal and ⅔ cup milk.

Serve with: Marinated cold green-and-yellow bean salad • Fresh fruit cup with mint sprig • Cookies

NEAR-EAST LAMB STEW

pictured on page 64

Time in Kitchen: 2 hours
Free Time: 1½ hours
Servings: 6

2 tablespoons all-purpose flour
seasoned salt
½ teaspoon seasoned pepper
4 pounds lamb stew meat
¼ cup salad oil
2 medium onions, chopped
2 garlic cloves, minced
½ teaspoon thyme leaves
4 medium tomatoes, cut into wedges
2 green peppers, cut into 1-inch squares
1 medium eggplant, cut into 1-inch chunks

About 2 hours before dinner: Combine flour with 1 tablespoon seasoned salt, seasoned pepper. Use to coat lamb pieces.

In Dutch oven, in hot oil, brown lamb; add onions and garlic and brown a few minutes more. Sprinkle with thyme; add 1 cup water. Simmer, covered, 1½ hours or until lamb is almost tender. Stir occasionally. If necessary, add a little more water.

Add tomatoes, green peppers and eggplant; sprinkle with 1½ teaspoons seasoned salt. Cook 15 minutes more or until vegetables are tender.

Serve with: Big green salad • Lemon meringue pie • Tea

YORKSHIRE HOT POT

Time in Kitchen: ½ hour
Free Time: 1 hour
Servings: 4

4 shoulder lamb chops
4 small whole onions
4 medium potatoes, halved
1 garlic clove, minced
1 9-ounce package frozen cut green beans
¼ teaspoon ground cloves
2 teaspoons salt
⅛ teaspoon pepper
1 10½-ounce can condensed cream-of-mushroom soup

About 1½ hours before dinner: Trim fat from chops. In Dutch oven, heat fat; brown chops on both sides. Tuck onions and potatoes around and under chops. Add garlic, beans, cloves, salt, pepper, undiluted soup and ½ soup-can water. Cover; cook slowly 1 hour or until all are fork-tender. Thicken gravy.

RIBLETS, ISLAND STYLE

Time in Kitchen: 40 minutes
Free Time: 1½ hours
Servings: 6 to 8

6 pounds lamb riblets
salt
1 13½-ounce can pineapple chunks
¼ cup honey
3 tablespoons vinegar
1 teaspoon Worcestershire
¼ teaspoon ginger
1 10-ounce package frozen peas, thawed

About 2 hours and 10 minutes before dinner: Preheat oven to 325°F. Place riblets on racks in 2 roasting pans; sprinkle with salt. Bake for 1½ hours.

In bowl, drain juice from pineapple (save pineapple); stir in honey, vinegar, 1 teaspoon salt, Worcestershire, ginger.

Remove riblets. Remove racks; discard fat. Return riblets to pans; pour on sauce; bake 40 minutes until tender; turn often. Add pineapple and peas last 10 minutes.

LAMB WITH LENTILS

Time in Kitchen: ½ hour
Free Time: 2 hours 15 minutes
Servings: 4

salad oil
3½ pounds lamb breast, in 2-rib pieces
3 large onions, sliced
2 garlic cloves, minced
1½ cups celery in ¾-inch pieces
1 tablespoon salt
¼ teaspoon pepper
¼ teaspoon oregano leaves
1 cup dried lentils
½ cup packaged precooked rice
3 large carrots, sliced ¼ inch thick

About 2 hours and 45 minutes before dinner: In Dutch oven, in a little oil, brown lamb well. Pour off drippings. Add 1 cup water, onions and next 5 ingredients. Cook, covered, 1 hour and 15 minutes.

Rinse lentils in cold water; add with 2 cups water, rice and carrots to lamb; cook, covered, 1 hour or until tender.

Serve with: Spinach-Orange salad • Sponge cake • Tea

LAMB STROGANOFF

Time in Kitchen: ½ hour
Free Time: 1 hour
Servings: 6

2 tablespoons salad oil
1 medium onion, chopped
1 tablespoon curry powder
2½ pounds boneless lamb shoulder, cubed
½ cup canned pineapple juice
4 teaspoons salt
¼ teaspoon dry mustard
1 bay leaf
1 tablespoon all-purpose flour
2 cups fresh pineapple chunks
1 cup sour cream

About 1½ hours before dinner: In large skillet, in hot oil, sauté onion and curry until onion is tender. Add lamb; brown well. Stir in pineapple juice, salt, mustard and bay leaf; cover; simmer 1 hour or until meat is fork-tender. Discard bay leaf.

In cup, combine flour with 2 tablespoons cold water; stir into liquid in skillet; cook, stirring constantly, until mixture thickens slightly. Reduce heat; add pineapple chunks and sour cream, stirring until well blended. (Do not boil sour cream.)

Serve with: Hot rice • Mixed green salad • Spice cake

TRADITIONAL CASSOULET

pictured on page 57

Do-Ahead Dish
Time in Kitchen: 1½ hours
Free Time: 2½ hours
Servings: 10

3 cups packaged dried pea or navy beans
2 teaspoons salt
½ pound salt pork, cut into 5 slices
1 garlic clove
4 parsley sprigs, 1 stalk celery, diced, 2 bay leaves, ½ teaspoon thyme leaves (tied in doubled cheesecloth bag)
2 tablespoons salad oil
2 pounds lean pork, cut into 1½-inch chunks
1 pound lean lamb, cut in 1½-inch chunks
1 cup white wine or canned chicken broth
1 8-ounce can tomato sauce
5 large carrots, halved crosswise
2 medium onions
1 cup sliced celery
4 whole cloves
1 Kielbasa sausage, cut in 1-inch slices
½ cup chopped green onions

Early in day: In large kettle, boil beans in 2 quarts water and salt 2 minutes. Remove from heat; let stand 1 hour; add salt pork, garlic, bag of seasonings; simmer, covered, 40 minutes; skim if needed.

Meanwhile, in large skillet, in hot oil, sauté lean pork and lamb, a few chunks at a time, until golden. Add to beans with wine, next 6 ingredients and all but 1 tablespoon green onions. Simmer, covered, 40 minutes. Discard bag. Transfer all to 4- to 6-quart casserole; refrigerate, covered.

About 2½ hours before dinner: Preheat oven to 350°F. Bake cassoulet 2½ hours. Garnish with rest of green onions.

MEAT-AND-VEGETABLE CASSEROLE

Time in Kitchen: ½ hour
Free Time: 2 hours
Servings: 4

¼ cup salad oil
1 pound onions, thinly sliced
1 pound boneless pork shoulder, cubed
4 or 5 tomatoes, sliced ½-inch thick
salt
pepper
1 cup cut-up green beans
1 carrot, sliced
2 cups diced green peppers
2 cups pared, cubed eggplant
½ cup regular white rice

About 2½ hours before dinner: In skillet, in oil, sauté onions until tender; remove onions from skillet; in same oil, sauté pork until browned.

Preheat oven to 375°F. Lightly grease 12″ by 8″ baking dish; on bottom, arrange half of onions, then layer of sliced tomatoes; sprinkle with 1 teaspoon salt, dash pepper; cover with half of beans, carrots, green peppers and eggplant. Top with rice, then pork; sprinkle with 1 teaspoon salt, dash of pepper; top with rest of onions, beans, carrots, green peppers, eggplant and tomatoes. Sprinkle with ½ teaspoon salt and dash of pepper.

Over all, pour ¾ cup water and any oil left in skillet; cover; bake 2 hours, removing cover for last ½ hour.

SKILLET PORK-CHOP DINNER

Time in Kitchen: 20 minutes
Free Time: 1 hour
Servings: 4

4 loin pork chops
salt
pepper
1 tablespoon salad oil
1 garlic clove, split
2 tablespoons granulated sugar
2 tablespoons cornstarch
½ teaspoon rosemary
½ teaspoon salt
2 to 3 tablespoons lemon juice
¼ cup orange juice
4 ¼-inch-thick orange slices
1 10-ounce package frozen peas, thawed
1 16-ounce can small whole potatoes, drained

About 1 hour and 20 minutes before dinner: Sprinkle pork chops with salt and pepper. In skillet, in hot oil, add garlic; brown chops on both sides. Set chops aside; discard garlic.

To drippings in skillet, add sugar, cornstarch, rosemary and ½ teaspoon salt. Gradually stir in 1¼ cups hot water; cook, stirring, until thick and glossy. Stir in lemon juice and orange juice. Set 1 orange slice on each pork chop; arrange in sauce. Cover; cook over low heat ½ hour.

Add peas and drained potatoes; cook, covered, basting occasionally with sauce, 20 minutes. Uncover and cook 10 minutes longer.

Serve with: Cucumber and stuffed celery salad • Bread sticks • Strawberry ripple ice cream

PORK CHOPS-AND-MACARONI MADRAS

Time in Kitchen: ½ hour
Free Time: ½ hour
Servings: 6

shortening
6 shoulder pork chops, ½-inch thick
¼ cup butter or margarine
2 small onions, minced
¼ cup all-purpose flour
3 teaspoons curry powder
2 teaspoons salt
2 small apples, chopped, unpared
2 tablespoons orange marmalade
1 tablespoon raisins
1 teaspoon granulated sugar
2 tablespoons lemon juice
1 cup elbow macaroni

1. *About 1 hour before dinner:* In large skillet, in small amount of shortening, brown chops well on both sides; remove. Pour off fat. In same skillet, melt butter. Stir in onions; sauté until golden, about 5 minutes. Stir in flour, curry powder and salt until well blended. Add apples, marmalade, raisins, sugar, lemon juice, 2 cups water; stir until thickened.
2. Add chops; simmer, covered, 45 minutes, or until chops are tender.
3. Last 15 minutes cook macaroni as label directs; drain.
4. Remove chops from skillet. To sauce, add cooked macaroni; toss; top with chops.

Serve with: Lettuce and escarole with French dressing • Applesauce • Tea

For more Family Dinners see page 65

Traditional Cassoulet, page 55

Swiss Steak, page 42

Left to right: Beef-and-Onion Stew, page
43; Chili Beans and Meatballs, page 49;
Macaroni-Tuna Loaf, page 71
Upper left: Accompaniments—Chopped
Green Pepper, Sliced Red Onion Rings,
Shredded Lettuce, Shredded Cheese

Beef-and-Vegetable Casserole, page 42
Bean-and-Bacon Bake, page 68
Philippine Pork-Shrimp Mold, page 67

Near-East Lamb Stew, page 53

PORK-CHOP CASSEROLE

Time in Kitchen: 15 minutes
Free Time: 1 hour 15 minutes
Servings: 6

6 shoulder pork chops, ½-inch thick
1 teaspoon salt
¾ teaspoon thyme leaves
¼ teaspoon pepper
3 tablespoons shortening
1 cup regular white rice
1 bay leaf, crushed
1 9-ounce package frozen cut green beans
1 10½-ounce can condensed onion soup

About 1½ hours before dinner: Preheat oven to 350°F. Sprinkle both sides of chops with salt, thyme and pepper.

In large skillet, in hot shortening, brown chops; set aside. Sprinkle rice in greased 13″ by 9″ baking dish. Add chops, bay leaf, beans. Pour on undiluted soup and 1½ soup-cans water. Cover; bake 1 hour and 15 minutes or until meat is tender.

Serve with: Cabbage-pepper slaw • Chilled pears • Tea

PORK-CHOP-AND-NOODLE TREASURE

Do-Ahead Dish
Time in Kitchen: 45 minutes
Free Time: 1½ hours
Servings: 6

¼ cup all-purpose flour
1½ teaspoons seasoned salt
¼ teaspoon seasoned pepper
6 loin pork chops, ¾-inch thick
½ cup butter or margarine
¼ cup chopped onion
1 13-ounce can undiluted evaporated milk
1 cup shredded Cheddar cheese
¼ cup chopped pimientos
1 8-ounce package medium noodles
1 16-ounce can whole baby carrots, drained

1. *Day before or early in day:* Combine flour, seasoned salt and seasoned pepper; lightly coat both sides of chops; reserve remaining flour.
2. In large skillet, in ¼ cup of the butter, brown pork chops with onion very well on both sides. Remove chops from skillet; set aside.
3. In same skillet, melt ¼ cup butter. Stir in reserved flour, then slowly add evaporated milk, stirring constantly. Cook over medium heat about 15 minutes or until sauce thickens, stirring constantly. Add cheese and pimientos; remove sauce from heat.
4. Meanwhile, cook noodles as label directs; combine with sauce. Place in 13″ by 9″ buttered baking dish. Place browned chops on top. Cover; refrigerate.
5. *About 1 hour and 45 minutes before dinner:* Preheat oven to 375°F. Bake casserole, covered, 1 hour and 15 minutes. Uncover; add carrots; bake 15 minutes longer or until carrots are hot.

HUNTERS' STEW

Do-Ahead Dish
Time in Kitchen: 20 minutes
Free Time: 2½ hours
Servings: 8

2 pounds shredded cabbage
1 27-ounce can sauerkraut
2 pounds shoulder pork chops
1 bay leaf
4 dried mushrooms (optional)
2 teaspoons salt
¼ teaspoon pepper
1 pound Kielbasa sausage
1 8-ounce can tomato sauce

Day before or early in day: In large Dutch oven, place cabbage, sauerkraut, chops, bay leaf, 2 cups water, mushrooms; sprinkle with salt, pepper; cook, covered, about 1½ hours, or until chops are almost tender. Cool; remove bones from chops; cut into bite-size pieces; refrigerate all.

About 1 hour before dinner: Peel, then slice Kielbasa about ¼-inch thick; add to cabbage with chops and tomato sauce. Cook, covered, 1 hour or until pork is tender.

Serve with: Boiled potatoes • Spinach salad • Butterscotch pudding

EASY PORK STEW

pictured on page 81

Time in Kitchen: 15 minutes
Free Time: 1 hour 45 minutes
Servings: 8

¼ cup all-purpose flour
salt
¼ teaspoon pepper
¼ teaspoon ground ginger
3 pounds pork stew meat, cut in 1½-inch pieces
¼ cup salad oil
½ cup cooking sherry
½ teaspoon granulated sugar
1¼ pounds tiny white onions
2 10-ounce packages frozen lima beans, thawed
1½ pounds yellow straight-neck squash, cut in 1½-inch chunks

About 2 hours before dinner: On waxed paper, mix flour, 1 tablespoon salt, pepper and ginger; coat pork with mixture.

Preheat oven to 350°F. In Dutch oven over medium heat, in hot oil, brown pork well, pushing pieces aside as they brown. Spoon off any excess fat. Add ¾ cup water, cooking sherry, sugar and onions. Bring to boiling, stirring to loosen brown bits in pan. Place in oven. Bake, covered, 1 hour, stirring occasionally.

Add lima beans, squash and 2 teaspoons salt. Bake 45 minutes or until squash is tender-crisp, stirring occasionally. Skim any excess fat from surface.

Serve with: Green salad • Baked apples with cream • Milk

PHILIPPINE PORK-SHRIMP MOLD

pictured on page 63

Do-Ahead Dish
Time in Kitchen: ½ hour
Free Time: ½ hour
Servings: 4

salad oil
1 cup chopped onions
1 garlic clove, minced
1 pound boned pork shoulder, cut into
   ½-inch pieces
½ pound raw shrimp, shelled,
   deveined, split in half
1 to 1½ teaspoons salt
soy sauce
¼ teaspoon pepper
3 cups hot cooked rice
½ cup cooked peas (optional)
2 pimientos, cut into strips
1 hard-cooked egg, sliced
2 eggs, well beaten

Early in day: In large skillet, in 3 tablespoons hot oil, lightly brown onions, garlic, pork; add ¼ cup water; cook, covered, 20 minutes; add shrimp; cook 5 minutes. Add salt, 1 teaspoon soy sauce, pepper, rice and peas. Refrigerate.

About 45 minutes before dinner: Preheat oven to 350°F. Generously grease 1½-quart casserole. On bottom, arrange pimientos and sliced egg.

Into rice mixture, with fork, toss beaten eggs; turn into casserole; cover. Set casserole in shallow pan, with about 1 inch hot water; bake ½ hour. Remove from water; let stand 5 minutes; remove cover. Loosen sides of mixture carefully with broad spatula, then invert a serving dish on top of casserole, invert both and lift off casserole. Pass soy sauce.

BAKED PORK CHOPS AND GREEN BEANS

Time in Kitchen: ½ hour
Free Time: 45 minutes
Servings: 6

6 pork chops, cut ¾-inch thick
salt and pepper
2 tablespoons salad oil
1 cup chicken broth
1 cup regular white rice
2 9-ounce packages frozen cut green
   beans, partially thawed
1 10½-ounce can condensed cream-
   of-mushroom soup
½ teaspoon dill seed

About 1 hour and 15 minutes before dinner: Preheat oven to 350°F. Sprinkle pork chops with ½ teaspoon salt and ⅛ teaspoon pepper. In large ovenproof skillet, in oil, brown chops. Remove from pan; pour off drippings.

In same skillet, bring broth and 1 teaspoon salt to boiling. Remove from heat; stir in rice; add green beans in a layer, then undiluted soup and dill seed; top with pork chops. Cover and bake 45 minutes or until chops are fork-tender.

Serve with: Canned fruits-for-salad in lettuce cups • Brownies (from mix) • Walnut ice cream • Coffee

HAM-AND-NOODLE BAKE

Time in Kitchen: 15 minutes
Free Time: 1 hour 15 minutes
Servings: 10

1 16-ounce package medium noodles
butter or margarine
½ teaspoon salt
¼ teaspoon pepper
1½ pounds cooked ham, cut into ½-inch cubes
6 eggs, slightly beaten
2 cups milk

About 1½ hours before dinner: Preheat oven to 375°F. Cook noodles as label directs; drain and quickly toss with ¼ cup butter until butter is melted. Stir in salt, pepper and ham. Pour mixture into a greased 13″ by 9″ baking dish.

In medium bowl, mix eggs and milk and pour over noodles. Dot with 2 tablespoons butter. Bake 1 hour and 15 minutes or until light brown. Remove from oven; let stand 10 minutes.

Serve with: Green salad with tarragon dressing • Lime sherbet • Tea

BEAN-AND-BACON BAKE

pictured on pages 62–63

Do-Ahead Dish
Time in Kitchen: 15 minutes
Free Time: 50 minutes
Servings: 8

3 16-ounce cans pork-and-beans in tomato sauce, lightly drained
¼ cup instant minced onion
1 teaspoon chili powder
½ cup catchup
1 tablespoon horseradish
1 tablespoon prepared mustard
2 teaspoons Worcestershire
4 unpeeled orange slices, ¼-inch thick
8 Canadian bacon slices, ¼-inch thick
¼ cup packed light brown sugar
melted butter or margarine

Early in day: In large bowl, combine pork-and-beans with next 6 ingredients; turn into 2½-quart shallow casserole.

On top of beans, in ring, arrange orange and Canadian bacon slices. Cover; chill.

About 1 hour before dinner: Preheat oven to 350°F. Sprinkle casserole with brown sugar; bake 50 minutes or until hot; brush orange slices lightly with melted butter.

SCALLOPED HAM AND POTATOES

Time in kitchen: 15 minutes
Free Time: 1 hour 10 minutes
Servings: 4

6 slices cooked ham
1 small onion, minced
4 to 6 potatoes pared, thinly sliced
3 tablespoons all-purpose flour
½ teaspoon salt
¼ teaspoon pepper
1 cup shredded process sharp Cheddar cheese
1 cup milk
2 tablespoons butter or margarine
¼ cup catchup

About 1 hour and 25 minutes before dinner: Preheat oven to 350°F. In greased 2-quart casserole, arrange ham; top with onion, half of potatoes; sprinkle with half of flour, salt, pepper, cheese; repeat.

Meanwhile, heat milk with butter; pour over all. Bake, covered, 40 minutes. Uncover; dot with catchup. Bake ½ hour or until potatoes are tender. (Milk will curdle.)

Serve with: Molded lime pear salad • Chocolate cake • Tea

SAVORY SMOKED BUTT WITH VEGETABLES

Time in Kitchen: 40 minutes
Servings: 6

1 tablespoon salad oil
2½-pound smoked pork butt, cut into ¾-inch-thick slices
1 garlic clove
⅔ cup orange juice
1 tablespoon dry mustard
¼ cup packed brown sugar
1 large yellow turnip, cut into long thin wedges
6 medium white onions
6 small whole new potatoes
½ to 1 teaspoon salt
chopped parsley for garnish

About 40 minutes before dinner: In pressure cooker, in hot oil, brown meat with garlic. Combine orange juice with dry mustard and brown sugar; add to meat. Bring to 15 pounds pressure, as manufacturer directs. Cook 10 minutes. Remove from heat and reduce pressure quickly as manufacturer directs before uncovering.

On top of meat, arrange turnip,

onions and potatoes in layers, sprinkling each layer with salt. Bring to 15 pounds pressure; cook 8 minutes. Reduce pressure, following above directions. To serve, spoon some of broth over meat and sprinkle all with parsley.

Serve with: Big green salad • Chilled cherries • Cookies

SEAFOOD STUFFED PEPPERS

Time in Kitchen: ½ hour
Free Time: ½ hour
Servings: 6

6 small green peppers
½ cup packaged dried bread crumbs
¼ cup salad oil
1 cup shredded process Cheddar cheese
1 6½- or 7-ounce can tuna, drained
2 tablespoons mayonnaise
2 tablespoons India relish
salt
¼ teaspoon seasoned pepper
12 cooked, shelled, deveined shrimp
1 teaspoon butter
1 8-ounce can tomato sauce
1 teaspoon Worcestershire
¼ teaspoon each: oregano leaves, dill seed, celery seed and thyme leaves

About 1 hour before dinner: Cut tops from peppers; remove seeds; cook, covered, in boiling water 5 minutes; drain.

In small bowl, mix crumbs, salad oil, cheese. In another bowl, combine tuna, mayonnaise, relish, ¼ teaspoon salt, seasoned pepper. Arrange peppers in 2- or 2½-quart oval or oblong baking dish; in each pepper, layer crumb and tuna mixtures, ending with crumbs. Top each with 2 shrimp; dot with butter.

Preheat oven to 350°F.

Combine tomato sauce with Worcestershire, ¼ teaspoon salt, oregano, dill seed, celery seed and thyme. Pour ½ cup of this sauce in baking dish with peppers. Bake ½ hour. Last 10 minutes of baking, spoon rest of tomato sauce over peppers.

Serve with: Parslied carrots • Mocha cake • Coffee

SHRIMP AND MACARONI

Time in Kitchen: 35 minutes
Free Time: 55 minutes
Servings: 4

1 10½-ounce can condensed cream-of-chicken soup
1 cup milk
¼ cup sherry
2 tablespoons chopped parsley
1½ teaspoons curry powder
½ teaspoon salt
1 pound frozen raw, shelled, deveined shrimp
2 cups cooked shell macaroni, page 10
1 10-ounce package frozen peas, partially thawed

About 1½ hours before dinner: Preheat oven to 375°F.

In large saucepan, over medium heat, heat undiluted soup, milk, sherry, parsley, curry powder and salt just to boiling, stirring occasionally.

In greased, 2-quart shallow casserole, combine soup mixture, shrimp, macaroni and peas. Bake 55 minutes or until shrimp is pink and tender.

Serve with: Sliced tomatoes • Apple pie with Cheddar cheese • Coffee • Milk

CODFISH STEW
pictured on page 82

Time in Kitchen: 15 minutes
Free Time: ½ hour
Servings: 4

3 bacon slices, cut up
1 onion, thinly sliced
1 16-ounce can tomatoes
1 16-ounce can potatoes, drained, halved
¼ cup catchup
1 teaspoon Worcestershire
¼ teaspoon seasoned pepper
⅛ teaspoon thyme leaves
1 16-ounce package frozen cod fillets, thawed, cut into chunks

About 45 minutes before dinner: In medium saucepan, cook bacon until just limp; add onion and cook until browned.

Stir in tomatoes, potatoes, catchup, Worcestershire, seasoned pepper and thyme. Simmer 20 minutes. Add thawed cod fillets; cook 10 minutes more.

Serve with: Escarole, chicory, radish-rose salad • Poundcake • Peaches

---

SALMON SCALLOP DIVAN

Time in Kitchen: 20 minutes
Free Time: 25 minutes
Servings: 4

1 10-ounce package frozen
  broccoli spears, thawed enough
  to separate
3 tablespoons butter or margarine
3 tablespoons all-purpose flour
½ teaspoon salt
⅛ teaspoon pepper
2 cups milk
1 16-ounce can tomatoes, drained
½ cup shredded process Cheddar
  cheese
1½ cups day-old bread crumbs
1 16-ounce can salmon, broken into
  chunks
2 hard-cooked eggs, sliced lengthwise

About 45 minutes before dinner: Preheat oven to 375°F. Place broccoli in 2-
quart casserole; cover; bake about 10
minutes.

Meanwhile, in saucepan, melt butter;
blend in flour, salt and pepper; blend in
milk. Cook, stirring, until smooth and
thickened; remove from heat. Carefully
fold in tomatoes, cheese and bread
crumbs.

Remove casserole from oven; arrange salmon over broccoli; pour on
tomato mixture. Arrange egg slices on
top; press gently into sauce. Bake 25
minutes.

Serve with: Boston lettuce with garlic
dressing • Bread sticks • Angel-food
cake

MACARONI-TUNA LOAF
pictured on page 61

Do-Ahead Dish
Time in Kitchen: 40 minutes
Free Time: 1 hour 55 minutes
Servings: 6 to 8

½ 8-ounce package elbow macaroni
butter or margarine
½ cup diced celery
¼ cup minced onion
¼ cup all-purpose flour
1⅔ cups milk
1 teaspoon salt
1 teaspoon Worcestershire
⅛ teaspoon pepper
1 13-ounce can tuna, drained, flaked
2 tablespoons diced pimiento
3 eggs, slightly beaten
onion rings for garnish

1. *Day before or early in day:* Cook
macaroni as label directs; drain; toss
with 1 tablespoon butter; set aside.
2. Meanwhile, in large skillet over medium heat, in ¼ cup hot butter, cook
celery and onion until tender, about 5
minutes. Stir in flour to make a smooth
paste. Gradually add milk, salt, Worcestershire and pepper, stirring constantly,
until mixture thickens and begins to
boil; remove from heat.
3. Stir in macaroni, tuna and pimiento;
add eggs, stirring until well blended.
Pour mixture into well-greased 9″ by 5″
loaf pan. Cover; refrigerate.
4. *About 2 hours before dinner:* Preheat oven to 350°F. Place loaf pan in
shallow baking pan of hot water and
bake 1 hour and 45 minutes. Cool 10
minutes; gently loosen sides and bottom with pancake turner and carefully
invert onto platter. Garnish with onion.

Serve with: Baked tomatoes with
cheese • Coffee ice cream

SAVORY TUNA CASSEROLE

pictured on page 83

Do-Ahead Dish*
Time in Kitchen: 15 minutes
Free Time: ½ hour
Servings: 6

3 6½- or 7-ounce cans tuna, drained
2 10¾-ounce cans condensed Cheddar-cheese soup
1 8¼-ounce can sliced carrots, drained
1 8-ounce can mushroom stems and pieces, drained
¼ cup sliced pimiento-stuffed olives
2 tablespoons chopped parsley
1 teaspoon grated lemon peel
⅛ teaspoon hot pepper sauce
pastry for one 9-inch pie
2 tablespoons butter or margarine, melted

About 45 minutes before dinner: In large bowl, combine tuna, undiluted soup and next 6 ingredients. Spoon into six 10-ounce individual baking dishes or one 8″ by 8″ baking dish. Preheat oven to 450°F.

On lightly floured surface, with stockinette-covered rolling pin, roll pastry into large circle ⅛ inch thick. With cookie or canape cutters, cut 6 fish or other designs to fit over individual casseroles or baking dish; brush with melted butter. Bake ½ hour or until crust is golden and filling is hot and bubbly.

To Freeze: Prepare recipe, using freezerproof-and-ovenproof baking dish but do not bake; wrap dish and freeze. To serve, preheat oven to 450°F.; uncover dish and bake 45 minutes, or until hot and bubbly.

Serve with: Tomato aspic • Rolls • Fresh fruit

CHICKEN POT ROAST

Time in Kitchen: 45 minutes
Free Time: 1½ hours
Servings: 6

6 slices day-old bread, cubed
¼ cup finely diced celery
¼ cup minced onion
½ teaspoon salt
⅛ teaspoon pepper
½ teaspoon poultry seasoning
¼ cup butter or margarine
1 3½- to 4-pound roasting chicken
2 teaspoons salt
1 teaspoon monosodium glutamate
3 tablespoons butter or margarine
8 small new potatoes, scrubbed
8 small whole white onions
1 10-ounce package frozen mixed vegetables, thawed enough to separate
1 teaspoon salt

About 2 hours 15 minutes before dinner: In large bowl, combine bread cubes, celery, onion, ½ teaspoon salt, pepper, poultry seasoning, ¼ cup butter, 2 tablespoons hot water; stuff body cavity of chicken. Combine 2 teaspoons salt, monosodium glutamate; rub into skin of chicken.

In Dutch oven, in 3 tablespoons hot butter, brown chicken on all sides 20 to 25 minutes. Add ¼ cup water; simmer, covered, 1 hour or until nearly tender, adding more water if necessary.

Add potatoes, onions, mixed vegetables, ¾ cup water, 1 teaspoon salt; cook, covered, ½ hour, or until vegetables are tender. Remove chicken to heated platter; arrange vegetables around chicken.

Serve with: Grapefruit-avocado salad • Chocolate pie

CHICKEN FRICASSEE

Time in Kitchen: ½ hour
Free Time: 1½ hours
Servings: 6

1 4½-pound stewing chicken, cut up
½ cup all-purpose flour
1 teaspoon salt
⅛ teaspoon pepper
salad oil
¼ teaspoon thyme leaves or rosemary

About 2 hours before dinner: Coat chicken pieces, giblets and neck with combined flour, salt and pepper. In Dutch oven, in thin layer of oil, brown chicken slowly, turning with tongs. Remove chicken; drain off fat.

Return chicken to Dutch oven. Add 1 cup water and thyme. Simmer, covered, about 1½ hours, or until fork-tender. Season to taste.

CHICKEN CASSEROLE

pictured on page 83

Do-Ahead Dish*
Time in Kitchen: 25 minutes
Free Time: ½ hour
Servings: 6

3 cups cooked chicken, in chunks
1 10½-ounce can condensed cream-of-chicken soup
1 10-ounce package frozen peas and carrots
½ cup diced celery
¼ cup diced green pepper
¼ cup chopped pimientos
¼ cup chopped onion
1 4-ounce can mushrooms, drained
2 hard-cooked eggs, sliced

About 55 minutes before dinner: Preheat oven to 350°F. In greased 2-quart casserole, thoroughly mix chicken, undiluted soup and next 6 ingredients. Arrange overlapping egg slices on top. Bake, covered, ½ hour or until hot.

*To Freeze: Prepare recipe using a covered, freezerproof-and-ovenproof casserole but omit egg slices and do not bake. Freeze up to 1 month. To serve, thaw overnight in refrigerator. Preheat oven to 350°F. and add egg slices. Bake covered 1 hour or until hot.

Serve with: Fruit salad • Butterscotch pudding • Tea

ROSE'S CHICKEN

Time in Kitchen: ½ hour
Free Time: 45 minutes
Servings: 4

½ cup olive or salad oil
1 2½-pound broiler-fryer, cut up
1 teaspoon salt
dash pepper
1 tablespoon oregano leaves
1 teaspoon thyme leaves
2 chicken-bouillon cubes
4 medium onions, thinly sliced
4 medium potatoes

About 1 hour and 15 minutes before dinner: In Dutch oven, in hot oil, brown chicken on all sides. Sprinkle with salt, pepper, oregano, thyme. Add bouillon cubes, ½ cup water, onions, potatoes.

Simmer, covered, 45 minutes, or until chicken and vegetables are fork-tender.

Serve on heated platter with sauce over all. Makes 4 servings.

Serve with: Spinach-bacon salad • Hot biscuits • Toasted poundcake à la mode

CHICKEN-MACARONI STEW

pictured on page 86

Time in Kitchen: ½ hour
Free Time: 45 minutes
Servings: 6

¼ cup all-purpose flour
2 teaspoons paprika
salt
½ teaspoon pepper
1 3-pound broiler-fryer, cut up
¼ cup salad oil
2 medium onions, thickly sliced
1 28-ounce can tomatoes
¼ bunch parsley
2 teaspoons poultry seasoning
2 garlic cloves
¼ teaspoon hot pepper sauce
2 cups elbow macaroni
1 10-ounce package frozen peas,
    partially thawed

About 1 hour and 15 minutes before dinner: On waxed paper, combine flour, paprika, 2 teaspoons salt, and pepper; coat chicken with flour mixture. In Dutch oven, in hot oil, brown chicken until golden; remove chicken. Add onions to Dutch oven and cook until tender-crisp, stirring occasionally.

Return chicken to Dutch oven with tomatoes, parsley (tied in a bunch), 2 teaspoons salt, poultry seasoning, garlic, hot pepper sauce and 1 cup water. Cook over low heat, covered, about 45 minutes, until chicken is tender. Remove from heat; discard parsley and garlic; skim off fat. Add macaroni; cover and cook over medium heat 10 minutes, stirring occasionally. Add peas; cover and cook over low heat 10 minutes or until tender.

Serve with: Orange Gelatin Mold, page 200 • Hot rolls

CHICKEN WITH PEAS

Time in Kitchen: 25 minutes
Free Time: ½ hour
Servings: 4

1 2½-pound broiler-fryer, quartered
salt
ground thyme
marjoram leaves
pepper
3 tablespoons salad oil
½ head lettuce, sliced
1 bay leaf
3 onions, sliced
5 carrots, thinly sliced
1 10-ounce package frozen peas
4 whole cloves

About 55 minutes before dinner: Coat chicken with 1 teaspoon salt, ⅛ teaspoon each thyme, marjoram, pepper. In Dutch oven, in oil, sauté until golden.

Then add lettuce, bay leaf, onions, carrots, peas, 2 teaspoons salt, ⅛ teaspoon each thyme, marjoram, pepper, then cloves. Cover; simmer ½ hour.

CHICKEN AL POMIDÒRO

Time in Kitchen: ½ hour
Free Time: ½ hour
Servings: 6

1 teaspoon paprika
salt and pepper
1 3-pound broiler-fryer, cut up
3 tablespoons butter or margarine
1 pint Do-Ahead Tomato Sauce,
    thawed, page 9
3 cups sliced carrots
1 10-ounce package frozen peas
1 8-ounce package medium noodles
¼ cup grated Parmesan cheese

About 1 hour before dinner: Combine paprika, 1 teaspoon salt and ¼ teaspoon pepper; use to coat chicken. In medium skillet, in hot butter, fry chicken until golden brown. Add tomato sauce; simmer, covered, 30 minutes, basting occasionally. Add carrots, peas and 1 teaspoon salt; simmer, covered 20 minutes or until carrots and chicken are fork-tender.

Meanwhile, cook noodles as label directs; drain; toss with cheese. Arrange noodles around chicken on platter; top with vegetables and sauce.

Serve with: Green salad • Fruit-topped custard • Tea

SPANISH CHICKEN

Time in Kitchen: ½ hour
Free Time: 1 hour
Servings: 4

6 tablespoons all-purpose flour
1¼ teaspoons salt
½ teaspoon pepper
2 bacon slices, diced
2 tablespoons butter or margarine
1 2½-pound broiler-fryer, cut up
2 tomatoes, peeled, sliced (2 cups)
2 onions, sliced
2 green peppers, cut in rings
1 chicken-bouillon cube

About 1½ hours before dinner: Combine 4 tablespoons flour, salt, pepper. Coat chicken.

In large skillet, sauté bacon until crisp; drain on paper towels. Add butter to drippings; brown chicken well. Place chicken and bacon in 2½-quart baking dish. Top with tomatoes, onions, green peppers. Preheat oven to 350°F.

Add remaining flour to fat in skillet; stir until smooth; gradually add 1⅓ cups hot water and bouillon cube; bring to boiling, stirring; pour over chicken. Cover, bake 1 hour or until chicken is fork-tender.

Serve with: Lettuce wedges with garlic dressing • Chocolate bread pudding with whipped cream or topping

---

HOT CHICKEN-SALAD PIE

Time in Kitchen: 20 minutes
Free Time: 40 minutes
Servings: 6

1 9-inch unbaked pie shell
1 2½-pound broiler-fryer, simmered (page 8), diced
1 teaspoon monosodium glutamate
1 teaspoon salt
1½ cups chopped celery
1½ cups fine fresh bread cubes
1 cup chopped walnuts or pecans
¾ cup mayonnaise
2 tablespoons lemon juice
1 teaspoon dry mustard
1 teaspoon Worcestershire
¼ teaspoon hot pepper sauce
½ cup shredded Cheddar cheese

About 1 hour before dinner: Bake pie shell as piecrust-mix label or your recipe directs, then reduce heat to 350°F. Meanwhile, toss chicken with monosodium glutamate, salt, celery, bread cubes and nuts.

Blend mayonnaise, lemon juice, mustard, Worcestershire, hot pepper sauce; toss with chicken; spoon into pie shell; sprinkle with cheese. Bake pie 40 to 45 minutes.

CHICKEN-IN-A-SKILLET

Time in Kitchen: 20 minutes
Free Time: 40 minutes
Servings: 4

¼ cup butter or margarine
4 chicken legs
2 small onions, chopped
1 cup chopped celery stalks
½ cup chopped celery leaves
2 4-ounce cans button mushrooms
½ teaspoon sage leaves
½ teaspoon thyme leaves
½ teaspoon marjoram leaves
1 teaspoon seasoned salt
1 cup regular white rice
2 10¾-ounce cans condensed
　vegetable soup

About 1 hour before dinner: In medium skillet, in hot butter, brown chicken. Add onion, celery stalks, leaves, mushrooms. Sauté a few minutes; stir in herbs, seasoned salt and 3 cups water; simmer, covered, 20 minutes. Stir in rice, undiluted soup; simmer, covered, 20 minutes or until tender.

BAKED CHICKEN BREASTS

Time in Kitchen: 45 minutes
Free Time: 1 hour
Servings: 6

6 celery stalks, cut in chunks
6 large carrots, cut in chunks
12 small white onions, peeled
4 whole chicken breasts, halved,
　skinned
¼ cup chopped parsley
2 10½-ounce cans condensed cream-
　of-mushroom soup
paprika

About 1 hour and 45 minutes before dinner: Preheat oven to 350°F. In covered, medium saucepan, in 1 cup boiling salted water, cook celery, carrots and onions 15 minutes; drain.

　Place chicken in 13" by 9" baking dish, sprinkle with parsley. Arrange vegetables around chicken.

　In small bowl, stir undiluted soup until smooth; pour over chicken and vegetables. Sprinkle with paprika. Cover; bake 1 hour or until fork-tender.

SAUCY FRANK DINNER
pictured on page 88

Time in Kitchen: 20 minutes
Servings: 8

2 pounds frankfurters
2 tablespoons butter or margarine
1 cup chopped onions
2 10¾-ounce cans condensed tomato
　soup
2 8-ounce cans tomato sauce
2 tablespoons Worcestershire
2 teaspoons granulated sugar
few dashes hot pepper sauce
1 16-ounce package bow-tie noodles
chopped parsley

About 20 minutes before dinner: Cut frankfurters lengthwise into quarters.

　In large saucepan, in butter, sauté onions until tender; stir in undiluted tomato soup, tomato sauce, 1 cup water, Worcestershire, sugar, pepper sauce. Add franks; simmer 10 minutes, stirring. Meanwhile, cook noodles as label directs.

　Serve franks surrounded with noodles; sprinkle with parsley.

Serve with: Romaine-cucumber salad
• Peach crisp • Tea

TANGY MEAT PATTIES AND FRANKS

pictured on page 87

Time in Kitchen: ½ hour
Free Time: ½ hour
Servings: 10

1 cup fresh bread crumbs
½ cup milk
2 eggs
2 pounds beef chuck, ground
2 teaspoons salt
1 teaspoon instant minced onion
¼ teaspoon pepper
2 tablespoons shortening
1 cup chili sauce
¾ cup grape jelly
1 tablespoon lemon juice
1 teaspoon Worcestershire
½ teaspoon dry mustard
½ pound frankfurters, cut diagonally

About 1 hour before dinner: In large bowl, soak crumbs in milk 2 or 3 minutes. Stir in eggs. Add chuck, salt, onion and pepper; shape into 16 to 18 small patties.

In large skillet, over high heat, in hot shortening, brown patties on both sides, half at a time; drain on paper towels. Pour off excess fat from skillet. Stir in chili sauce, grape jelly, lemon juice, Worcestershire, mustard and ¼ cup water. Add meat patties.

Simmer, covered, ½ hour, stirring occasionally. Add franks; cook 5 minutes or until heated.

Serve with: Broiled grapefruit halves • Bean and celery salad • Baked apples with cream • Tea

MACARONI-STUFFED GREEN PEPPERS

Time in Kitchen: 20 minutes
Free Time: 25 minutes
Servings: 6

1 8-ounce package elbow macaroni
6 medium green peppers
salt
1 3-ounce package cream cheese, softened
1 cup sour cream
¼ cup milk
2 tablespoons minced onion
½ teaspoon dry mustard
½ pound frankfurters, sliced
¼ cup shredded Cheddar cheese

About 45 minutes before dinner: Cook macaroni as label directs; drain. Cut green peppers in halves lengthwise; remove seeds. In large saucepan, cook peppers in boiling salted water 5 minutes; drain on paper towels. Preheat oven to 350°F.

In large bowl, blend cream cheese with sour cream and milk until smooth; stir in onion, ½ teaspoon salt and mustard; stir in frankfurters and macaroni. Spoon macaroni mixture into pepper halves and arrange in large, shallow baking dish.

Cover and bake 25 minutes; uncover; sprinkle with cheese; bake a few minutes to melt cheese.

Serve with: Tomato-lettuce salad • Mint-chip ice cream

BAVARIAN KRAUT CASEROLE

pictured on page 84

Time in Kitchen: ½ hour
Free Time: 2½ hours
Servings: 8

2 27-ounce cans sauerkraut
1 16-ounce can white potatoes, drained
1 carrot, sliced
2 pounds smoked boneless shoulder pork butt
¼ pound bacon in 1 piece
3 bay leaves
¼ teaspoon peppercorns
8 juniper berries (optional)
2 tablespoons instant minced onion
1 10½-ounce can condensed consommé
¾ to 1 cup white wine
6 frankfurters or 4 knackwurst

1. *About 3 hours before dinner:* Preheat oven to 400°F. Drain and rinse sauerkraut. Place half of sauerkraut in shallow 4-quart casserole. Top with half the potatoes, then half the carrot slices.
2. Cut butt into ¾-inch crosswise slices; arrange half of them on top of carrots; cover with rest of sauerkraut.
3. Next, arrange rest of butt slices, then potatoes and carrot slices on top.
4. Cut bacon into ¼-inch slices, place on top.
5. Tuck bay leaves in sauerkraut; sprinkle whole peppercorns, juniper berries and instant minced onion over it.
6. Pour consommé, 1 soup-can water and wine over kraut. Cover tightly with foil; bake 2 hours.
7. Remove a paper-thin layer of skin from knackwurst (use franks as is), then arrange them on top. Cover with foil again and bake ½ hour longer.

FRANK-SPAGHETTI-CHEESE CASSEROLE

Time in Kitchen: ½ hour
Free Time: ½ hour
Servings: 3

¼ pound spaghetti, in pieces
3 tablespoons butter or margarine
2 tablespoons chopped celery
2 tablespoons chopped green pepper
2 tablespoons minced onion
3 tablespoons all-purpose flour
1 16-ounce can tomatoes
1 teaspoon salt
¼ teaspoon pepper
¼ teaspoon granulated sugar
½ cup shredded natural sharp Cheddar cheese
4 frankfurters, diagonally sliced
green pepper rings (optional)

1. *About 1 hour before dinner:* Cook spaghetti in boiling salted water as label directs; drain. Preheat oven to 350°F.
2. Meanwhile, in large saucepan over low heat, in hot butter, cook celery, green pepper and onion until lightly browned.
3. Stir in flour. Add tomatoes, salt, pepper, sugar and cheese, stirring just until cheese is melted; remove from heat. Stir in cooked spaghetti, sliced frankfurters.
4. Turn mixture into greased 1½-quart casserole; bake ½ hour or until bubbly and golden. Garnish top of casserole with green pepper rings, if desired.

Serve with: Ripe olives • Hard rolls • Tortoni • Coffee

SAUSAGE CASSEROLE DELUXE

Time in Kitchen: 15 minutes
Free Time: 45 minutes
Servings: 4

8 pork-sausage links
1 18-ounce can sweet potatoes, drained
3 medium apples, peeled
1 tablespoon all-purpose flour
½ teaspoon salt
1 tablespoon brown sugar
¼ cup canned pineapple juice

About 1 hour before dinner; Preheat oven to 375°F. In large skillet, lightly brown sausage links.

Into 2-quart casserole, slice potatoes and apples. In small bowl, blend flour, salt, brown sugar, pineapple juice and ¼ cup water; pour over potatoes and apples; top with sausages. Bake 45 minutes, or until apples are tender.

Serve with: Green salad • Prunes • Vanilla ice cream

WINTER CASSEROLE

Time in Kitchen: 15 minutes
Free Time: 1 hour 15 minutes
Servings: 4

1 pound pork-sausage links
3 cups thinly sliced raw potatoes
1 cup thinly sliced onions
½ teaspoon salt
½ cup milk
1 17-ounce can cream-style corn
8 green pepper rings

About 1½ hours before dinner: Preheat oven to 375°F. In large skillet, lightly brown sausage links; drain.

In 10″ by 6″ baking dish, layer potatoes and onions. Sprinkle with salt, then pour on milk. Spoon corn over potato mixture; top with pepper rings and sausage links. Cover with foil; bake 55 minutes; uncover; bake 20 minutes.

HERB-STUFFED PEPPERS WITH SAUSAGES

Time in Kitchen: 20 minutes
Free Time: 20 minutes
Servings: 4

2 large green peppers
1 large onion, minced
¼ cup butter or margarine
4 slices white bread, crumbled
½ teaspoon marjoram leaves
½ teaspoon thyme leaves
1 celery top, chopped
½ teaspoon salt
⅛ teaspoon pepper
1 egg, beaten
2 8-ounce cans tomato sauce
1 8-ounce package brown-and-serve sausage links

About 40 minutes before dinner: Preheat oven to 400°F. Halve peppers lengthwise; remove seeds; in large kettle, in boiling, salted water, cook, covered, 5 minutes.

Sauté onion in butter until tender; add bread and next 6 ingredients; blend.

In 10″ by 6″ baking dish, place tomato sauce; set pepper halves in it; heap bread mixture in peppers. In pie plate, place sausages. Bake both 20 minutes.

EGG-AND-MUSHROOM-DINNER CASSEROLE

Time in Kitchen: 20 minutes
Free Time: 20 minutes
Servings: 4

5 hard-cooked eggs, sliced
1 3-ounce can sliced mushrooms, undrained
milk
butter or margarine
2 tablespoons all-purpose flour
¼ teaspoon salt
¼ teaspoon onion salt
½ cup minced celery
½ cup packaged herb-seasoned stuffing mix
½ cup shredded process Cheddar cheese

1. *About 40 minutes before dinner:* Preheat oven to 375°F. Place eggs in shallow 10″ by 6″ baking dish.
2. Drain mushroom juice into measuring cup; add milk to make 1 cup.
3. In saucepan, in 1 tablespoon butter, heat mushrooms 2 or 3 minutes; scatter mushrooms over eggs.
4. Melt 2 tablespoons butter in saucepan; stir in flour, salts, then milk mixture. Cook, stirring, until thickened. Add celery; pour over eggs. Scatter stuffing, mixed with cheese, over top. Bake 20 minutes, or until bubbly.

Serve with: Mixed greens with herb dressing • Cantaloupe wedges

ASPARAGUS-CHEESE PIE

Time in Kitchen: 1 hour
Servings: 6

¾ cup shredded natural sharp Cheddar cheese
1 10-ounce package piecrust mix
2 10-ounce packages frozen asparagus spears
2 tablespoons butter or margarine
¼ cup all-purpose flour
1½ cups milk
4 ounces shredded natural Swiss cheese
¼ teaspoon salt
⅛ teaspoon pepper
dash each: nutmeg and paprika

About 1 hour before dinner: Preheat oven to 425°F. Add ½ cup of the Cheddar cheese to piecrust mix. Follow piecrust-package directions. On lightly floured surface, roll out pastry 1½ inches wider than greased 10-inch pie plate. Fit into plate. Roll overhang under; flute. Prick pastry. Bake 15 minutes or until golden.

Meanwhile, cook asparagus as label directs. From 12 stalks, cut tips (including 3 inches of stalk); reserve. Chop remainder; drain on paper towels; place in slightly cooled shell.

In medium saucepan, melt butter; add flour, stirring until smooth; gradually add milk; continue stirring until sauce boils. Stir in Swiss cheese, salt, pepper, nutmeg. Pour over asparagus in pie shell. Sprinkle with remaining ¼ cup Cheddar cheese, dash paprika. Broil under medium heat until cheese melts. Garnish with asparagus spears. Broil two minutes or until asparagus is hot. Cool 10 minutes; serve.

Easy Pork Stew, page 66

Codfish Stew, page 70

Clockwise: Chicken Casserole, page 73; Manicotti, page 48; Savory Tuna Casserole, page 72

Bavarian Kraut Casserole, page 78

Orange Gelatin Mold, page 200
Chicken-and-Macaroni Stew, page 74

Tangy Meat Patties and Franks, page 77

Saucy Frank Dinner, page 76

COMPANY FEASTS

The easiest possible way to entertain—one superb main dish plus a special bread and salad

PAELLA PRONTO
pictured on page 105

Time in Kitchen: ½ hour
Servings: 4

3 medium frozen rock-lobster tails, thawed
2 6-ounce packages curried-rice mix
8 cherrystone clams in their shells, scrubbed
1 green pepper, cut into eighths
1 15-ounce can asparagus, drained
4 pimientos, quartered

About ½ hour before dinner: Cut lobster tails while still in shell into 1-inch pieces. In Dutch oven, prepare both packages rice as labels direct, reducing total amount of water by 1 cup, and adding lobster, clams, green pepper. When rice is done, add asparagus, pimientos. Heat.

Serve with: Jellied madrilène with lemon twist • Head Lettuce with Foamy Dressing, page 196

OYSTER-AND-RICE BAKE

Time in Kitchen: 45 minutes
Free Time: ½ hour
Servings: 6

¼ cup butter or margarine
1 cup chopped onions
½ pound mushrooms, thinly sliced
seasoned salt
pepper
1 cup dry white wine
1 cup regular white rice
2 dozen shucked, raw oysters, drained
½ cup grated Parmesan cheese

About 1 hour and 15 minutes before dinner: In skillet, melt butter; sauté onions and mushrooms with 1½ teaspoons seasoned salt and ⅛ teaspoon pepper, 15 minutes; add wine; simmer slowly, uncovered, 15 minutes.

Meanwhile, cook rice as package label directs. Preheat oven to 350°F. Combine rice with onion-mushroom mixture. In 12″ by 8″ baking dish, layer oysters and rice mixture. Sprinkle with seasoned salt, pepper and cheese. Bake ½ hour. Place casserole under broiler a few minutes.

Serve with: Spinach salad • Frozen peaches and cream

SHRIMP-AND-MUSHROOM DINNER

Time in Kitchen: 35 minutes
Servings: 6

6 green onions
2 teaspoons salt
¼ teaspoon peppercorns
2 large stalks celery with leaves, cut in large chunks
1 large onion, quartered
8 parsley sprigs
1 medium carrot, sliced lengthwise
2 garlic cloves
1 bay leaf
3 tablespoons cornstarch
1½ pounds peeled, deveined frozen shrimp
1 cup sliced mushrooms
dash pepper
2 tablespoons lemon juice

1. *About 35 minutes before dinner:* Chop 2 tablespoons green-onion tops; set aside for use in step 4.
2. In medium saucepan, bring 2½ cups water, salt and peppercorns to

boiling. Add all remaining green onions, celery, and next 5 ingredients; cover; simmer 15 minutes.

3. Into medium bowl, strain liquid from pan through sieve; discard vegetables; pour liquid back into saucepan. Blend ½ cup cold water and cornstarch. Gradually add cornstarch mixture to hot liquid; cook, stirring constantly.

4. Stir in shrimp, mushrooms and pepper; cook over medium heat, stirring constantly, until thickened and shrimp turn pink. Stir in reserved green-onion tops and lemon juice just before serving.

Serve with: Beef bouillon • Lettuce-and-avocado salad

CRAB MARYLAND

Time in Kitchen: ½ hour
Free Time: 15 minutes
Servings: 6

butter or margarine
3 tablespoons all-purpose flour
2 cups milk
2 tablespoons minced onion
½ teaspoon celery salt
⅛ teaspoon grated orange peel
1 tablespoon chopped parsley
1 tablespoon minced green pepper
1 pimiento, minced
dash hot pepper sauce
2 tablespoons sherry
1 egg, beaten
1 teaspoon salt
dash pepper
3 cups flaked, cooked or canned crab
½ cup fresh bread crumbs

About 45 minutes before dinner: In double boiler, melt ¼ cup butter; stir in flour, then milk; cook, stirring, until

sauce is thickened. Add minced onion, celery salt, orange peel, parsley, green pepper, pimiento, and hot pepper sauce. Remove from heat; add sherry. Preheat oven to 350°F.

Stir some of sauce slowly into beaten egg; then stir egg mixture back into rest of sauce. Add salt, pepper and crab; turn into greased 1½-quart casserole. Melt 1 tablespoon butter; toss with bread crumbs. Sprinkle over casserole. Bake casserole 15 minutes.

SHRIMP-AND-TUNA GOURMET

Time in Kitchen: 25 minutes
Servings: 6

3 tablespoons butter or margarine
1 4-ounce can mushrooms, drained
⅓ cup chopped green onions
1 10½-ounce can condensed cream-of-chicken soup
1 teaspoon Worcestershire
¼ teaspoon salt
4 drops hot pepper sauce
¼ cup diced pimientos
½ cup pitted ripe olives
1 cup cooked, shelled, deveined shrimp
1 6½- or 7-ounce can chunk-style tuna
½ cup light cream

About 25 minutes before dinner: In medium skillet, in butter, sauté mushrooms and green onions, stirring occasionally, for 5 minutes.

Stir in undiluted soup, Worcestershire, salt, hot pepper sauce; continue cooking, stirring occasionally, until mixture is hot. Reduce heat; stir in remaining ingredients; heat.

SEAFOOD ESPAÑOL

pictured on page 136

Time in Kitchen: ½ hour
Servings: 8

salad oil
2 6-ounce packages yellow-rice mix
1 cup minced onions
1 garlic clove, crushed
2 green peppers, seeded, quartered
1 16-ounce package frozen, shelled, deveined shrimp
1 cup sliced mushrooms
½ teaspoon salt
¼ teaspoon pepper
2 7-ounce packages frozen Alaska King crab, thawed
1 7-ounce can lobster
1 4-ounce can pimientos, drained, sliced
1 3½-ounce can pitted ripe olives

About ½ hour before dinner: In Dutch oven over medium heat, in 4 tablespoons oil, sauté rice mix, onion and garlic 3 minutes. Add 1 quart water; bring to boiling; cover; simmer 15 minutes. Meanwhile, in medium saucepan, in 2 tablespoons oil, cook green peppers, covered, until tender.

Add shrimp, mushrooms to rice; bring to boiling; cover; simmer 5 minutes. Add green peppers, salt and rest of ingredients. Simmer 3 minutes.

Serve with: Greens and avocado-onion salad • Coffee

PIQUANT CRAB

Do-Ahead Dish
Time in Kitchen: 25 minutes
Free Time: 40 minutes
Servings: 4

1 pound fresh spinach, washed
1½ cups shredded process sharp Cheddar cheese
1 6½-ounce can crab, drained
1 tablespoon lemon juice
1 small onion, minced
1 6-ounce can tomato paste
1 cup sour cream
½ teaspoon salt
dash pepper
dash nutmeg
1 tablespoon cooking sherry

Early in day: Cook spinach in small amount of salted water until barely tender; drain. Chop spinach coarsely; spread in greased 1-quart casserole. Sprinkle with half of cheese. Sprinkle with crab, then lemon juice. Mix onion and rest of ingredients; pour over all. Sprinkle with rest of cheese; chill.

About 50 minutes before dinner: Preheat oven to 350°F. Bake casserole about 40 minutes or until hot.

SHRIMPALAYA CASSEROLE

Do-Ahead Dish
Time in Kitchen: ½ hour
Free Time: 1 hour
Servings: 4

6 ounces elbow macaroni (1½ cups)
2 bacon slices, diced
½ cup minced onions
½ cup minced green pepper
½ garlic clove, minced
1 19-ounce can tomatoes (2½ cups)
1 teaspoon salt
½ pound cooked ham, cubed (about 1¼ cups)
1 cup cooked, shelled, deveined shrimp
½ cup day-old bread crumbs
2 tablespoons grated Parmesan cheese
2 tablespoons melted butter or margarine

Early in day: Cook macaroni as label directs. Meanwhile, in skillet, sauté bacon until crisp. Add onions, peppers, garlic; sauté until tender. Add tomatoes and salt; heat. Add macaroni, ham and shrimp; pour into 1½-quart casserole. Refrigerate.

About 1 hour before dinner: Preheat oven to 350°F. Combine bread crumbs, cheese and butter; sprinkle on top of mixture in casserole. Bake 1 hour or until hot and bubbly.

CRAB-ASPARAGUS CASSEROLE

Time in Kitchen: 25 minutes
Free Time: 45 minutes
Servings: 4

butter or margarine
¼ cup all-purpose flour
1¼ cups milk
seasoned salt
seasoned pepper
4 teaspoons grated Parmesan cheese
2 7-ounce packages frozen Alaska King crab, thawed
2 15-ounce cans colossal white asparagus spears, drained

About 1 hour and 10 minutes before dinner: Preheat oven to 375°F. In small saucepan, melt ¼ cup butter; stir in flour until smooth. Slowly add milk, stirring constantly to avoid lumps. Add 1 teaspoon seasoned salt, ⅛ teaspoon seasoned pepper and grated cheese. Cook, stirring, until smooth and thickened.

In buttered 1½-quart casserole, place crab; sprinkle lightly with seasoned salt and seasoned pepper; add 6 tablespoons of the cheese sauce; mix lightly with fork.

Arrange asparagus spears on top of crab mixture. Spoon remaining cheese sauce over asparagus, covering it entirely. Bake 40 minutes or until hot.

BAKED FLOUNDER SUPREME
pictured on page 107

Time in Kitchen: 40 minutes
Servings: 6

6 large flounder fillets (about 2 pounds)
seasoned salt
1 medium tomato, cut into 6 slices
6 slices natural Swiss cheese
2 tablespoons butter or margarine
1 3- or 4-ounce can sliced mushrooms, drained (reserve liquid)
2 small onions, sliced
1½ tablespoons all-purpose flour
chopped parsley
1 cup light cream
6 tablespoons sherry
2 cups packaged precooked rice

1. *About 40 minutes before dinner:* Sprinkle fillets lightly on both sides with seasoned salt, then roll each up.
2. Arrange rolls, seam side down, in 13″ by 9″ baking dish; alternate with tomato slices and cheese slices folded in half. Preheat oven to 400°F.
3. In large skillet, in butter, sauté mushrooms and onions until golden. Stir in flour, 1½ teaspoons seasoned salt and ¼ cup parsley; stir in cream, mushroom liquid plus water to make ½ cup, and sherry. Bring to boiling; pour over fish. Bake 20 minutes, or until easily flaked with fork.
4. Meanwhile, prepare rice as label directs. Stir in ½ cup parsley. When fish is done, spoon rice along its sides.

BAKED FISH WITH VEGETABLES

Time in Kitchen: ½ hour
Free Time: ½ hour
Cooking time: 1 hour
Servings: 6

3 cups cooked rice
¼ cup olive oil
2 garlic cloves, minced
½ pound small white onions
2 medium green peppers, cut into 1½-inch pieces
1½ pounds zucchini (unpared), cut into 1-inch, diagonal slices
1 teaspoon all-purpose flour
salt
1 teaspoon basil
½ teaspoon oregano leaves
⅛ teaspoon pepper
seasoned salt
½ cup dry white wine
6 large flounder fillets
6 slices natural Swiss cheese
2 tablespoons butter or margarine
few radish roses for garnish
6 lemon wedges for garnish
fresh dill sprigs for garnish

1. *About 1 hour before dinner:* Arrange rice along center of 13″ by 9″ greased baking dish to within 2 inches of edges.
2. In large skillet, in olive oil, sauté garlic, onions, green peppers and zucchini slices 5 minutes. Sprinkle with flour, 1¼ teaspoons salt, basil, oregano, pepper and 1 teaspoon seasoned salt; mix well. Add 1 cup water and white wine; cover; bring to boiling; simmer 10 minutes.
3. Preheat oven to 350°F. Around rice in baking dish, arrange zucchini mixture, with its juices. Sprinkle flounder fillets with ¾ teaspoon salt, ¾ teaspoon seasoned salt. Fold one end of each fillet over about one-third of the way; fold cheese slices in half crosswise. Arrange fillets and cheese, alternately, over rice. Dot with butter.
4. Bake 15 minutes, then turn heat to 400°F. Bake 15 minutes, or until fish is easily flaked with fork and cheese is melted and golden.
5. Garnish with radish roses, lemon wedges and dill.

Serve with: Baked herbed-tomato halves • Mixed green salad • Sponge-cake with orange glaze

TUNA ROMANOFF

Do-Ahead Dish
Time in Kitchen: 15 minutes
Free Time: 1 hour 15 minutes
Servings: 6

1 8-ounce package ziti macaroni
1 cup sour cream
1 8-ounce container creamed cottage cheese
1 13-ounce can tuna, drained, flaked
¼ cup chopped pitted ripe olives
2 tablespoons chopped pimientos
2 tablespoons minced onion
1 9-ounce package frozen French green beans with toasted almonds, thawed
2 teaspoons Worcestershire
¼ teaspoon hot pepper sauce
1 teaspoon seasoned salt
¼ teaspoon seasoned pepper
1 10½-ounce can condensed cream-of-celery soup
½ cup milk

1. *Day before or early in day:* Cook macaroni as label directs; drain.

2. Meanwhile, in bowl, combine sour cream, cottage cheese. Stir in ziti, tuna and next 8 ingredients.

3. In small bowl, combine undiluted soup and milk. Turn tuna mixture into greased 2-quart casserole; pour on soup; cover; refrigerate.

4. *About 1 hour 15 minutes before dinner:* Preheat oven to 400°F. Bake tuna 1 hour; uncover; bake 15 minutes longer.

Serve with: Celery-lettuce salad • Pecan pie • Coffee

TUNA-STUFFED ACORN SQUASH

Time in Kitchen: ½ hour
Free Time: ½ hour
Servings: 4

2 medium acorn squash, halved lengthwise
butter or margarine
¼ cup minced onion
¼ cup minced celery
1 6½- or 7-ounce can tuna, drained
1 teaspoon salt
¼ teaspoon pepper
¼ teaspoon thyme leaves
packaged dried bread crumbs
paprika

About 1 hour before dinner: Preheat oven to 400°F. Remove seeds from squash. Spread 1 tablespoon butter on cut surfaces of squash; place, cut side down, in shallow baking dish. Bake ½ hour or until very tender. Scoop cooked squash from shells into bowl; mash. Combine with onion, celery, 1 table-spoon melted butter, tuna, salt, pepper and thyme; mix well.

Pile mixture into shells. Sprinkle with

crumbs and 2 tablespoons melted but-ter; dust with paprika. Bake 10 minutes.

FRENCH BEEF STEW
pictured on page 108

Time in Kitchen: ½ hour
Free Time: 1 hour
Servings: 8

3 bacon slices, cut into pieces
2 pounds beef stew meat, cut in 1½-
  inch chunks
1 cup dry red wine
1 bouillon cube
2 garlic cloves, chopped
1 tablespoon instant minced onion
2 teaspoons salt
¼ teaspoon thyme leaves
1 strip orange peel
18 small white onions
¾ pound small mushrooms
2 tablespoons cornstarch
1 10-ounce package frozen peas
½ cup pitted ripe olives, drained

About 1½ hours before dinner: In large Dutch oven, fry bacon until crisp; push to side of pan. Add meat and brown. Stir in 1 cup water, wine and next 6 ingredients. Cover; simmer 1 hour or until meat is fork-tender.

In covered medium saucepan, in 1 inch boiling salted water, cook onions 10 minutes; add mushrooms and con-tinue cooking 5 minutes more; drain.

Mix cornstarch and 2 tablespoons water; stir into stew; heat to boiling, stirring constantly until thickened. Add onions, mushrooms, peas and olives; cover; cook 10 minutes or until tender.

BOEUF BOURGUIGNON

Do-Ahead Dish
Time in Kitchen: 1½ hours
Free Time: 1½ hours
Servings: 6

1 pound beef round steak, cut in 1-inch
    cubes
all-purpose flour
2 tablespoons butter or margarine
3 tablespoons cognac
1 garlic clove, minced
2 carrots, thinly sliced
2 cups thinly sliced celery
1 cup chopped onions
1 tablespoon parsley flakes
1 bay leaf, crumbled
½ teaspoon thyme leaves
2 teaspoons bottled sauce for gravy
salt
½ teaspoon hickory-smoked salt
1 pound small white onions
1 pound mushrooms
1 teaspoon lemon juice

Day before or early in day: Preheat
oven to 350°F. Roll beef cubes in flour
until completely covered. In Dutch oven,
in 1 tablespoon butter, brown beef. Add
cognac and ignite; when flames have
subsided, add garlic, carrots, celery,
chopped onions, parsley, bay leaf,
thyme, 2 cups water, sauce for gravy, 2
teaspoons salt and hickory salt. Stir to
distribute spices; simmer 2 to 3 minutes; cover tightly, then bake 2 hours,
or until meat is fork-tender.

One-half hour before meat is done:
Wash and peel small white onions
(halve those more than 1 inch in diameter); boil, in salted water to cover, until tender, about 20 minutes. Meanwhile,
wash and stem mushrooms (halve caps
more than 1½ inches in diameter);
sauté caps and stems in 1 tablespoon
butter and lemon juice until brown,

about 15 minutes. Make a smooth paste
from 2 tablespoons flour and ¼ cup
water. To meat mixture, add drained
onions, mushrooms, paste and ¾ cup
water; simmer until gravy has thickened; stir to prevent sticking.

About 20 minutes before dinner: Reheat, stirring frequently, until hot.

Serve with: Endive salad • Peach tart

POT ROAST POLYNESIAN

Time in Kitchen: ½ hour
Free Time: 1½ hours
Servings: 8

3-pound boneless beef chuck roast,
    rolled, tied
1½ teaspoon meat tenderizer
1 large onion, sliced in rings
1 cup canned pineapple juice
3 tablespoons soy sauce
1½ teaspoons ginger
½ teaspoon salt
4 stalks celery, sliced diagonally
4 whole carrots, sliced thin lengthwise
½ pound washed spinach
1 tablespoon cornstarch

Day before or early in day: Sprinkle
meat with tenderizer as label directs.
Place onion slices in bottom of 3-
quart casserole or bowl. Set meat on
top. Combine pineapple juice, soy
sauce, ginger and salt; pour over meat,
cover; refrigerate.

About 2 hours before dinner: In
Dutch oven, place onions and meat;
pour on marinade; cover; simmer 1½
hours, or until meat is fork-tender. Add
celery and carrots; cook 8 minutes.
Add spinach and cook untli tender-
crisp, and spinach wilts.

Remove meat and vegetables to
heated platter; keep warm. Blend corn-

starch with 2 tablespoons water; stir into gravy; cook, stirring, until it thickens, about 3 minutes; serve with meat.

Serve with: Orange muffins • Lime sherbet

STEAK LASAGNA

Do-Ahead Dish*
Time in Kitchen: 1 hour 15 minutes
Free Time: 1 hour 20 minutes
Servings: 6

8 thinly sliced, 2½-ounce beef round
　steaks
seasoned instant meat tenderizer
½ cup butter or margarine
1 small onion, minced
1 medium carrot, chopped
⅓ cup minced celery
¼ pound fresh mushrooms, sliced
1 small garlic clove, minced
¼ cup dry white wine
1 8-ounce can tomato sauce
¼ teaspoon basil
6 lasagna noodles
¼ cup all-purpose flour
⅛ teaspoon freshly ground black
　pepper
2 cups milk
½ cup grated Parmesan cheese

*1. *Make and freeze up to one month ahead:* Sprinkle steaks with tenderizer as label directs.
2. In large skillet, in ¼ cup butter, sauté onion, carrot, celery, mushrooms and garlic until golden; remove from pan; set aside. Brown steaks, a few at a time, 4 minutes; return to pan; add wine, tomato sauce, basil; simmer, uncovered, 10 minutes. Meanwhile, cook noodles as label directs.
3. In saucepan, melt remaining ¼ cup

butter; with wire whisk stir in flour, pepper, milk; stir until boiling; remove.
4. In 12″ by 8″ baking dish, layer half of noodles, half of steaks in their sauce with half of white sauce, half of cheese; repeat. Cool; freezer-wrap and freeze.
5. *About 1 hour and 20 minutes before dinner:* Unwrap lasagna; bake 1 hour 20 minutes or until hot.

BOILED BEEF-RIB DINNER

Time in Kitchen: 45 minutes
Free Time: 1½ hours
Servings: 6

2½ pounds beef short ribs
4 teaspoons salt
1 teaspoon pepper
2 large onions, halved
3 carrots, halved crosswise
3 cabbage wedges (about ½ pound)
3 sweet or hot Italian sausages
2 or 3 garlic cloves, minced
2 large potatoes, halved
1 yellow summer squash, sliced
1 green pepper, cut into strips
2 ears corn
2 tomatoes, quartered
1 20-ounce can chick peas, drained

1. *About 2 hours and 15 minutes before dinner:* In large kettle, place short ribs, 2 quarts water, salt, pepper. Bring to boiling; skim surface with spoon. Cover; simmer 1½ hours.
2. Add onions and next 5 ingredients; bring to boiling; cover; simmer 20 minutes. Add squash, green pepper, cook 10 minutes more.
3. With sharp knife, scrape kernels from corn; add, with tomatoes and chick peas, to soup. Simmer 5 minutes.
4. Serve vegetables and meat. Reserve broth for another day.

BEEFSTEAK-AND-MUSHROOM PIE

Do-Ahead Dish
Time in Kitchen: ½ hour
Free Time: 1½ hours
Servings: 4

¼ cup bacon fat
1½ pounds beef (round or chuck), cut into 2-inch strips, ¼-inch thick
salt
¼ teaspoon pepper
2 cups sliced onions
1 bay leaf
¼ teaspoon marjoram leaves
1 3- or 4-ounce can sliced mushrooms, undrained
1½ tablespoons all-purpose flour
3 tablespoons chili sauce
½ teaspoon Worcestershire
¼ teaspoon hot pepper sauce
Pastry for One-Crust Pie, page 9
1 egg, beaten

1. *Early in day or about 2 hours before dinner:* In large skillet, in hot fat, brown meat. Sprinkle with 2 teaspoons salt, pepper; add onions, bay leaf, marjoram, 1 cup hot water, liquid drained from mushrooms; cover; simmer 1 hour.
2. Into 1½-quart shallow baking dish spoon meat pieces, onions, mushrooms, none of gravy. Blend flour with 2 tablespoons water; stir into gravy still in skillet; add chili sauce, Worcestershire, hot pepper sauce, ½ teaspoon salt; bring to boiling; pour over meat; cool.
3. *About 1 hour before dinner:* Preheat oven to 450°F. Make Pastry. On lightly floured surface, roll into circle ⅛ inch thick that fits top of baking dish, with ½-inch overhang.
4. Fold pastry in half; make several slits near center fold; unfold over meat mixture in baking dish; turn overhang under; press firmly to top edge of dish all the way around. Brush pastry with beaten egg. Bake pie 10 minutes; turn heat to 350°F.; bake ½ hour or until golden and hot.

TAMALE PIE

pictured on page 109

Time in Kitchen: 55 minutes
Free Time: 1 hour 5 minutes
Servings: 8

2 13¾-ounce cans chicken broth
1½ cups yellow cornmeal
1 pound beef round, ground
1 large onion, minced
1 green pepper, minced
⅛ teaspoon instant minced garlic
½ teaspoon salt
1½ tablespoons chili powder
3 medium tomatoes, cut in wedges
1 13-ounce can Mexican-style corn, drained
1 4¾-ounce can pitted ripe olives
2 eggs, beaten
½ cup grated Parmesan cheese
2 16-ounce cans sliced, whole tomatoes, drained
¼ cup minced parsley

1. *About 2 hours before dinner:* In medium saucepan, bring 3 cups broth to boiling. In bowl, place cornmeal; stir in remaining ⅔ cup broth and ⅓ cup water; pour on boiling broth; stir; return to saucepan. Cook, gently stirring, until thick. Place saucepan of cornmeal in large skillet containing 1 inch simmering water. Cover; cook, 20 minutes.
2. In skillet, brown beef; stir often; add onion and next 6 ingredients. Cover; simmer 10 minutes. Add olives.
3. Grease 3-quart round baking dish;

line bottom with waxed paper; grease well. Stir a little hot cornmeal into eggs; beat well; add remaining cornmeal and cheese. Preheat oven to 350°F. Spread ⅔ of cornmeal over bottom and sides of dish; fill with meat; spread with rest of cornmeal; seal edges. Bake 1 hour 5 minutes. Cool on rack 10 minutes.

4. Run metal spatula around pie to loosen. Invert round platter over dish; invert both; lift off dish; peel off paper; place tomatoes around pie; sprinkle with parsley. Cut into wedges.

CURRIED MEATBALL BAKE

pictured on page 132

Time in Kitchen: 35 minutes
Free Time: 25 minutes
Servings: 8

1½ pounds small white onions
1 bunch small carrots, halved crosswise
1 10-ounce package frozen peas, thawed
2 pounds lean beef chuck, ground
1 egg
1 cup day-old bread crumbs
¾ teaspoon marjoram leaves
2½ teaspoons salt
¾ teaspoon Worcestershire
⅔ cup milk
⅓ to ½ cup salad oil
1½ pounds small mushrooms
1 10½-ounce can condensed cream-of-mushroom soup
¾ teaspoon nutmeg
¾ teaspoon bottled sauce for gravy
¾ teaspoon onion salt
3 cups hot cooked rice
1 teaspoon curry powder

1. *One hour before dinner:* In saucepan, to 1 inch boiling salted water, add onions, carrots. Cover; cook 20 minutes. Add peas; cover; turn off heat.
2. Meanwhile, mix chuck with next 6 ingredients. In skillet, in oil, drop meat by tablespoonfuls; brown; remove.
3. In same skillet, sauté mushrooms about 5 minutes; remove. In same skillet, heat undiluted soup with nutmeg, sauce for gravy and onion salt.
4. Preheat oven to 400°F. Put drained vegetables and meatballs in 3-quart casserole. Pour on soup. Bake, uncovered, 25 minutes.
5. Meanwhile, toss rice with curry; arrange on casserole. Bake 10 minutes.

BEEFY NOODLE BAKE

Do-Ahead Dish
Time in Kitchen: ½ hour
Free Time: 45 minutes
Servings: 6

1 8-ounce package noodles
butter or margarine
1 pound beef chuck, ground
2 8-ounce cans tomato sauce
1 8-ounce container cottage cheese
1 8-ounce package cream cheese, softened
¼ cup sour cream
⅓ cup chopped green onions
1 tablespoon minced green pepper

Early in day: Cook noodles as label directs. In skillet, in 1 tablespoon butter, brown chuck. Add tomato sauce. In bowl, mix cottage cheese and next 4 ingredients. In 2-quart casserole, put half of noodles. Cover with cheese mixture, then rest of noodles, 2 tablespoons melted butter, meat mixture. Chill.

One hour before dinner: Preheat oven to 375°F. Bake casserole 45 minutes.

HAMBURGER-MACARONI TREAT

pictured on page 111

Time in Kitchen: 1 hour
Servings: 4

4 large green peppers
1 large onion, chopped
2 pounds beef chuck, ground
1 cup cooked rice
¼ cup chopped parsley
salt and pepper
2 tablespoons horseradish
1 teaspoon prepared mustard
½ teaspoon nutmeg
¼ cup milk
salad oil
2 eggs, well beaten
2 15-ounce cans macaroni and cheese
4 large tomatoes
Worcestershire
paprika
watercress for garnish

1. *About 1 hour before dinner:* Cut tops from peppers; seed them, then cook in boiling salted water, tightly covered, 5 minutes; drain. Preheat oven to 350°F.
2. In bowl, combine onion, chuck, rice, parsley, 1 teaspoon salt, ¼ teaspoon pepper, horseradish, mustard, nutmeg and milk. Divide mixture in half. In skillet, in 2 tablespoons hot oil, cook half of meat until meat loses its red color. Use to fill pepper shells. Arrange down one side of a 13″ by 9″ baking dish.
3. To remaining meat mixture, add beaten eggs; shape into tiny meatballs. In same skillet, in 2 tablespoons hot oil, sauté meatballs until browned. Top each filled pepper with 3 meatballs, then place remaining meatballs down center of baking dish. Bake 15 minutes.
4. Meanwhile, heat macaroni and cheese in saucepan. Scoop out centers of tomatoes; season with salt, pepper and Worcestershire, then fill with hot macaroni and sprinkle with paprika. Arrange beside peppers in baking dish; return all to oven for about 10 minutes. Garnish with watercress.

Serve with: Escarole salad • Pudding

SWEET-AND-SOUR CABBAGE

pictured on page 134

Do-Ahead Dish
Time in Kitchen: 1 hour
Free Time: 45 minutes
Servings: 6

2 tablespoons butter or margarine
1 large onion, chopped
salt and pepper
½ teaspoon paprika
1 16-ounce can tomatoes
2 6-ounce cans tomato paste
2 to 4 tablespoons granulated sugar
¼ cup lemon juice
1 head green cabbage
1 pound beef chuck, ground
1 cup cooked rice
3 tablespoons instant minced onion
1 fresh white-bread slice, crumbled
3 tablespoons milk
1 teaspoon Worcestershire

1. *Early in day:* In skillet, in butter, sauté chopped onion lightly. Stir in 1 teaspoon salt, ¼ teaspoon pepper, paprika, tomatoes, tomato paste, sugar and lemon juice. Simmer, covered, ½ hour; cool; refrigerate.
2. While sauce cooks, in large kettle, heat to boiling enough water to cover cabbage head; immerse cabbage, upside down, for 10 minutes; drain. Carefully remove 12 leaves. (If leaves are

too stiff to remove easily, immerse cabbage in boiling water again until enough leaves are freed.) With sharp knife, carefully trim wide center vein in each cabbage leaf, near its base, so it bends easily.

3. In large bowl, with fork, toss together chuck, 1 teaspoon salt, rice, ¼ teaspoon pepper, instant minced onion, crumbled bread, milk and Worcestershire. Divide mixture among cabbage leaves, then roll up each snugly, forming a bundle. Place the bundles, seam side down, on tray; cover; refrigerate.

4. *About 50 minutes before dinner:* In 12-inch skillet, place sauce; top with cabbage bundles, seam side down; bring to boiling; cover; simmer 45 minutes or until tender. Serve, right from skillet; or transfer to chafing dish.

Serve with: Frozen mixed fruit on vanilla ice cream

NEW YORK TAMALE PIE

Time in Kitchen: 35 minutes
Free Time: 25 minutes
Servings: 6

2 tablespoons butter or margarine
1½ pounds beef chuck, ground
2 tablespoons chopped onion
1 10½-ounce can condensed consommé
5 tablespoons chopped parsley
1 teaspoon salt
⅛ teaspoon pepper
2 tablespoons Worcestershire
1 9½-ounce package corn-muffin mix

About 1 hour before dinner: Preheat oven to 400°F. In large skillet, in hot butter, sauté beef and onion just until beef is brown. Stir in undiluted con-

sommé, parsley, salt, pepper, Worcestershire; pour into 12″ by 8″ baking dish. Prepare mix as label directs; spoon over beef. Bake 25 minutes or until golden. Let stand 5 minutes before serving.

BEEF AND MACARONI

Do-Ahead Dish
Time in Kitchen: 45 minutes
Free Time: 2 hours
Servings: 8

1 8-ounce package shell macaroni
½ cup butter or margarine
2 pounds beef chuck, ground
3 medium onions, minced
1 green pepper, minced
3 garlic cloves, minced
4 8-ounce cans tomato sauce
1 12-ounce can whole-kernel corn
1 3-ounce can mushrooms, undrained
4 ounces sharp natural Cheddar cheese, shredded (1 cup)
1 tablespoon brown sugar
1 tablespoon Worcestershire
1 tablespoon chili powder
½ cup cooking sherry
2 teaspoons salt
¼ teaspoon pepper

Day before: Cook macaroni as label directs. In skillet, in half of butter, sauté half of meat with half of onions, green pepper, garlic until meat browns. Transfer to 3-quart casserole. Repeat; stir in tomato sauce and next 9 ingredients. Add macaroni; toss. Cover; refrigerate.

About 2 hours before dinner: Preheat oven to 350°F. Bake casserole, covered, about 2 hours or until bubbling.

BURGER TRITTINI
pictured on page 129

Time in Kitchen: ½ hour
Free Time: ½ hour
Servings: 10

2 pounds beef round, ground
½ cup minced onions
2 6-ounce cans tomato paste
1 15-ounce can tomato sauce
2 teaspoons basil
2 teaspoons parsley flakes
salt
2 teaspoons granulated sugar
1 teaspoon oregano leaves
dash garlic salt
¼ teaspoon pepper
2 3-ounce cans mushroom slices, drained
2 10-ounce packages frozen chopped spinach, thawed
1 16-ounce container creamed cottage cheese
1 8-ounce package mozzarella cheese

1. *About 1 hour before dinner:* In large skillet, sauté meat and onion until meat loses its pink color and onion becomes transparent. Add tomato paste, tomato sauce, basil, parsley, 1 teaspoon salt, sugar, oregano, garlic salt and pepper.
2. Set aside 15 canned mushroom slices; add rest of slices to meat mixture. Simmer, uncovered, 10 minutes, stirring often, until thickened.
3. Meanwhile, squeeze out as much liquid as possible from thawed spinach. Then, in medium bowl, with fork, combine spinach, cottage cheese and a dash of salt.
4. With sharp knife, slice twelve 2½″ by ½″ by ½″ strips from mozzarella cheese; dice rest of cheese.
5. Preheat oven to 375°F. In 13″ by 9″ baking dish, arrange alternately, in lengthwise rows, ⅔ of spinach mixture and ⅓ of meat mixture, covering bottom of baking dish; sprinkle on diced mozzarella cheese. Then, on top of cheese, arrange alternately, in lengthwise rows, remaining meat mixture and spinach mixture.
6. With the cheese strips, make 4 rows on top of meat mixture, using 3 strips, placed end to end, for each row. Garnish with reserved mushroom slices. Bake ½ hour or until bubbling hot. Serve at once.

Serve with: Orange, apple, grape compote • Cream-filled ladyfingers

ENCHILADA CASSEROLE

Do-Ahead Dish
Time in Kitchen: ½ hour
Free Time: 45 minutes
Servings: 12

2 teaspoons salad oil
1 medium onion, finely chopped
2 pounds beef chuck, ground
2 1⅝-ounce packages enchilada-sauce mix (or 1 1¼-ounce package taco-sauce mix)
2 8-ounce cans tomato sauce
1 10½-ounce can condensed cream-of-mushroom soup
2 9-ounce packages frozen tortillas
1 or 2 bottled hot chili peppers, seeded, minced
16 ounces shredded Cheddar cheese (4 cups)

Day before or early in day: In large skillet, in hot oil, sauté onion 5 minutes or until lightly browned; add beef and brown well. Drain off any excess fat; refrigerate.

In large saucepan, prepare sauce mix as label directs, adding canned tomato sauce and 6 cups water; stir in undiluted mushroom soup; simmer 15 minutes; refrigerate.

About 1 hour before dinner: Preheat oven to 350°F. Prepare tortillas as label directs. In greased 15½″ by 10½″ roasting pan, place 6 tortillas. Layer ⅓ of meat mixture, ⅓ of chili peppers, about 2 cups sauce and 1 cup cheese on tortillas. Repeat layering 2 more times; pour remaining sauce over top; sprinkle with remaining cheese. Cover pan with foil; bake 45 minutes. Uncover; bake 15 minutes more. Remove from oven, let stand 10 minutes before serving.

Serve with: Melon balls • Chilled coleslaw • Corn chips • Yellow cake with chocolate frosting

dinner: Preheat oven to 350°F. Sprinkle eggplant with salt, using 1 teaspoon salt in all.

2. In skillet, in 3 tablespoons hot butter, sauté onions and tomatoes until onions are tender; stir in 1 tablespoon salt, paprika, basil, nutmeg, pepper, chuck and pork. Cook 5 minutes, or until meat is lightly browned.

3. Rinse salted eggplant in cold water. In 12″ by 8″ baking dish, place half of meat mixture, then all of eggplant slices; top with rest of meat mixture.

4. Cover with foil; bake 40 minutes.

5. Toss bread crumbs with 2 tablespoons melted butter and cheese. Remove foil from baking dish; sprinkle with crumbs. Bake 15 minutes more, or until browned.

Serve with: Lettuce with Italian dressing • Banana cake

HAMBURGER-EGGPLANT CASSEROLE

Time in Kitchen: 40 minutes
Free Time: 40 minutes
Servings: 8

1 medium eggplant, pared, sliced ½ inch thick
salt
butter or margarine
1½ cups chopped onions
2 cups diced fresh tomatoes
1 teaspoon paprika
1 teaspoon basil
1 teaspoon nutmeg
¼ teaspoon pepper
1 pound beef chuck, ground
½ pound lean pork, ground
1 cup fresh bread crumbs
½ cup sharp Cheddar cheese, shredded

1. *About 1 hour and 20 minutes before*

TURKEY DIVAN

pictured on page 110

Time in Kitchen: 20 minutes
Servings: 6

12 slices cooked turkey or chicken
2 10-ounce packages frozen broccoli spears
1 6-ounce jar hollandaise
shredded process Cheddar cheese

About 20 minutes before dinner: In chafing dish, over boiling water, heat turkey in 1 tablespoon water. Meanwhile, cook broccoli as label directs.

Arrange broccoli on turkey; top with hollandaise; sprinkle with cheese. Cover; heat. Serve from chafing dish.

Serve with: Brioche à la Maxim, page 218 • Apples

WILD-RICE-AND-TURKEY CASSEROLE

Do-Ahead Dish
Time in Kitchen: ½ hour
Free Time: 45 minutes
Servings: 8

1½ cups wild rice
1 teaspoon salt
1 pound bulk pork sausage
1 3-ounce can whole mushrooms, undrained
2 10½-ounce cans condensed cream-of-mushroom soup
1 teaspoon Worcestershire
12 slices roast turkey
1½ cups day-old bread crumbs
¼ cup melted butter or margarine

Early in day: Wash rice several times in lukewarm water. In large saucepan, bring 4 cups water to boiling; add salt; gradually sprinkle rice on water so water does not stop boiling. Cover; reduce heat and cook gently ½ hour, or until rice is tender and water is absorbed. Meanwhile, in skillet over medium heat, cook sausage until browned, stirring, breaking sausage into bits and draining off fat as it accumulates. Stir in mushrooms, undiluted soup and Worcestershire; lightly stir this mixture into cooked, drained rice. Spoon half of rice mixture into greased 12″ by 8″ baking dish; layer turkey slices on top; spoon on rest of rice mixture; refrigerate.

About 1 hour before dinner: Preheat oven to 375°F. Mix crumbs with butter; sprinkle over rice, making 1-inch border along edge of casserole. Bake about 45 minutes, or until hot and golden. (If made and baked at one time, bake ½ hour.)

CHICKEN-AND-APPLE

pictured on page 107

Time in Kitchen: 1 hour
Free Time: 1 hour 15 minutes
Servings: 4

¾ cup all-purpose flour
¾ teaspoon ginger
1½ teaspoons nutmeg
4 large red apples
butter or margarine
¾ pound small white onions (8 to 10)
1 2½-pound broiler-fryer, cut up
1½ teaspoons salt
2 chicken-bouillon cubes

1. *About 2 hours and 15 minutes before dinner:* In small bowl, combine flour, ginger and nutmeg. Core apples; cut into rings ¾ inch thick. Dip in ginger mixture. In skillet, in ¼ cup butter, sauté rings until lightly browned on both sides. Make 2 layers of overlapping rings in 12″ by 8″ baking dish.
2. In same skillet, sauté onions until browned on all sides; set aside. Preheat oven to 350°F.
3. Sprinkle chicken pieces on all sides with salt; dip in all but 2 tablespoons of remaining ginger mixture. In same skillet, in ¼ cup butter, sauté chicken pieces until browned; arrange with onions on either side of apple rings.
4. Stir 2 tablespoons ginger mixture into drippings in skillet; add bouillon cubes. Stir in 1½ cups water, a little at a time, blending well. Bring to boiling, stirring constantly, then cook 2 minutes or until slightly thickened. Pour over apples, chicken and onions.
5. Cover with foil; bake 1 hour and 15 minutes or until fork-tender.

*For more Company Feasts
see page 113*

Paella Pronto, page 90
Head Lettuce with Foamy Dressing, page 196

Chicken-and-Apple, page 104
Baked Flounder Supreme,
page 93

French Beef Stew, page 95

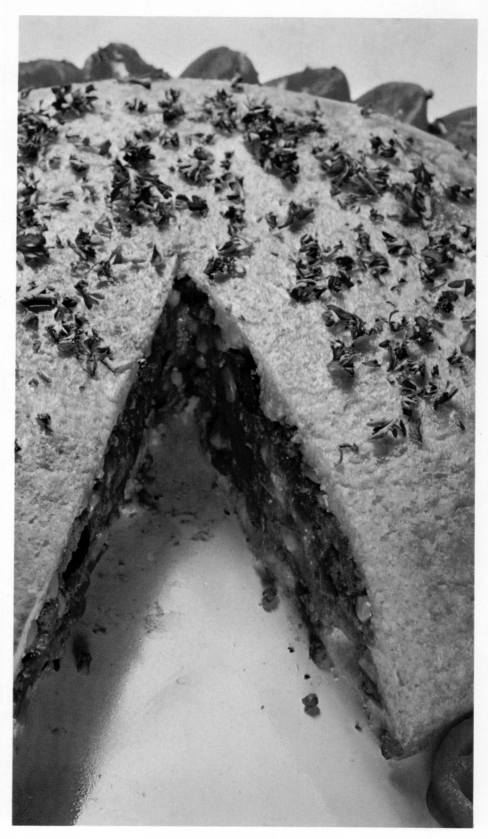

Tamale Pie, page 98

Turkey Divan, page 103
Brioche à la Maxim, page 218

Hamburger-Macaroni Treat, page 100

Chicken Parmigiana, page 113

CHICKEN-HERBED-RICE CASSEROLE

Do-Ahead Dish
Time in Kitchen: 25 minutes
Free Time: 50 minutes
Servings: 6

1 6-ounce package long-grain-and-wild-rice mix
2 tablespoons butter or margarine
3 large whole chicken breasts, boned, skinned, cut in half
1 10½-ounce can condensed cream-of-chicken soup
½ cup sauterne
½ cup diced celery
1 3-ounce can sliced mushrooms, drained

Early in day: Cook rice mix as label directs. Meanwhile, in large skillet, in hot butter, sauté chicken breasts until golden; remove from skillet.

Into drippings in skillet, stir undiluted soup, sauterne, celery and mushrooms; bring to boiling.

Spoon rice into 12″ by 8″ baking dish. Arrange chicken on top; pour on sauce; cover; refrigerate.

One hour before dinner: Preheat oven to 375°F. Bake chicken 35 minutes; uncover; bake 15 minutes more or until chicken is fork-tender.

Serve with: Marinated green bean salad • Basket of warm crackers • Blueberry pie à la mode

---

CHICKEN PARMIGIANA

pictured on page 112

Time in Kitchen: ½ hour
Free Time: ½ hour
Servings: 4

dry instant potato flakes for 4 servings
1 teaspoon salt
¼ teaspoon pepper
1 egg
2 large whole chicken breasts, halved
butter or margarine
4 ounces spaghetti
4 slices Swiss cheese
1 16-ounce can stewed tomatoes
¼ cup grated Parmesan cheese
parsley sprigs for garnish

1. *About 1 hour before dinner:* Preheat oven to 350°F. Mix potato flakes, salt, pepper. Beat egg with 2 tablespoons water; in it, dip chicken breasts; coat well with potato flakes.
2. In oven, in large, shallow baking dish, heat ¼ cup butter until hot. In it, lay chicken, skin side down. Bake 25 minutes; turn over, then bake until golden, about 20 minutes.
3. Meanwhile, cook spaghetti as label directs. Increase oven heat to 500°F. Remove chicken from oven; top each with a cheese slice, folded in half. Return to oven for 10 minutes, or until cheese is melted.
4. Meanwhile, heat stewed tomatoes. Toss spaghetti with Parmesan cheese, 3 tablespoons butter; arrange on serving dish. Top with chicken; spoon tomatoes around; garnish with parsley sprigs.

Serve with: Romaine-mushroom salad with green goddess dressing • Homemade gingerbread with whipped cream or topping

CHICKEN-AND-CRAB

Time in Kitchen: 15 minutes
Free Time: ½ hour
Servings: 6

½ cup butter or margarine
1 7-ounce can water chestnuts,
    drained, sliced
1 10-ounce can bamboo shoots,
    drained, sliced
¼ pound fresh mushrooms, sliced
1 10-ounce package frozen peas,
    slightly thawed
1 10½-ounce can condensed chicken
    broth
1 teaspoon salt
¼ cup cornstarch
2 tablespoons soy sauce
1 large whole chicken breast,
    simmered tender, boned, cut up
1 7½-ounce can Alaska King crab,
    drained
2 3-ounce cans chow-mein noddles

About 45 minutes before dinner: Preheat oven to 350°F. In 12-inch skillet, in hot butter, sauté chestnuts, shoots, mushrooms and peas 3 minutes. Add undiluted broth, salt; cook 1 minute. In bowl, mix cornstarch, ¼ cup water and soy sauce until smooth; add to vegetables, stirring; cook until thickened. Pour into 13″ by 9″ baking dish; top with chicken and crab. Sprinkle with noodles. Bake ½ hour.

CHICKEN SANTA FÉ

Time in Kitchen: ½ hour
Free Time: 2 hours
Servings: 8

¼ cup salad oil
1 5-pound stewing chicken, cut up
2 onions, sliced
5 teaspoons salt
½ to 1 teaspoon pepper
½ teaspoon sage leaves
1 8-ounce package elbow macaroni
2 17-ounce cans kidney beans, drained
1 12-ounce can whole-kernel corn
1 16-ounce can cut green beans
1 16-ounce can tomatoes
4 dashes hot pepper sauce

About 2½ hours before dinner: In 7-quart kettle, in hot oil, brown chicken. Add onions; sauté until golden. Add 2 cups water, salt, pepper, sage. Cover; cook 2 hours or until fork-tender.

    Meanwhile, cook macaroni as label directs. Add to chicken with beans and rest of ingredients; heat.

CHEESY CHICKEN

Time in Kitchen: ½ hour
Free Time: ½ hour
Servings: 6

1 4-pound stewing chicken
2 10-ounce packages frozen broccoli
    spears
2 cups milk
2 8-ounce packages cream cheese
1 teaspoon salt
¾ teaspoon garlic salt
1½ cups grated Parmesan cheese

1. *Early in day:* Simmer chicken as directed on page 8. Cool; remove skin. Slice thinly; cover; refrigerate.
2. *About 1 hour before dinner:* Preheat oven to 350°F. Lightly grease 2-quart oblong casserole. Cook broccoli as label directs; cut into bite-size pieces; arrange in casserole.
3. In double boiler, over hot, not boil-

ing water, blend milk, cream cheese, salt, garlic salt. Stir in ¾ cup Parmesan.
4. Pour 1 cup sauce over broccoli; top with chicken. Spoon on rest of sauce. Top with ¼ cup cheese. Bake ½ hour; remove; let stand 5 minutes. Pass cheese.

MEXICAN CHICKEN CASSEROLE

Time in Kitchen: 20 minutes
Free Time: 40 minutes
Servings: 8

1 4- to 5-pound stewing chicken, cut up
2 tablespoons shortening
2 small onions, chopped
1 green pepper, chopped
¼ cup all-purpose flour
1 16-ounce can tomatoes
24 pitted ripe olives (about 1 cup)
½ teaspoon garlic salt
salt
½ teaspoon seasoned pepper
¼ teaspoon sage leaves
1 12-ounce can whole-kernel corn, drained
¼ teaspoon seasoned salt

1. *Early in day:* Simmer chicken as directed on page 8. Remove chicken from broth; cool; refrigerate both.
2. *About 1 hour before dinner:* Remove sizable pieces of chicken from bones; skin pieces. Preheat oven to 350°F.
3. In medium skillet, in shortening, sauté onions and green pepper 5 minutes; stir in flour, tomatoes, olives, garlic salt, 1 teaspoon salt, seasoned pepper, sage.
4. Grease 2-quart casserole; in it, arrange half of corn, sprinkled with half of seasoned salt, half of chicken and olive sauce. Repeat. Bake 40 minutes.

SAVORY VEAL STEW

pictured on page 133

Time in Kitchen: 40 minutes
Free Time: 50 minutes
Servings: 8

6 bacon slices
3 pounds veal shoulder, cut in 1½-inch cubes
3 large onions, sliced
2 garlic cloves
½ teaspoon curry powder
1 10½-ounce can condensed tomato soup
1 teaspoon salt
⅛ teaspoon thyme leaves
⅛ teaspoon rosemary leaves, crushed
2 tablespoons butter or margarine
½ pound fresh mushrooms, sliced
⅓ cup sherry
½ cup chopped parsley for garnish

1. *About 1½ hours before dinner:* In Dutch oven, fry bacon until crisp; drain on paper towels; crumble and set aside. Remove all but 3 tablespoons bacon fat.
2. In fat, brown veal lightly. Add onions and garlic; continue cooking, stirring, until veal is well browned. Add curry powder and 1½ cups boiling water; stir to scrape up brown bits from bottom and sides of Dutch oven.
3. Add crumbled bacon, undiluted soup, salt, thyme and rosemary; blend thoroughly. Cover and simmer over low heat for 1 hour.
4. About 10 minutes before the hour is up, in medium skillet, melt butter; add mushrooms and sauté about 5 minutes. Stir into stew, with sherry; remove garlic; sprinkle with parsley.

Serve with: Tossed avocado salad • Fresh peach sundae

LAMB FRICASSEE

Time in Kitchen: ½ hour
Free Time: 1½ hours
Servings: 8

½ cup all-purpose flour
1 tablespoon salt
½ teaspoon pepper
3 pounds boneless lamb, cut in 1-inch cubes
⅓ cup butter or margarine
3 medium onions, chopped
1½ teaspoons garlic salt
½ teaspoon paprika
½ teaspoon rosemary
2 tablespoons lemon juice
2 9-ounce packages frozen artichoke hearts

1. *About 2 hours before dinner:* In large bowl, combine flour, salt and pepper; coat lamb cubes with flour mixture.
2. In large skillet or Dutch oven, in butter, sauté lamb cubes until brown.
3. Add onions, garlic salt, paprika, rosemary, lemon juice and 1½ cups water; cover; simmer 1½ hours.
4. Add artichoke hearts; cover; simmer about 10 minutes or until hot.

Serve with: Buttered noodles • Fresh fruit • Tea

SWISS VEAL ROAST

Time in Kitchen: 35 minutes
Free Time: 2 hours
Servings: 8

1 3-pound shoulder veal roast, boned, rolled
2 teaspoons salt
½ teaspoon pepper
1 bay leaf
5 onions
4 whole cloves
3 tablespoons salad oil
1½ tablespoons all-purpose flour
1 beef-bouillon cube
¼ teaspoon rosemary
8 small potatoes, pared
4 carrots, cut into 1-inch diagonal slices

1. *About 2 hours and 35 minutes before dinner:* Rub veal with salt and pepper. Attach bay leaf to one onion with cloves. In Dutch oven, or large heavy kettle, in hot oil, sauté veal until well browned on all sides; remove from heat.
2. To drippings in Dutch oven, add flour. Brown, while stirring, then add 1¾ cups water, bouillon cube and rosemary. Bring to boiling, while stirring. Add studded onion and browned veal.
3. Cover; simmer 1½ hours; turn roast once.
4. Add potatoes, carrots and remaining 4 onions, halved. Bring to boiling; cover; simmer ½ hour, or until meat is fork-tender.

Serve with: Cheese-stuffed celery • Hot rolls • Rice pudding with frozen mixed fruit, thawed

CURRIED VEAL PAPRIKA

Time in Kitchen: 50 minutes
Free Time: 40 minutes
Servings: 8 to 10

½ cup butter or margarine
4 pounds boned veal shoulder, in 1½-inch cubes
2 teaspoons salt
1 tablespoon granulated sugar
4 teaspoons curry powder
1¼ teaspoons pepper
¼ teaspoon paprika
1 10½-ounce can condensed beef broth
2½ cups sour cream
⅔ cup all-purpose flour
1 cup chopped parsley
1 8-ounce package broad noodles
¼ cup toasted slivered almonds
½ tablespoon poppy seed

About 1½ hours before dinner: In Dutch oven, in hot butter, brown veal cubes one-third at a time, then return all to Dutch oven.

Sprinkle veal with salt, sugar, curry, pepper, paprika; add undiluted broth, sour cream. Blend flour with ⅔ cup water; stir into veal; add parsley. Simmer, covered, 1 hour, or until veal is tender, stirring often. About 20 minutes before end of hour, cook noodles as label directs.

About 20 minutes before dinner: Preheat oven to 350°F. Arrange noodles in ring around edge of shallow baking dish. Spoon veal into center; top with almonds, poppy seed. Cover with foil; bake 15 minutes.

Serve with: Romaine salad with cherry tomatoes • Crusty hard rolls • Honeydew melon

VEAL À LA PARMIGIANA

Time in Kitchen: ½ hour
Free Time: 15 minutes
Servings: 8

1 egg
⅓ cup all-purpose flour
¾ cup grated Parmesan cheese
1 teaspoon salt
⅛ teaspoon pepper
8 veal cutlets
⅓ cup salad oil
1 pint Do-Ahead Tomato Sauce, thawed (page 9)

About 45 minutes before dinner: In pie plate, with fork, beat egg with 1 tablespoon water. Mix flour, ¼ cup Parmesan cheese, salt and pepper. Dip each cutlet first in egg mixture, then in flour mixture, coating evenly.

In large skillet, in hot oil, brown cutlets well on both sides, a few at a time. Return all cutlets to skillet; pour on tomato sauce. Sprinkle with ½ cup Parmesan cheese; cover; cook 15 minutes.

Serve with: Chicory-cucumber salad with Italian dressing • Spumoni or tortoni • Black coffee

LAMB STEW

Time in Kitchen: 25 minutes
Free Time: 45 minutes
Servings: 6

2 tablespoons butter or margarine
2 pounds boned lamb shoulder, diced
2 bacon slices, diced
1 medium onion, minced
½ teaspoon salt
dash pepper
3 tablespoons all-purpose flour
½ cup dry white wine
2 egg yolks
1 tablespoon lemon juice
2 tablespoons chopped parsley
½ teaspoon marjoram leaves

About 1 hour and 10 minutes before dinner: In Dutch oven, in hot butter, brown lamb, bacon, onion. Add salt, pepper, flour, wine; cook, stirring, until liquid thickens and boils. Add ½ cup water; simmer, covered, 45 minutes.

   With fork, beat yolks with juice. Stir in a little liquid from Dutch oven; add parsley, marjoram; remove from heat; stir in egg mixture. Cover; let stand 5 minutes.

LAMB CHOP CASSEROLE
pictured on page 131

Do-Ahead Dish
Time in Kitchen: ½ hour
Free Time: ½ hour
Servings: 6 to 8

1 pound small white onions (about 18)
12 loin lamb chops, ¾ inch thick
onion salt
3 large baking apples, halved, cored
half lemon
1 pound cooked whole young carrots
1 10-ounce jar currant jelly

1. *Day before or early in day:* In saucepan, in boiling salted water, cook onions, covered, until almost tender.
2. Meanwhile, sprinkle chops with onion salt; in large skillet, brown them, a few at a time, on both sides.
3. Rub cut surface of apples with lemon.
4. Around sides of large shallow casserole, stand 10 chops; lay 2 on bottom; place apples, onions and carrots.
5. In small saucepan, melt half of jelly. Spoon over food in casserole, then cover casserole with foil; refrigerate.
6. *About 40 minutes before dinner:* Preheat oven to 350°F. Bake casserole, uncovered, about ½ hour or until apples are tender and all are glazed. Melt rest of jelly in small saucepan; brush apples once during baking.

PORK WITH DUMPLINGS

Time in Kitchen: 45 minutes
Free Time: 45 minutes
Servings: 8

2 tablespoons salad oil
1½ cups chopped onions
1 tablespoon paprika
3 pounds pork shoulder, in 1½-inch cubes
1 teaspoon salt
1 10½-ounce can condensed beef broth
Dumplings (below)
3 tablespoons all-purpose flour
½ cup heavy or whipping cream

About 1½ hours before dinner: In large deep skillet, in oil, fry onions until golden. Stir paprika into onions; cook a few minutes. Add pork; cook 10 minutes or until coated with onions. Stir in salt and undiluted beef broth; simmer, covered, 1 hour 15 minutes or until meat is tender. Meanwhile, make Dumplings.

Just before serving, blend flour with cream until smooth; pour over meat in skillet; bring to boiling, while stirring.

Dumplings

5 slices white bread
¼ cup butter or margarine
3 cups sifted all-purpose flour
1½ teaspoons salt
6 teaspoons double-acting baking powder
1 cup milk
2 eggs, beaten

About 45 minutes before dinner: Cut crusts from bread. Cut slices into ½-inch cubes. In skillet, melt butter; sauté bread cubes until golden and crisp; set aside.

In medium bowl, mix flour, salt and baking powder. Beat in milk and eggs until smooth; fold in cubes.

Into kettle of gently boiling, salted water, drop dough by tablespoonfuls. Simmer, uncovered, 20 minutes or until done. With slotted spoon, transfer to platter.

Serve with: Chilled pineapple juice • Pickled beet-and-cucumber salad • Apple strudel

PEPPER-PORK STEW

Time in Kitchen: 25 minutes
Free Time: 1½ hours
Servings: 6

¼ cup salad oil
2 pounds lean pork, in 1½-inch pieces
3 tablespoons regular white rice
4 medium onions, coarsely chopped
3 garlic cloves, minced
1 10½-ounce can condensed beef consommé
3 medium tomatoes, coarsely chopped
¼ teaspoon saffron (optional)
1½ teaspoons salt
¼ teaspoon red pepper, crushed
¼ teaspoon cinnamon
3 medium potatoes, quartered
¼ cup chopped salted peanuts
¼ cup heavy or whipping cream
1 tablespoon molasses
1 green banana, quartered

About 1 hour and 55 minutes before dinner: In large Dutch oven, in hot oil, brown pork; add rice, onions, and garlic; sauté 5 minutes, stirring. Stir in undiluted consommé and next 5 ingredients. Simmer, covered, 1 hour.

Stir in potatoes; simmer 15 minutes. Add peanuts, cream, molasses, banana; simmer 15 minutes or until fork-tender.

Serve with: Rye bread and butter • Fresh pears and grapes with cheese • Coffee

PORK CHOPS MAJESTIC

Time in Kitchen: ½ hour
Free Time: 1 hour
Servings: 4

6 loin pork chops, 1½ inches thick
⅓ cup packaged seasoned bread crumbs
3 tablespoons salad oil
1 garlic clove
1 chicken-bouillon cube
4 medium onions, sliced
6 tablespoons sherry
¼ cup soy sauce
1 tablespoon granulated sugar
2 10-ounce packages frozen broccoli spears, thawed
1 tablespoon cornstarch (optional)

About 1½ hours before dinner: Coat chops with crumbs. In large skillet, heat oil and garlic; in it, sauté chops until golden brown. Remove garlic and excess fat. Turn heat low. Dissolve bouillon cube in 1 cup boiling water; add to chops with onions, sherry, soy sauce and sugar. Cover; simmer 1 hour or until fork-tender, turning once. Uncover skillet; lay broccoli around chops; cover; boil 5 minutes. Uncover; remove chops to heated platter; arrange broccoli around them. If desired, blend cornstarch with 3 tablespoons water; gradually stir into broth in skillet until thickened. Pour sauce over chops.

Serve with: Hot cooked rice • Spinach salad • Chilled fruit cocktail • Tea

SWEET-SOUR PORK CHOPS

Time in Kitchen: 45 minutes
Servings: 4

4 loin pork chops, ½ inch thick
salt and pepper
6 to 8 peeled, cooked sweet potatoes
3 tablespoons syrup drained from crushed pineapple
2 tablespoons minced onion
1 teaspoon cornstarch
1 cup canned, crushed pineapple
2 tablespoons vinegar
1 tablespoon soy sauce

About 45 minutes before dinner: In large skillet, brown chops; sprinkle with salt and pepper; pour off fat; set aside; return 2 tablespoons to skillet. Arrange sweet potatoes around chops; add pineapple syrup; cover; cook over low heat about ½ hour; turn potatoes.

Meanwhile, measure 1 tablespoon fat into small saucepan; add onion; sauté 3 minutes. Sprinkle with cornstarch; stir in pineapple, vinegar, soy sauce; cook, stirring, until thickened and clear. Pour over chops.

SAUERKRAUT GARNI

Time in Kitchen: 35 minutes
Free Time: 1 hour and 25 minutes
Servings: 8

4 shoulder pork chops
2 17-ounce cans sauerkraut, drained
4 bacon slices, halved
1 pound frankfurters
½ teaspoon coriander seed
¼ teaspoon pepper
¼ cup dry white wine
4 medium potatoes, halved
2 carrots, sliced

About 2 hours before dinner: Cut each chop into 2 pieces. Turn one can of sauerkraut into 4-quart Dutch oven; top with half of pork chops, half of bacon. Add rest of sauerkraut; top with rest of pork and bacon, then with two frankfurters, sliced ¼ inch thick, coriander, pepper, wine. Simmer, covered, 45 minutes.

Top with potatoes, carrots; cook, covered, 40 minutes more, or until potatoes are almost tender. Top with remaining frankfurters, halved. Cover; simmer until heated through.

Serve with: Tomato juice • Warm apple pie • Coffee

PARTY BEANS AND FRANKS

Time in Kitchen: 20 minutes
Free Time: 20 minutes
Servings: 10

⅓ cup salad oil
2 medium onions, sliced
1 garlic clove, minced
1½ pounds frankfurters, sliced ½ inch thick
¾ cup chopped pitted ripe olives
1 16-ounce can kidney beans, drained
1 29-ounce can hominy, drained
1 tablespoon chili powder
2 teaspoons salt
1¾ cups tomato juice
6 ounces shredded Cheddar cheese (1½ cups)
buttered French-bread slices

About 40 minutes before dinner: Preheat oven to 400°F. In large skillet, in hot oil, fry onions and garlic until golden; add frankfurters and heat 5 minutes. Stir in olives, beans, hominy, chili powder, salt and tomato juice; bring to boiling; stir in cheese. Pour

into 12″ by 8″ baking dish. Place bread on top; bake, uncovered, 20 minutes.

Serve with: Lettuce wedges with mayonnaise • Watermelon

SPICY EGGS AND HAM

Time in Kitchen: 20 minutes
Free Time: ½ hour
Servings: 4

3 tablespoons butter or margarine
3 tablespoons all-purpose flour
1 teaspoon dry mustard
¾ teaspoon salt
⅛ teaspoon pepper
1½ cups milk
1 teaspoon horseradish
1 tablespoon Worcestershire
1 tablespoon chili sauce
dash hot pepper sauce
6 hard-cooked eggs, sliced
2 cups diced, cooked ham
½ cup cut-up ripe olives
¾ cup diced process sharp Cheddar cheese

About 50 minutes before dinner: Preheat oven to 400°F. In saucepan, melt butter; stir in flour, mustard, salt, pepper, then milk; cook, stirring, until smooth and thickened. Stir in horseradish, Worcestershire, chili sauce and hot pepper sauce.

In 1½-quart casserole, arrange layers of eggs, ham, olives, cheese and sauce. Bake ½ hour.

Serve with: Toasted corn muffins • Big green salad • Cinnamon cookies • Coffee

CHEESE-BACON CROWN
pictured on page 135

Time in Kitchen: 50 minutes
Free Time: 1 hour 40 minutes
Servings: 8

butter or margarine
1 cup all-purpose flour
2½ teaspoons salt
¼ teaspoon pepper
⅛ teaspoon nutmeg
2 cups milk
½ cup heavy or whipping cream
8 ounces shredded natural Swiss cheese (2 cups)
½ cup chopped chives
8 eggs, separated
about 9 slices white bread
6 lean bacon slices
1 small mushroom, cut in thin slices

1. *About 2½ hours before dinner:* In large saucepan, melt ½ cup butter; stir in flour, salt, pepper and nutmeg. Slowly stir in milk and cream, blending well. Cook, while stirring constantly, until smooth and thickened. Blend in grated cheese (reserve 2 tablespoons) and chives.
2. Remove from heat; turn into large bowl, then stir in egg yolks one at a time. Let cool slightly. Preheat oven to 350°F.
3. Butter a china soufflé dish which holds 10 cups to brim. Line bottom of dish with about 3 bread slices cut to fit. Cut 6 more bread slices in half lengthwise. Place them upright and side by side, around inner edge of dish. Lace a strip of bacon, in figure-eight fashion, around every two of these slices, as pictured.
4. Fold 35-inch length of foil, 12 inches wide, in half lengthwise; wrap around outside of dish, to make collar 3 inches higher than rim; fasten with cellophane tape.
5. In large bowl, beat egg whites until stiff; carefully fold into cooled cheese mixture; pour into soufflé dish.
6. Lay mushroom slices in circle and one in center on top of soufflé mixture; sprinkle reserved grated cheese over top. Bake 1 hour 40 minutes or until golden. Carefully remove foil collar.

Serve with: Green salad • Blueberry-orange compote with sugar cookies • Coffee

TRIPLE-TREAT CHEESE PIE

Time in Kitchen: 25 minutes
Free Time: 1½ hours
Servings: 6

1 tablespoon butter or margarine
8 thin slices Canadian-style bacon
1 10-inch unbaked pie shell, page 9
4 packaged process Swiss cheese slices
1 3-ounce package cream cheese, softened
3 ounces crumbled blue cheese (½ cup)
3 eggs
1½ cups light cream
1½ tablespoons all-purpose flour
dash cayenne

About 1 hour and 55 minutes before dinner: Preheat oven to 325°F. In skillet, melt butter; brown bacon on both sides. Arrange in pie shell; top with Swiss cheese. Mix cream cheese, blue cheese; spread over bacon-cheese layer. In bowl, beat eggs, cream, flour, cayenne. Pour over cheeses. Bake 1½ hours or until firm.

CURRIED EGGS

Time in Kitchen: 25 minutes
Servings: 6

2 tablespoons butter or margarine
2 tablespoons minced onion
2 tablespoons all-purpose flour
1 teaspoon curry powder
2 cups milk
1 teaspoon salt
¼ teaspoon pepper
2 teaspoons grated orange peel
¼ cup orange juice
6 hard-cooked eggs, quartered
3 cups hot cooked rice

About 25 minutes before dinner: In skillet, in butter, sauté onion until tender. Stir in flour, curry powder until smooth and bubbly. Stir in milk. Cook, stirring, until thickened. Add salt, pepper, orange peel and juice. Add eggs. Heat, stirring gently. Spoon over rice.

Serve with: Sliced oranges • Tea

BAKED EGGS

Time in Kitchen: ½ hour
Servings: 4

¼ cup butter or margarine
3 medium potatoes, cooked, cubed
½ pound bologna, in ½-inch cubes
salt and pepper
1 cup drained cooked or canned peas
1 pimiento, slivered (optional)
2 tomatoes, slivered
2 tablespoons chopped parsley
4 eggs
2 tablespoons light cream

About ½ hour before dinner: Preheat oven to 425°F. In skillet, in butter, sauté potatoes until lightly browned. Add bologna, 1 teaspoon salt, ¼ teaspoon pepper, peas, pimientos; cook 3 minutes. Add tomatoes, parsley; heat.

Turn bologna mixture into 1½-quart baking dish; make 4 depressions in top; into each, break an egg; sprinkle with salt, pepper. Bake 10 minutes or until done; pour on cream.

Serve with: Green salad • Brownies à la mode • Tea

CHILI-NESTED EGGS

Time in Kitchen: 20 minutes
Servings: 4

4 hard-cooked eggs
¾ teaspoon onion salt
¼ teaspoon pepper
1 egg, separated
1 15-ounce can chili con carne, without beans
all-purpose flour
packaged dried bread crumbs
salad oil

1. *About 20 minutes before dinner:* Chop eggs very fine; add onion salt, pepper, egg yolk; mix well, mashing with spoon. Form egg mixture into 4 half-inch patties.
2. Heat chili, stirring occasionally.
3. With fork, beat egg white until frothy; dip patties first into flour, next into egg white, then into crumbs. In skillet, in hot oil, brown patties on both sides.
4. Spoon chili into 4 individual casseroles; top each with 1 patty.

EGGS DIVAN

Time in Kitchen: 25 minutes
Free Time: 20 minutes
Servings: 6

12 hard-cooked eggs
½ cup mayonnaise
1 tablespoon instant minced onion
½ teaspoon salt
2 10-ounce packages frozen broccoli
    spears
2 8-ounce jars pasteurized process
    cheese spread

About 45 minutes before dinner: Halve eggs crosswise; remove yolks. In small bowl, mix yolks, mayonnaise, onion, salt; fill egg halves. Preheat oven to 400°F. Cook broccoli as label directs.

In 13″ by 9″ baking dish, arrange spears in 6 piles; place eggs in between. Spoon on cheese spread. Bake 20 minutes or until cheese is hot.

BAKED-EGGS-AND-SPINACH CASSEROLE

Time in Kitchen: 15 minutes
Free Time: ½ hour
Servings: 4

2 10-ounce packages frozen chopped
    spinach, thawed and drained
salt
3 tablespoons butter or margarine
3 tablespoons all-purpose flour
1 cup milk
1 4-ounce package shredded Cheddar
    cheese (1 cup)
6 eggs
⅛ teaspoon pepper
toast points

About 45 minutes before dinner: Preheat oven to 325°F. In 8-inch shallow baking dish, toss spinach with salt and spread in even layer; with spoon, make 6 indentations in spinach.

In small saucepan, melt butter; stir in flour until smooth; gradually stir in milk and cook, stirring constantly, until sauce is thickened; stir in cheese and heat just until melted.

Break one egg into each indentation; sprinkle eggs with pepper and ¼ teaspoon salt. Pour sauce over eggs. Bake ½ hour or until eggs are of desired doneness. Place on toast points.

Serve with: Tomato bisque • Fresh peaches • Macaroons

FRANKFURTER QUICKIE

Time in Kitchen: ½ hour
Free Time: ½ hour
Servings: 25

½ cup butter, margarine, salad oil or
    shortening
2 cups sliced onions
25 franks (3 pounds), sliced into ½-
    inch circles
1 cup minced green peppers
6 15¼-ounce cans spaghetti in tomato
    sauce with cheese
3 12-ounce cans vacuum-packed
    whole-kernel corn
2 teaspoons salt
1 teaspoon pepper
2 cups grated Parmesan cheese

About 1 hour before dinner: Preheat oven to 350°F. In large kettle, in butter, sauté onions and franks, tossing frequently, until onions are tender. Add green peppers; cook few minutes longer. Add spaghetti, corn, salt, pepper. Turn into 2 shallow roasting pans, about 15″ by 11″. Sprinkle top of each with Parmesan cheese. Bake ½ hour or until hot.

Serve with: Tossed green salad • Canned purple plums

WIENER-CORN-AND-POTATO BAKE

Time in Kitchen: ½ hour
Free Time: 1½ hours
Servings: 16

8 unpared small sweet potatoes
8 medium white potatoes
16 ears corn, halved
2 teaspoons salt
½ teaspoon pepper
32 frankfurters
½ cup melted butter or margarine
¼ cup chopped parsley

1. *About 2 hours before dinner:* Preheat oven to 425°F.
2. Scrub potatoes. Halve both the sweet and white potatoes; score surfaces.
3. In each of 2 large roasting pans, make single layer of potatoes. Place corn on top. Into each pan, pour 1½ cups boiling water. Sprinkle vegetables with 1 teaspoon salt and ¼ teaspoon pepper. Cover with foil; bake about 1 hour or until potatoes are nearly tender.
4. Place franks on top. Bake, covered, ½ hour more. Uncover; pour butter, with parsley added, over all.

Serve with: Waldorf salad • Devil's food cake • Coffee

MACARONI AND CHEESE, FRANK STYLE

Time in Kitchen: 50 minutes
Free Time: 40 minutes
Servings: 25

2 16-ounce packages elbow macaroni
2 quarts milk
¾ cup butter or margarine
1 cup all-purpose flour
1 tablespoon salt
1½ teaspoons dry mustard
2 pounds natural sharp Cheddar cheese, shredded (8 cups)
¼ cup minced onion
2 teaspoons Worcestershire
25 tomato slices, sliced ¼ inch thick
25 frankfurters, halved lengthwise (3 pounds)

About 1½ hours before dinner: Cook macaroni as label directs; drain. Meanwhile, in double boiler, heat milk. In large kettle, melt butter; stir in flour, salt, mustard; cook, stirring often, 10 minutes. Stir in heated milk; cook, stirring constantly, until thickened. Add cheese, onion, Worcestershire; stir gently until cheese is melted. Remove from heat; stir in macaroni.

Preheat oven to 400°F. Pour macaroni mixture into 2 shallow pans, about 15″ by 11″. Bake, uncovered, 20 minutes. On top of macaroni in each pan, arrange tomato slices, then franks. Bake 15 minutes more, or until franks are golden brown. Let stand about 5 minutes before serving.

Macaroni and Cheese: Just omit franks.

Serve with: Tomato juice with cheese crackers • Spiced peach salad • Gingerbread squares with lemon sauce

CHICKEN TETRAZZINI

Time in Kitchen: 1 hour 15 minutes
Servings: 25

18 to 20 cups cooked chicken or turkey, in large pieces
1¼ cups butter or margarine
3 pounds mushrooms, sliced
¾ cup all-purpose flour
pepper
salt
½ teaspoon nutmeg
2 quarts chicken broth
1 cup heavy or whipping cream
3 8-ounce packages fine noodles
½ cup melted butter or margarine
2 tablespoons lemon juice
2 ounces grated Parmesan cheese (⅔ cup)

Day before: Prepare chicken as in Simmered Chicken (page 8); refrigerate.

1. *About 1 hour and 15 minutes before dinner:* In large skillet, in ¾ cup butter, sauté mushrooms (¾ pound at a time); set aside.
2. In large kettle, melt ½ cup of the butter; stir in flour, ¼ teaspoon pepper, 5 teaspoons salt, nutmeg. Gradually stir in chicken broth and cream; cook until thickened, stirring occasionally.
3. Meanwhile, cook noodles as label directs (you'll need about 8 quarts water and 2 tablespoons salt); drain. To cooked noodles add ½ cup melted butter; season with salt and pepper.
4. Combine sauce, chicken and sliced mushrooms, heat through.
5. *Just before dinner:* Add lemon juice to chicken mixture. Arrange servings of noodles on each dinner plate; top with some chicken mixture; sprinkle with cheese.

CHICKEN CURRY ON PARSLEY RICE

Time in Kitchen: 1½ hours
Servings: 25

18 to 20 cups cooked chicken, in large pieces
1½ cups butter or margarine
4 pounds mushrooms, sliced ¼ inch thick
1⅓ cups minced onions
4 cups diced, pared apples
¾ cup all-purpose flour
4 teaspoons salt
⅛ teaspoon pepper
2 tablespoons curry powder
3 cups milk
3 cups chicken broth
4 cups regular white rice
¾ cup chopped parsley

Day before: Prepare and refrigerate chicken as in Simmered Chicken (page 8).

About 1½ hours before dinner: In large kettle, over medium heat, in ¾ cup butter, sauté mushrooms until browned; remove mushrooms; reserve. In same kettle, in remaining ¾ cup butter, sauté onions and apples until tender. Remove kettle from heat; stir in flour, salt, pepper, curry. Slowly stir in milk and chicken broth; cook over low heat, stirring, until thickened. Cover; cook over low heat, 20 minutes, stirring often. Meanwhile, cook rice as label directs, using 2 large pots; toss with parsley. Then add mushrooms and chicken to curry mixture; heat thoroughly. Spoon chicken over rice.

Serve with: Bowls of chutney, raisins, salted peanuts • Green salad • Fruit-filled watermelon • Iced tea

CALICO HAM CASSEROLE

Do-Ahead Dish
Time in Kitchen: 1 hour
Free Time: 40 minutes
Servings: 25

4 10-ounce packages frozen mixed
  vegetables
1 cup butter or margarine
3 cups fresh bread squares, in ½-inch
  cubes
1 cup all-purpose flour
1 teaspoon salt
¼ teaspoon pepper
2 teaspoons dry mustard
2 teaspoons Worcestershire
6 cups milk
1 medium onion, grated
2 to 3 cups process sharp Cheddar
  cheese, shredded (½ to ¾ pound)
2 pounds cooked ham, cut into strips
  1½ inches long and ¼ inch wide

Day before: Cook vegetables as label
directs. Meanwhile, in large kettle, melt
¼ cup of the butter; add bread
squares; toss well; remove bread; set
aside.

In bowl, mix flour with salt, pepper,
mustard, Worcestershire; slowly stir in
about 2 cups milk. Heat rest of milk in
same large kettle used for bread; stir
in flour mixture and remaining ¾ cup
butter. Cook over low heat, stirring
often, until smooth and thickened; add
onion and cheese. Cook, stirring often,
until cheese is melted. Add drained
vegetables and ham. Pour into two 12″
by 8″ baking dishes. Refrigerate along
with bread.

About 1 hour before dinner: Preheat
oven to 350°F. Sprinkle top of each
baking dish with buttered bread. Bake,
uncovered, 40 minutes or until hot.

SPAGHETTI WITH MEAT SAUCE

Do-Ahead Dish
Time in Kitchen: 1 hour
Free Time: 3½ hours
Servings: 25

1 cup salad or olive oil
2 cups minced onions
4 pounds beef chuck, ground
8 garlic cloves, minced
8 3-ounce cans sliced mushrooms, undrained
1 cup chopped parsley
2 cups sliced stuffed olives
4 8-ounce cans tomato sauce
4 19-ounce cans tomatoes (10 cups)
2 tablespoons salt
2 teaspoons pepper
1 teaspoon granulated sugar
6 pounds spaghetti
1 pound sharp Cheddar cheese, diced
2 2-ounce jars grated Parmesan
  cheese

Day before: In large kettle, in hot oil,
simmer onions 5 minutes. Add beef,
garlic; cook, stirring, until beef is
slightly browned. Add mushrooms,
parsley, olives, tomato sauce. Force
tomatoes through sieve; add to beef,
with salt, pepper, sugar. Simmer, covered, 1 hour. Uncover; simmer 2 hours
longer, stirring occasionally. Cool; refrigerate.

About ½ hour before dinner: In very
large pot, cook spaghetti as label
directs; drain. Meanwhile, heat sauce;
add diced cheese; heat, stirring occasionally, until cheese is melted.

To serve: Arrange spaghetti on individual plates or platters; pour on
sauce; top with grated Parmesan
cheese, or pass grated cheese in small
bowls.

ITALIAN SPAGHETTI MODERNO

Time in Kitchen: 1 hour 15 minutes
Servings: 25

1 cup salad oil
6 pounds beef chuck, ground
6 medium onions, sliced
6 garlic cloves, minced
1 teaspoon oregano leaves
7 teaspoons salt
1½ teaspoons pepper
1½ cups chopped parsley
1½ pounds spaghetti, broken into thirds
3 quarts tomato juice
3 cups chili sauce
3 6-ounce cans sliced mushrooms, undrained
grated Parmesan cheese

About 1 hour and 15 minutes before dinner: In large kettle, in hot oil, brown beef, onions, garlic; stir often. Add oregano and next 7 ingredients; stir with fork. Cover; cook over low heat, stirring occasionally, 45 minutes or until spaghetti is done. Serve with cheese.

NEW ENGLAND BOILED DINNER

Time in Kitchen: 1½ hours
Free Time: 4 hours
Servings: 50

22 to 25 pounds corned-beef brisket
1 pound onions, sliced
12 pounds medium potatoes
10 pounds small carrots, scraped
15 pounds cabbage, cut in wedges

1. *About 5½ hours before dinner:* Wash brisket; cut into pieces. Place in 17-quart kettle; add onions. Cover with water; simmer; covered, 5½ hours, or until fork-tender.
2. About 50 minutes before meat is done, peel potatoes; add to meat; cover; simmer until tender.
3. During last 25 minutes, in 8-quart covered kettle, in boiling salted water to cover, cook carrots until tender.
4. During last 12 minutes, in 8-quart kettle, in boiling salted water to cover, cook cabbage until tender. Serve meat and vegetables with horseradish.

CORN-CHEESE BAKE

Do-Ahead Dish
Time in Kitchen: 1 hour
Free Time: 1 hour
Servings: 24

2 1-pound loaves sliced white bread
2 20-ounce cans cream-style corn
¼ cup minced onion
2 pounds process Cheddar cheese, sliced
12 eggs
2 tablespoons salt
2 teaspoons paprika
2 teaspoons dry mustard
¼ teaspoon pepper
2½ quarts milk
½ cup melted butter or margarine

About 2 hours before dinner: Trim bread crusts; quarter each slice. In each of six 1½-quart casseroles, put layer of bread, corn mixed with onion, then cheese. Repeat. Beat eggs and seasonings; stir in milk, butter; pour on each casserole; refrigerate.

About 1 hour and 10 minutes before dinner: Preheat oven to 325°F. Bake 1 hour or until set.

Burger Trittini, page 102

Lamb Chop Casserole, page 118

Curried Meatball Bake, page 99

Savory Veal Stew, page 115

Sweet-and-Sour Cabbage, page 100

Cheese-Bacon Crown, page 122

Avocado-Spinach Salad, page 188
Seafood Español, page 92

BUSY-DAY SPECIALS

Quick, easy, and all in one dish, these are meant for those times you must prepare meals in minutes

CURRIED SPAGHETTI

*variations pictured
on pages 154–5*

Time in Kitchen: 35 minutes
Servings: 10

1 8-ounce package spaghetti
1½ 10½-ounce cans condensed cream-of-chicken soup
1 10½-ounce can condensed cream-of-mushroom soup
½ cup milk
2 teaspoons curry powder
1 3-ounce can whole mushrooms, undrained
1½ teaspoons grated onion
¼ teaspoon thyme leaves
⅛ teaspoon basil
⅛ teaspoon oregano
¼ cup grated Parmesan cheese

1. *About 35 minutes before dinner:* Cook spaghetti until barely tender, as label directs; drain. Meanwhile, in saucepan, stir together undiluted soups, milk and ¼ cup water; simmer, stirring, 10 minutes.
2. Add curry, mushrooms, onion, thyme, basil and oregano. Simmer, stirring, 10 minutes.
3. Arrange spaghetti in 2-quart casserole; pour on soup mixture; toss lightly with fork. Sprinkle with cheese and serve. (Or keep it warm in 300°F. oven up to 1 hour; for creamy casserole, cover dish.)
Gourmet's Choice: Omit basil, oregano; increase thyme to ½ teaspoon. In step 2, with curry, etc., add ½ package frozen peas. In skillet, sauté ¼ pound fresh link sausages, cut into 1-inch pieces, 12 minutes; just before they're done, add ¼ pound chicken livers and sauté until they lose their red color. Cut into large pieces. Add, with 1 cup slivered cooked ham, to spaghetti-soup mixture, then sprinkle with cheese.
Tuna-Tomato Spaghetti: Make as in steps 1 to 3, using 3-quart casserole and substituting ¼ teaspoon dried mint for thyme and oregano. Before topping with cheese in step 3, toss spaghetti-soup mixture with 1 cup diced Cheddar cheese, two 6½- or 7-ounce cans tuna, drained, and 1 large tomato, sliced and sprinkled with salt and pepper.
Seafood Supreme: With curry, etc., in step 2, add 1 pound raw shelled, deveined shrimp, ¼ pound scallops, halved and one 6-ounce package frozen Alaska King crab, thawed and well drained.

SPAGHETTI CASSEROLE

Time in Kitchen: ½ hour
Free Time: ½ hour
Servings: 8

1 16-ounce package spaghetti
1 pound beef chuck, ground
3 pints Do-Ahead Tomato Sauce, thawed (page 9)
1 8-ounce package process cheese, cut into pieces
1½ cups halved, pitted ripe olives

About 1 hour before dinner: Cook spaghetti as label directs. Preheat oven to 350°F. In skillet, brown meat. Add tomato sauce, cheese, olives; cook, stirring, until cheese melts. Stir in spaghetti. Pour into greased 3-quart casserole. Bake ½ hour.

FORTY-MINUTE CHILI

Time in Kitchen: 35 minutes
Servings: 6

2 tablespoons salad oil
1 medium onion, minced
1 or 2 garlic cloves, minced
½ to 1 pound beef chuck, ground
½ pound beef liver, diced
2 10¾-ounce cans condensed tomato
   soup
2 16-ounce cans kidney beans, drained
1 to 2 tablespoons chili powder
½ teaspoon salt
⅛ to ¼ teaspoon cayenne
dash pepper

About 35 minutes before dinner: In skillet, in oil, sauté onion, garlic, chuck and liver until browned. Stir in undiluted soup, beans, chili powder, salt, cayenne, pepper. Cover; simmer ½ hour; stir often.

  Serve with: Saltines • Lettuce with cheese dressing

HAMBURGER CHOP SUEY

Time in Kitchen: 20 minutes
Servings: 6

2 tablespoons butter or margarine
1 pound beef chuck, ground
2 onions, sliced
1 cup sliced celery
1 16-ounce can bean sprouts, drained
1 10½-ounce can condensed beef
   broth
2 3-ounce cans mushrooms, undrained
3 tablespoons cornstarch
¼ cup soy sauce

About 20 minutes before dinner: In skillet, in butter, sauté chuck, onions, celery. Add bean sprouts, undiluted beef broth, mushrooms. Simmer, covered, 10 minutes.

  Blend cornstarch with soy sauce; stir into chuck mixture; simmer, stirring, until thickened.

  Serve with: Hot rice • Tomato salad • Cherry-flavor gelatin

DUTCH HASH

Time in Kitchen: ½ hour
Free Time: ½ hour
Servings: 6

¼ cup butter or margarine
2 large green peppers, cut in chunks
2 large onions, sliced
1 pound beef chuck, ground
1 19-ounce can tomatoes (2½ cups)
2 cups crushed pretzels
¼ cup chopped parsley
1 teaspoon dill seed
½ teaspoon salt
½ teaspoon seasoned pepper
½ teaspoon dry mustard

About 1 hour before dinner: Preheat oven to 350°F. In large skillet, in butter, sauté green peppers and onions until just fork-tender. Stir in beef and continue to cook until meat just loses its red color. Remove one-third of mixture. Into meat left in skillet, stir tomatoes and rest of ingredients. Turn mixture into 2½-quart casserole. Top with reserved meat mixture. Cover with lid or foil. Bake ½ hour or until heated through.

CARAWAY MEATBALLS

Time in Kitchen: ½ hour
Free Time: 1 hour
Servings: 8

2 pounds beef chuck, ground
½ cup minced onions
2 teaspoons salt
caraway seed
¼ teaspoon pepper
2 tablespoons salad oil
1 27-ounce can sauerkraut, well-
   drained (3½ cups)
2 large apples, cut in wedges
2 tablespoons brown sugar
1 cup apple juice

About 1½ hours before dinner: In large bowl, combine meat, onions, salt, 1 teaspoon caraway seed and pepper; shape into 20 meatballs. In large skillet, in hot oil, brown meatballs.

Preheat oven to 375°F. In 3-quart casserole, toss sauerkraut with 1 teaspoon caraway seed. Top with apples; sprinkle with sugar; top with meatballs. Pour on juice; cover; bake 1 hour.

SAVORY SPAGHETTI

Time in Kitchen: 20 minutes
Servings: 4

1 pound pork-sausage meat
1 3-ounce can sliced mushrooms,
   drained
1 medium onion, sliced
1 garlic clove, minced
½ teaspoon salt
⅛ teaspoon pepper
2 15¼-ounce cans spaghetti in tomato
   sauce with cheese

About 20 minutes before dinner: In skillet, sauté sausage until nicely browned. Pour off all but 1 tablespoon drippings. Add mushrooms, onion, garlic, salt and pepper; sauté until onion is tender. Add spaghetti; cover; heat thoroughly over low heat, stirring occasionally.

Serve with: Mixed greens with red-onion slices and Italian dressing • Cheese • Pears • Black coffee

SAUSAGE SKILLET

Time in Kitchen: ½ hour
Servings: 6

1 pound pork-sausage meat
1 medium onion, chopped
1 green pepper, chopped
1 16-ounce can tomatoes
1 cup uncooked elbow macaroni
1 tablespoon granulated sugar
½ teaspoon salt
¼ teaspoon pepper
1 cup sour cream

About ½ hour before dinner: In large skillet over high heat, brown sausage with onion and green pepper, breaking sausage into small pieces as it browns; spoon off all fat. Stir in tomatoes, macaroni, sugar, salt and pepper. Cover and simmer, stirring occasionally, for 20 minutes. Remove from heat and stir in sour cream.

Serve with: Waldorf salad in lettuce cups • Frozen lemon cream pie, thawed • Milk

CURRIED FRANKS AND CORN

Time in Kitchen: 15 minutes
Servings: 4

3 tablespoons butter or margarine
4 frankfurters, quartered lengthwise
2 12-ounce cans vacuum-packed whole-kernel corn, drained
1¼ teaspoons curry powder
¾ teaspoon salt
¼ teaspoon pepper
¼ cup light cream
chopped parsley

About 15 minutes before dinner: In skillet, in butter, sauté frankfurters until lightly browned. Add corn, curry powder, salt, pepper, cream. Heat, stirring, until hot. Sprinkle with parsley.

Serve with: Garlic bread • Molded fruit ring • Tea

TWENTY-MINUTE BOILED DINNER

Time in Kitchen: 15 minutes
Servings: 6

1 head cabbage, cut into 6 wedges
1 pound frankfurters
salt
2 tablespoons butter or margarine
2 tablespoons all-purpose flour
1½ cups milk
2 to 3 tablespoons prepared mustard

About 15 minutes before dinner: In Dutch oven or large kettle, place cabbage wedges; top with franks. Add 1 quart boiling water and 1 teaspoon salt.

Cover; boil 10 minutes or until cabbage is tender-crisp.

Meanwhile, in saucepan, melt butter; add flour; stir until smooth. Remove from heat. Add milk, stirring constantly; add 1 teaspoon salt and mustard. Stir over low heat until smooth and thickened. Remove cabbage and franks to heated platter. Spoon on some of sauce; pass rest.

Serve with: Baked potatoes • Chocolate cake • Coffee

CREOLE FRANKS

Time in Kitchen: 15 minutes
Free Time: ½ hour
Servings: 4

3 tablespoons butter or margarine
½ cup coarsely chopped green pepper
½ cup coarsely chopped onions
1 garlic clove, minced
½ cup regular white rice
1 28-ounce can tomatoes
1½ teaspoons salt
1 tablespoon granulated sugar
⅛ teaspoon pepper
1 bay leaf
3 whole cloves
6 frankfurters, slashed
6 frankfurter buns

About 45 minutes before dinner: In Dutch oven or large covered skillet, in butter, brown green peppers, onions and garlic. Add rice, tomatoes, salt, sugar, pepper, bay leaf and cloves. Cover; simmer ½ hour. Top with franks. Cover; simmer 5 minutes more. Place on toasted split buns.

BROILED FRANK DINNER

pictured on page 159

Time in Kitchen: ½ hour
Servings: 4

2 16-ounce cans whole white potatoes
½ cup melted butter or margarine
paprika
salt
1 16-ounce can whole green beans
nutmeg
1 16-ounce can cling-peach halves
curry powder
5 frankfurters
prepared mustard
1 tablespoon instant minced onion

1. *About ½ hour before dinner:* Preheat broiler if manufacturer directs. Drain potatoes; place on broiling pan; brush potatoes with some of melted butter, then dust with paprika and lightly sprinkle with salt; broil, turning often, about 10 minutes; push to one side.
2. Toss drained green beans with 2 tablespoons melted butter, then season with salt and dash of nutmeg; place on broiling pan.
3. Brush 5 well drained peach halves (refrigerate rest for lunch next day) with melted butter; sprinkle with curry powder, then place on broiling pan.
4. Split frankfurters lengthwise, almost, but not quite through; brush with melted butter, spread inside with mustard; place, split side down, on broiling pan.
5. Broil all, turning once and sprinkling potatoes with instant minced onion, until franks are hot, about 7 minutes, brushing with butter as needed. Serve on trivet, right from broiling pan, or rearrange all on heated platter.

FRANKFURTER RICE PRONTO

Time in Kitchen: 25 minutes
Servings: 6

¼ cup butter or margarine
6 frankfurters, cut into strips
2 medium onions, thickly sliced
1 green pepper, diced
1⅓ cups packaged precooked rice
2 8-ounce cans tomato sauce
1 teaspoon salt
dash pepper
1 teaspoon prepared mustard
2 cups cooked or canned peas

About 25 minutes before dinner: In skillet, in butter, sauté frankfurters, onions, green pepper, rice; stir often until onions are soft. Stir in 1½ cups boiling water, tomato sauce and next 4 ingredients. Bring to boiling; simmer 5 minutes, stirring occasionally.

FRANK-AND-NOODLE BAKE

Time in Kitchen: 15 minutes
Free Time: ½ hour
Servings: 4

2 tablespoons butter or margarine
2 tablespoons minced onion
2 tablespoons minced green pepper
2 cups diced frankfurters (about 5)
⅛ teaspoon curry powder
½ to ¾ teaspoon salt
1 10½-ounce can condensed cream-of-chicken soup
2 cups cooked noodles
¾ cup shredded process Cheddar cheese

About 45 minutes before dinner: Preheat oven to 350°F. In skillet, in butter, sauté onion and pepper until tender; add franks, curry, salt, undiluted soup, noodles, ½ cup of the cheese. Turn into 2-quart casserole. Top with rest of cheese. Bake ½ hour or until hot and bubbly.

Serve with: Chicory and romaine with tart salad dressing • Spiced applesauce • Coffee

---

FRANKFURTERS PAPRIKA

Time in Kitchen: 20 minutes
Servings: 4

2 tablespoons butter or margarine
1 cup minced onions
1 beef-bouillon cube
4 teaspoons paprika
1 large green pepper, chopped
8 frankfurters, cut into diagonal slices
¼ teaspoon salt
⅛ teaspoon pepper
few dill seeds (optional)
few caraway seeds (optional)
2 medium tomatoes, cut up
hot cooked rice
green-pepper rings (optional)

About 20 minutes before dinner: In large skillet, in butter, sauté onions until soft. Stir in 1 cup hot water, then bouillon cube, paprika and green pepper; simmer 3 to 4 minutes.

Add frankfurters, salt, pepper, seeds; simmer, uncovered, 8 to 10 minutes. Fold in tomatoes; cook 2 minutes. Serve on heated platter with hot, cooked rice.

Serve with: Spinach • Hot canned peaches with oatmeal cookies • Milk

---

QUICK SKILLET ITALIENNE

Time in Kitchen: 20 minutes
Servings: 4

1 4-ounce can sliced mushrooms
2 tablespoons salad oil
1 medium onion, sliced
½ medium green pepper, chopped
¼ cup chopped celery
1 garlic clove, minced
¼ cup canned tomato juice
¾ teaspoon salt
⅛ teaspoon basil
1 15¼-ounce can spaghetti in tomato sauce with cheese
1 pound frankfurters, cut into diagonal chunks
grated Parmesan cheese

About 20 minutes before dinner: Drain mushrooms; reserve liquid. In large skillet, in hot oil, sauté onion, green pepper, celery, garlic and mushrooms until onion is transparent, about 5 minutes.

Into tomato juice, stir reserved mushroom liquid, salt and basil; add to onion mixture, along with spaghetti and franks. Cook over low heat, stirring occasionally, until heated through. Sprinkle with Parmesan cheese.

Serve with: Salted bread sticks • Sliced cooked zucchini • Ice-cream-sundae cups • Coffee

TUNA-EGG CURRY

Time in Kitchen: 15 minutes
Servings: 4

1 8-ounce package medium noodles
1 10½-ounce can condensed cream-
   of-celery soup
½ cup milk, cream, or white wine
1 to 3 teaspoons curry powder
1 6½- or 7-ounce can tuna, drained
2 hard-cooked eggs, quartered
chopped parsley

About 15 minutes before dinner: Cook noodles as label directs; drain. Meanwhile, in saucepan, combine undiluted soup, milk, curry powder. Cook, stirring, until well blended. Add tuna, eggs; heat. Serve over drained noodles. Sprinkle with parsley.

TUNA LASAGNA

Time in Kitchen: 15 minutes
Free Time: ½ hour
Servings: 8

9 packaged lasagna noodles
3 8-ounce cans tomato sauce with
   mushrooms
½ teaspoon basil
¼ teaspoon salt
⅛ teaspoon oregano leaves
1 8-ounce package sliced mozzarella
½ cup ricotta cheese
¼ cup grated Parmesan cheese
1 13-ounce can tuna, drained, flaked

About 45 minutes before dinner: Cook noodles as label directs. Meanwhile, combine tomato sauce, basil, salt and oregano. Preheat oven to 375°F. In

lightly greased 12″ by 8″ baking dish, arrange a lengthwise layer of 3 noodles, ¼ cup of tomato mixture, 2 mozzarella slices, ¼ cup ricotta cheese, 2 tablespoons grated Parmesan and tuna. Repeat with ¾ cup tomato mixture, 3 more noodles, 2 slices mozzarella, ¼ cup ricotta cheese, 2 tablespoons grated Parmesan, ¾ cup tomato sauce, then rest of noodles and tomato mixture.

Cut last slice of mozzarella into narrow strips; place on lasagna; bake ½ hour or until cheese melts. Remove; let stand a few minutes before serving.

TUNA PILAF

Time in Kitchen: 15 minutes
Servings: 6

2 6½- or 7-ounce cans tuna
1 cup sliced celery
⅓ cup minced onions
1 large green pepper, cut in thin strips
3 cups hot cooked rice
⅓ cup diced pimiento
1 3- or 4-ounce can sliced mushrooms
½ cup sliced Brazil nuts
1 teaspoon salt
½ teaspoon monosodium glutamate
¼ teaspoon pepper
1 teaspoon rosemary
1 teaspoon marjoram leaves

About 15 minutes before dinner: Drain oil from tuna into skillet; heat. Add celery, onion, green pepper; cook 5 minutes or until tender-crisp.

Add tuna, rice, pimiento, mushrooms with liquid, Brazil nuts, salt, monosodium glutamate, pepper, rosemary and marjoram. Cook about 10 minutes or until heated through.

TUNA ESPAÑOL

Time in Kitchen: 15 minutes
Free Time: ½ hour
Servings: 6

1 6-ounce package noodles with sour-cream and cheese-sauce mix
2 6½- or 7-ounce cans tuna, drained
1 3-ounce can sliced mushrooms, drained
2 pimientos, coarsely diced
½ cup grated Parmesan cheese
⅔ cup milk
2 tablespoons chopped parsley

About 45 minutes before dinner: Cook noodles as mix label directs; drain. Preheat oven to 350°F. Into noodles, stir sour-cream mix, tuna, mushrooms, pimientos, Parmesan and milk; turn into greased 1½-quart casserole.

Bake, uncovered, ½ hour or until hot and bubbly. Sprinkle with parsley.

Serve with: Toasted muffins • Banana-orange compote

TUNA-VEGETABLE CASSEROLE

Time in Kitchen: 10 minutes
Free Time: 15 minutes
Servings: 4

1 1¼-ounce envelope dehydrated noodle-soup mix
1 cup cooked or canned peas
1 8-ounce can small white onions, drained
1 7-ounce can tuna, drained, in large pieces
2 tablespoons all-purpose flour

About 25 minutes before dinner: Preheat oven to 400°F. Into 1 cup boiling water, in saucepan, stir noodle-soup mix; simmer gently 7 minutes.

In 1-quart casserole, arrange peas, onions, tuna. Stir a little water into flour to make smooth paste; stir into soup mixture; pour over tuna. Bake, covered, 15 minutes or until hot.

Serve with: Carrot coleslaw • Pears • Pecan cookies

TUNA-AND-RICE DINNER

Time in Kitchen: 15 minutes
Free Time: ½ hour
Servings: 6

1 6-ounce package long-grain-and-wild-rice mix
¼ cup butter or margarine
2 tablespoons all-purpose flour
dash pepper
1 cup chicken broth
1 16-ounce can French-style green beans, drained
2 6½- or 7-ounce cans tuna, drained and flaked
1 4-ounce can sliced mushrooms, drained

About 45 minutes before dinner: Cook rice as label directs but do not add seasoning package (use this with white rice another day). Meanwhile, in medium saucepan, melt butter; stir in flour and pepper until blended; gradually stir in broth and cook, stirring constantly, until thickened. Preheat oven to 350°F. Combine sauce with rice, beans, tuna and mushrooms; pour into greased 2-quart casserole. Bake, covered, ½ hour.

SAN FRANCISCO TUNA BAKE

Time in Kitchen: 20 minutes
Free Time: 40 minutes
Servings: 4

¼ pound medium noodles (about 2 cups)
1 medium onion, minced
2 tablespoons butter or margarine
1 16-ounce can tomatoes
¼ teaspoon garlic salt
1 teaspoon salt
¼ teaspoon pepper
¼ cup chopped parsley
1 6½-ounce can chunk-style tuna
1 8-ounce package process sharp Cheddar-cheese slices

About 1 hour before dinner: Cook noodles as package directs, adding onion; add butter. Preheat oven to 350°F. Combine tomatoes, salts, pepper, parsley. In 8″ by 8″ baking dish, place half of noodles, tuna, and cheese; pour on half of tomato mixture. Repeat. Bake 40 minutes.

TUNA-CASHEW CASSEROLE

Time in Kitchen: 10 minutes
Free Time: 40 minutes
Servings: 4

1 3-ounce can chow-mein noodles
1 10½-ounce can condensed cream-of-mushroom soup
1 6½- or 7-ounce can tuna
¼ pound cashew nuts
1 cup finely diced celery
¼ cup minced onion
dash each: pepper, salt

About 50 minutes before dinner: Preheat oven to 325°F. Set aside ½ cup of the noodles. In 1½-quart casserole, mix rest of noodles with undiluted soup, ¼ cup water, tuna, nuts, celery, onion, pepper, salt. Top with reserved noodles. Bake, uncovered, 40 minutes.

ONE-DISH TUNA DINNER

Time in Kitchen: 40 minutes
Free Time: 20 minutes
Servings: 4

14 small white onions, peeled
1 teaspoon salt
1 10-ounce package frozen peas
3 tablespoons butter or margarine
3 tablespoons all-purpose flour
milk
1 6½- or 7-ounce can tuna, drained
1 cup packaged buttermilk-biscuit mix
½ teaspoon ground sage

About 1 hour before dinner: In medium saucepan, in 2 cups boiling water, cook onions with salt until almost tender, about 5 minutes. Add peas; cover and cook until both vegetables are tender, about 5 minutes more. Drain, reserving liquid.

In medium saucepan, melt butter; stir in flour; gradually stir in 1 cup reserved vegetable liquid, then 1⅓ cups milk. Cook over low heat, until thickened. Remove from heat; fold in onions and peas, then tuna in large pieces. Turn into 2-quart casserole.

Preheat oven to 450°F. Combine biscuit mix with sage and ¼ cup milk; on lightly floured surface, knead about 10 times, then roll into circle ¼ inch thick. Cut into 4 rounds with large biscuit cutter. Place biscuits on top of onion-tuna mixture, brush with milk; bake 20 minutes or until golden. Let stand a few minutes before serving. Spoon some tuna mixture over each biscuit.

Serve with: Tossed salad with apple and pineapple chunks • Warm gingerbread squares • Lemon sauce

---

CASSEROLE FROM THE SEA

Time in Kitchen: 15 minutes
Free Time: ½ hour
Servings: 4

about 2 cups packaged ziti macaroni
1 10½-ounce can condensed cream-of-mushroom soup
⅓ cup mayonnaise
⅓ cup milk
1 5-ounce can cleaned shrimp
1 6½- or 7-ounce can tuna
1 7-ounce can water chestnuts, drained, sliced
1 cup minced celery
3 tablespoons chopped parsley
1 teaspoon minced onion
little curry powder

About 45 minutes before dinner: Cook ziti as label directs. Preheat oven to 350°F. Meanwhile, in 2-quart casserole, combine undiluted soup, mayonnaise and milk. Rinse shrimp under cold water; add to casserole with tuna, chestnuts, celery, parsley, onion and ziti. Sprinkle with curry powder; bake ½ hour or until hot.

Serve with: Broccoli with lemon and toasted almonds • Assorted hot breads • Buttery baked pears

---

SHRIMP-AND-RICE PARMESAN

Time in Kitchen: ½ hour
Servings: 4

2 tablespoons salad oil
⅔ cup regular white rice
2 teaspoons salt
⅛ teaspoon pepper
1 16-ounce can tomatoes
1 small onion, minced
¼ cup minced green pepper
1 cup coarsely shredded carrots
1 teaspoon Worcestershire
3 drops hot pepper sauce
1 20-ounce package frozen raw shelled, deveined shrimp
grated Parmesan cheese

About ½ hour before dinner: In pressure cooker, in hot oil, cook rice, stirring constantly, until lightly browned. Add 1½ cups water, salt, pepper, tomatoes, onion, green pepper, carrots, Worcestershire and hot pepper sauce.

Bring to 15 pounds pressure as manufacturer directs; cook 5 minutes. Remove from heat and reduce pressure quickly as manufacturer directs before uncovering. Add shrimp; bring to boiling; cook 5 minutes or until shrimp is tender. Serve with Parmesan cheese.

Serve with: Romaine-cucumber-radish bowl • Fresh peaches with cream • Iced tea

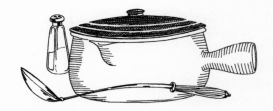

TWO-IN-ONE
ITALIAN DISH
pictured on page 158

Time in Kitchen: 15 minutes
Servings: 4

1 15-ounce can beef ravioli in sauce
½ teaspoon basil
½ teaspoon instant minced onion
1 15-ounce can spaghetti sauce with
    meatballs
1 tablespoon grated Parmesan cheese

About 15 minutes before dinner: Preheat oven to 425°F. Spoon ravioli into 8-inch skillet with metal or removable handles. Separate ravioli with fork; sprinkle with basil, onion. Top with spaghetti sauce. Heat. Sprinkle with cheese. Bake 10 minutes.

SWEET-SOUR CORNED
BEEF AND CABBAGE

Time in Kitchen: ½ hour
Servings: 4

4 cups finely shredded cabbage
salt
2 tablespoons butter or margarine
1 12-ounce can corned beef, chilled,
    quartered
1½ teaspoons all-purpose flour
1 tablespoon prepared mustard
2 teaspoons granulated sugar
2 tablespoons vinegar
1 tablespoon mayonnaise
2 tablespoons pickle relish
⅛ teaspoon hot pepper sauce
chopped parsley

About ½ hour before dinner: In large skillet, place cabbage; sprinkle with ¼ teaspoon salt; add ⅓ cup water; dot with 1 tablespoon butter. Cook, covered, 10 minutes; uncover; top with corned beef; cover; cook 5 minutes.

Meanwhile, in small saucepan, melt remaining butter; remove from heat; blend in flour, mustard, sugar, ¼ teaspoon salt, ¼ cup water and vinegar. Cook over low heat, stirring constantly, until mixture thickens and comes to boiling. Remove from heat; stir in mayonnaise, relish, hot pepper sauce.

Sprinkle corned beef and cabbage with parsley. Serve with sweet-sour sauce.

HASH-STUFFED
GREEN PEPPERS

Do-Ahead Dish
Time in Kitchen: ½ hour
Free Time: ½ hour
Servings: 6

6 medium green peppers
2 15½-ounce cans corned-beef hash
1 4-ounce package shredded Cheddar
    cheese (1 cup)
¼ teaspoon pepper
1 10½-ounce can spaghetti sauce with
    mushrooms
2 teaspoons granulated sugar

1. *Early in day:* Slice stem end from each green pepper; remove seeds. Cut thin slice from bottom of each so it stands level. In large saucepan, cover peppers with boiling water; simmer 5 minutes, uncovered; drain.
2. In medium bowl, combine corned-beef hash, half of cheese and pepper. Toss well, spoon into green peppers.

3. In 8″ by 8″ baking dish, combine spaghetti sauce, sugar. Set stuffed peppers in this sauce; cover dish; chill.
4. *About 1 hour before dinner:* Preheat oven to 375°F. Bake peppers, covered, ½ hour; uncover. With spoon, press down on top of each to form a slight indentation in center. Top each with some of remaining cheese; continue baking 15 minutes, uncovered; baste with sauce.

Serve with: Harvard beets • Fresh fruit • Cheese and crackers • Coffee

BEEF PIE À LA MODE

Time in Kitchen: 15 minutes
Free Time: 25 minutes
Servings: 4

2 19-ounce cans beef stew
1 8-ounce can white onions, drained
2 cups cooked or canned peas, drained
½ teaspoon thyme leaves
½ teaspoon garlic salt
¼ teaspoon salt
⅛ teaspoon pepper
1 8-ounce can refrigerated biscuits
½ tablespoon butter or margarine, softened

About 40 minutes before dinner: Preheat oven to 425°F. In 1½- or 2-quart casserole, combine stew, onions, peas, thyme, garlic salt, salt, pepper. Heat in oven, uncovered, 25 minutes.

Arrange biscuits on top of stew; bake 12 to 15 minutes or until biscuits are browned. Brush with butter.

Serve with: Cherry tomatoes and hearts of lettuce with blue-cheese dressing • Lemon meringue pie • Tea

SPAGHETTI-STUFFED PEPPERS

Time in Kitchen: 20 minutes
Free Time: 20 minutes
Servings: 6

6 medium green peppers
3 tablespoons salad oil
½ cup minced onions
1 garlic clove, minced
1 12-ounce can luncheon meat
¼ teaspoon basil
1 15½-ounce can spaghetti in tomato sauce with cheese
3 cups diagonally sliced carrots
½ teaspoon salt
3 tablespoons butter or margarine

1. *About 40 minutes before dinner:* Cut thin slice from stem end of each pepper; remove seeds.
2. In skillet, cook peppers with 2 cups boiling salted water, covered, 5 minutes; drain. Remove peppers. In same skillet, heat oil; add onions and garlic; sauté until tender but not brown.
3. Grate luncheon meat on coarse grater; add to onions; sauté until lightly browned. Add basil and spaghetti; use fork to avoid breaking up spaghetti. Lightly fill peppers with spaghetti mixture.
4. Arrange peppers along one side of skillet; arrange carrots along other side. Sprinkle salt on carrots; pour ⅓ cup water into bottom of skillet. Simmer, covered, 20 minutes or until carrots are tender. Spoon butter over carrots.

Serve with: Romaine-cucumber salad with onion dressing • Crescent rolls • Canned purple plums • Coffee

APPLE-SWEET-POTATO CASEROLE

Time in Kitchen: 10 minutes
Free Time: 25 minutes
Servings: 4

1 20-ounce can unsweetened sliced apples
1 23-ounce can vacuum-packed sweet potatoes
1 12-ounce can luncheon meat, cut into 4 slices
¼ cup packed brown sugar
½ teaspoon cinnamon

About 35 minutes before dinner: Preheat oven to 400°F. In greased 2-quart casserole, arrange alternate layers of apples and sweet potatoes, cutting large potatoes in half lengthwise. Arrange slices of luncheon meat on top. Sprinkle with brown sugar and cinnamon. Bake, uncovered, 25 minutes.

Serve with: Vegetable relishes • Cake

GRETCHEN'S CASSEROLE

Time in Kitchen: 10 minutes
Free Time: ½ hour
Servings: 6

1 16-ounce can sauerkraut
1 20-ounce can unsweetened apple slices
⅓ cup packed brown sugar
2 tablespoons vinegar
¼ cup minced onion
2 tablespoons butter or margarine
2 12-ounce cans luncheon meat
¼ cup packed brown sugar
2 teaspoons prepared mustard

About 40 minutes before dinner: Preheat oven to 400°F. In 2-quart casserole, combine sauerkraut and apples, undrained, with ⅓ cup brown sugar, vinegar, onion; dot with butter.

Slice meat into 8 to 12 slices; arrange on top of sauerkraut mixture. Combine ¼ cup brown sugar with mustard; spread on meat. Bake, uncovered, ½ hour or until meat is glazed and sauerkraut is heated through.

Serve with: Succotash • Cantaloupe

MACARONI AND CHEESE WITH MEAT

Time in Kitchen: 15 minutes
Free Time: ½ hour
Servings: 6

2 cups elbow macaroni
butter or margarine
3 tablespoons all-purpose flour
2½ cups milk
1½ teaspoons salt
¼ teaspoon pepper
1½ teaspoons horseradish
1 teaspoon prepared mustard
½ teaspoon Worcestershire
1 12-ounce can luncheon meat, cut in 1-inch-wide strips
1 cup cooked peas
2 tablespoons chopped parsley
½ cup shredded sharp Cheddar cheese

About 45 minutes before dinner: Cook macaroni as label directs. Preheat oven to 375°F. Meanwhile, in double boiler, melt 3 tablespoons butter; stir in flour, then gradually milk, salt, pepper, horseradish, mustard, Worcestershire; cook, stirring, until sauce is smooth and thickened.

In greased 2-quart casserole, combine macaroni, sauce, luncheon meat, peas and parsley. Sprinkle with cheese; dot with 1 tablespoon butter. Bake ½ hour or until bubbly.

DUTCH PANTRY PIE

Time in Kitchen: 25 minutes
Free Time: 35 minutes
Servings: 6

pastry for a 9-inch two-crust pie (page 10)
4 packaged process Cheddar cheese slices
1½ cups undiluted evaporated milk
2 cups cubed, raw potatoes
¼ cup chopped green onion
2 tablespoons chopped green pepper or pimiento
¼ teaspoon salt
¼ teaspoon pepper
1 12-ounce can luncheon meat, cubed
1 10½-ounce can condensed cream-of-mushroom, chicken or celery soup

1. *About 1 hour before dinner:* Roll half of pastry into 11-inch or 12-inch round; fit into 9-inch pie plate.
2. Preheat oven to 425°F. In saucepan, melt cheese in 1 cup of the evaporated milk, stirring. Add potatoes, green onions, green pepper, salt, pepper; spread in pastry-lined pie plate. Top with luncheon meat.
3. Roll out top crust; place top crust over pie; seal edges together; flute edges. Make 3 or 4 slashes in top crust. Bake 35 to 40 minutes.
4. Heat soup with remaining ½ cup evaporated milk; serve as sauce.

SPEEDY SQUARE MEAL

pictured on page 156

Time in Kitchen: 10 minutes
Free Time: 20 minutes
Servings: 4

2 12-ounce cans luncheon meat
whole cloves
1 8-ounce can refrigerated crescent rolls
1 tablespoon prepared mustard
½ cup apricot preserves
pickled watermelon slices for garnish

About ½ hour before dinner: Preheat oven to 375°F. Cut each luncheon loaf, almost to bottom, into 9 squares; stud with cloves. Place on ovenproof platter. Open can of dough; don't unroll. Cut dough into 9 slices; place around meat. Spread meat and rolls with mustard, then with preserves. Bake 20 minutes. Garnish with watermelon slices.

MEXICAN DINNER

Time in Kitchen: 10 minutes
Free Time: 15 minutes
Servings: 4

2 15½-ounce cans chili con carne with beans
1 12-ounce can whole-kernel corn, Mexican style, drained
butter or margarine
1 12-ounce package corn-muffin mix

About 25 minutes before dinner: Preheat oven to 450°F. In saucepan, heat chili with corn. Pour into buttered 12″ by 8″ baking dish. Prepare mix as label directs; spread on chili. Bake 15 minutes.

EAST-WEST CHILI BAKE

Time in Kitchen: 10 minutes
Free Time: ½ hour
Servings: 4

2 16-ounce cans pork and beans with tomato sauce
1 15-ounce can chili con carne without beans
1 15½-ounce can tamales in chili gravy
1 cup shredded process American cheese
½ cup minced onions

About 40 minutes before dinner: Preheat oven to 425°F. Spread pork and beans in 12" by 8" baking dish. With fork, break up chili; sprinkle on top.

Arrange tamales lengthwise down center; sprinkle with cheese. Bake ½ hour or until hot and bubbly.

Before serving, sprinkle minced onions between every two tamales.

BROILED LEMON-CHICKEN DINNER

pictured on page 153

Time in Kitchen: 50 minutes
Servings: 4

½ cup butter or margarine
¼ cup lemon juice
1½ teaspoons salt
1 teaspoon granulated sugar
¼ teaspoon pepper
1 3-pound broiler-fryer, quartered
4 medium tomatoes
1 10-ounce package frozen crispy processed fried potatoes
2 teaspoons grated lemon peel
2 teaspoons chopped parsley

About 50 minutes before dinner: Preheat broiler if manufacturer directs. In saucepan over low heat, melt butter with lemon juice, salt, sugar, pepper.

Place chicken, skin side down, on large broiling pan; broil 20 minutes, basting with butter mixture frequently. Meanwhile, cut tomatoes into 6 wedges about ¾ way through, gently spreading wedges apart.

Turn chicken pieces. Surround with tomatoes and potatoes. Broil 15 minutes or until chicken is tender; baste chicken and tomatoes with butter mixture. Sprinkle with lemon peel, parsley.

CHICKEN BREASTS SAUTÉ

Time in Kitchen: 25 minutes
Free Time: 25 minutes
Servings: 4 to 6

¼ cup butter or margarine
2 or 3 large whole chicken breasts, halved
1 sliced onion
1 garlic clove, minced
2 tablespoons all-purpose flour
½ teaspoon salt
¼ teaspoon pepper
1 chicken-bouillon cube
1 16-ounce can small white potatoes
¼ cup red wine

About 50 minutes before dinner: In large skillet, in hot butter, sauté chicken breasts until browned. Add onion, garlic; cook about 5 minutes. In small bowl, combine flour, salt, pepper. In 1 cup hot water, dissolve bouillon cube; slowly stir into flour; pour over browned chicken. Cover; cook slowly about 25 minutes or until chicken is tender. Add drained potatoes, wine; heat through.

Broiled Lemon-Chicken Dinner, page 152

Left: Tuna-Tomato Spaghetti, page 138
Center: Seafood Supreme, page 138
Right: Gourmet's Choice, page 138

Speedy Square Meal, page 151

Top: Calypso Pork Stew, page 166
Bottom: Deep-Dish Turkey Pie, page 169

Two-in-One Italian Dish, page 148

Broiled Frank Dinner, page 142

Front Center: Lemon-Cabbage Rolls, page
166
Upper Left: Ham-and-Rice Mold, page 163
Upper right: Franks Risotto, page 167

NEW LIFE FOR LEFTOVERS

A little bit of this plus a little of that can add up to the greatest dish you ever tasted

INDIAN CURRY

Sauté a chopped onion and apple in some butter or margarine. When they're soft, blend in one or two teaspoons curry powder, depending on how well your family likes curry. Stir in leftover gravy or a can of condensed cream-of-chicken soup and 1 to 2 cups cut-up cooked lamb or chicken. Cook until heated through. Season to taste with salt and pepper. Serve with steamed rice. Makes 4 servings.

CHINESE SWEET-AND-SOUR PORK

Chicken, beef or shrimp are good in this dish too. Sauté a chopped onion, diced green pepper and some sliced celery in salad oil until barely tender. Add ½ cup pineapple cubes, 1 to 2 cups meat or fish and a can of condensed beef bouillon, blended with two teaspoons cornstarch. Cook, stirring, until thickened. Season to taste with soy sauce. Makes 4 servings

ITALIAN MEAT SAUCE

Start with the same onion, green pepper and celery sautéed in oil; add garlic if desired. Instead of bouillon, add a can of tomatoes; simmer for about 20 minutes. Season with a dash of thyme and oregano and salt and pepper to taste. Add meat. Cook until heated through. Serve with steaming pasta and grated Parmesan cheese and you'll be cooking in the best Italian tradition.

ALL-AMERICAN BARBECUE

Barbecued spareribs, pork chops, hamburgers and hot dogs are traditional American favorites, but barbecued leftovers deserve a place on your list of family favorites too. The sauce that works its magic on the outdoor grill, will given an entirely new taste to yesterday's roast lamb, pork or pot roast.

Start with a chopped onion sautéed in butter or margarine until golden. Blend in ¼ cup each of brown sugar and cider vinegar; add a cup of catchup, half as much water and 2 teaspoons Worcestershire. Cover; let simmer 15 minutes. Add 2 cups thinly-sliced cooked meat; cook until heated. Serve on buns or over noodles. It's even better made ahead and rewarmed. Makes 4 servings.

As you can see, in planning a one-meal dish from leftovers, the possibilities are endless. Measurements need not be exact and substitutions are the rule of the day. If a recipe calls for peas and you have green beans, use the beans. No noodles?—try rice, stuffing mix or potatoes. Not quite enough meat?—add a hard-cooked egg, some nuts or cheese.

Experiment with different seasonings too, but do it with discretion. Start out with just a dash—you want to enhance the natural flavors, not bury them. Remember too that not all herbs and spices complement all foods. Consult our spice chart (page 12) before you get carried away.

Toppings are the final touch. They add eye as well as taste appeal. Instead of the usual buttered bread crumbs, try corn or potato chips, chow-mein noodles, nuts, grated cheese, flaky pastry or packaged stuffing mix, French-fried onion rings.

There is just one drawback to this kind of "fun" cooking. Every once in a while you come up with a real winner and the family keeps asking you to make it again. Then you may have a problem. It's not always easy to remember exactly what went into your masterpiece!

HAM SCALLOP

Time in Kitchen: 20 minutes
Free Time: 40 minutes
Servings: 4

1 10½-ounce can condensed cream-
  of-celery soup
½ cup milk
3 cups sliced, cooked, pared potatoes
1½ cups diced cooked ham
1 cup cooked peas
1 tablespoon grated Parmesan cheese

About 1 hour before dinner: Preheat
oven to 350°F. In small bowl, combine
undiluted soup with milk.

In greased 2-quart casserole, arrange in layers, potatoes, ham, peas
and soup mixture, ending with soup.
Sprinkle with cheese. Bake 40 minutes.

Serve with: Coleslaw • Lemon pie

HAM-AND-RICE MOLD

pictured on page 160

Time in Kitchen: 25 minutes
Free Time: 20 minutes
Servings: 4

1½ cups regular white rice
butter or margarine
½ cup minced green onions
¼ cup minced green pepper
2 cups ground leftover cooked ham
½ teaspoon prepared mustard
½ teaspoon salt
¼ teaspoon pepper
1 hard-cooked egg, sliced
2 eggs
½ cup shredded natural Cheddar
  cheese

About 45 minutes before dinner: Cook
rice as label directs; add 2 tablespoons
butter. Preheat oven to 350°F.

Meanwhile, in skillet in 2 tablespoons
butter, sauté onions and green pepper;
combine with ham, mustard, salt, pepper. Arrange sliced egg in bottom of
1½-quart greased casserole. Mix ham
mixture with 1 cup of rice. Spread on
top of egg slices.

Beat eggs; combine with cheese and
rest of rice. Pour into casserole. Press
down lightly; cover with foil. Place in
pan containing 2 inches of boiling
water. Bake 20 minutes; cool 5 minutes; unmold onto platter.

SWISS HAM AND EGGS

Time in Kitchen: ½ hour
Servings: 4

½ pound natural Swiss cheese, sliced
1 cup diced cooked ham
¾ cup heavy or whipping cream
4 eggs
¼ teaspoon salt
⅛ teaspoon pepper
dash paprika

About ½ hour before dinner: Preheat
oven to 425°F. Line well-buttered, 9-
inch-deep fluted pie plate or shallow
baking dish with overlapping cheese
slices. Top with half of ham. Pour half
of cream over ham. Carefully break
eggs into pie plate. Sprinkle with salt,
pepper. Arrange rest of ham around
eggs. Pour rest of cream over all.
Sprinkle with paprika. Bake 15 to 20
minutes or until eggs are of desired
doneness.

Serve with: Buttered toast • Green
salad • Spongecake

HAM-AND-GREEN-BEAN BAKE

Time in Kitchen: 10 minutes
Free Time: 20 minutes
Servings: 3

1 10½-ounce can condensed cream-of-mushroom soup
½ cup milk
2 cups cooked onions
1 cup slivered, cooked ham
1 cup cooked green beans
½ cup buttered fresh bread crumbs

About ½ hour before dinner: Preheat oven to 375°F. In 2-quart casserole, blend undiluted soup with milk; add onions, ham and green beans. Sprinkle top with buttered crumbs. Bake 20 minutes or until hot and bubbly.

Serve with: Marinated cucumbers • Ice-cream roll

HAM-TOMATO-CHEESE PIE

Time in Kitchen: 20 minutes
Free Time: 20 minutes
Servings: 8

1 baked 9-inch pie shell (page 9)
1 cup ground cooked ham
2 medium tomatoes, sliced
1 tablespoon instant minced onion
½ teaspoon oregano leaves
½ teaspoon salt
⅛ teaspoon pepper
¼ cup mayonnaise or salad dressing
1 8-ounce package process Cheddar cheese, shredded (2 cups)

About 40 minutes before dinner: Preheat oven to 350°F. Line pie shell with ground ham; cover with tomatoes. Sprinkle with onion, oregano, salt, pepper. Bake 20 minutes.

Meanwhile, combine mayonnaise with shredded cheese. Spread over baked ham-tomato filling; bake pie 5 minutes longer or until cheese melts.

BANANA-HAM CASSEROLE, CHEESE SAUCE

Time in Kitchen: 15 minutes
Free Time: ½ hour
Servings: 4

1½ tablespoons butter or margarine
2½ tablespoons all-purpose flour
¾ cup milk
1½ cups shredded process sharp Cheddar cheese
4 slightly green-tipped bananas, peeled
1½ tablespoons melted butter or margarine
1 tablespoon prepared mustard
1 cup diced, cooked ham
½ cup fresh bread crumbs

About 45 minutes before dinner: Preheat oven to 350°F. In saucepan, melt 1½ tablespoons butter; gradually stir in flour and milk. Add cheese; cook over low heat, stirring, until sauce is smooth and thickened.

In greased shallow baking dish, arrange bananas; brush with 1½ tablespoons melted butter; spread with mustard. Top with ham, then with cheese sauce; sprinkle with crumbs. Bake ½ hour or until bananas are done.

SAVORY HAM

Time in Kitchen: 15 minutes
Free Time: ½ hour
Servings: 4

1 medium head cauliflower
1 10½-ounce can condensed cream-of-chicken soup
¼ cup milk
2 cups cut-up, leftover, cooked ham
⅛ teaspoon savory
4 ounces process sharp Cheddar cheese, shredded (1 cup)

About 45 minutes before dinner: Break cauliflower into flowerets; cook in 1 inch boiling salted water until tender-crisp; drain. Preheat oven to 350°F.

Combine soup and milk in 10″ by 6″ baking dish. Fold in cauliflowerets, ham, savory, ½ cup of cheese. Top with remaining cheese. Bake ½ hour.

DEVILED-HAM CASSEROLE

Time in Kitchen: 15 minutes
Free Time: 1 hour 15 minutes
Servings: 6

½ cup ground cooked ham
2 tablespoons chili sauce
1 teaspoon prepared mustard
1 teaspoon minced onion
1 teaspoon Worcestershire
1 teaspoon horseradish
4 slices day-old bread
¼ cup shredded process sharp Cheddar cheese
2 teaspoons butter or margarine
3 eggs, beaten
½ teaspoon salt
2 cups milk

About 1½ hours before dinner: Preheat oven to 350°F. Combine ham with next 5 ingredients; spread ¼ of mixture on each bread slice; cut into ½-inch cubes.

In greased 1½-quart casserole, alternate layers of bread cubes and cheese, ending with bread; dot with butter.

Combine eggs, salt, milk; pour over all. Set casserole in pan of warm water; bake 1 hour 15 minutes.

EGGPLANT STUFFIES

Time in Kitchen: 15 minutes
Free Time: ½ hour
Servings: 4

1 large eggplant, halved lengthwise
1 cup cubed cooked ham
2 tablespoons butter or margarine
¾ cup soft bread crumbs
¼ cup chopped onion
¼ cup each: chopped cooked celery, carrots, turnips
½ teaspoon salt
⅛ teaspoon pepper
buttered bread crumbs

About 45 minutes before dinner: Preheat oven to 350°F. Parboil eggplant 10 minutes. Scoop out pulp, leaving ½-inch shell. Chop pulp fine.

In skillet, brown ham in butter. Add eggplant pulp, soft bread crumbs, onion, celery, carrots, turnips, salt and pepper. In shallow baking dish, place eggplant shells; fill with ham mixture; top with buttered bread crumbs. Bake ½ hour. To serve, cut each in half.

Serve with: Baked tomatoes • Ice-cream sundae • Coffee

CALYPSO PORK STEW
pictured on page 157

Time in Kitchen: 45 minutes
Free Time: 1 hour
Servings: 10

2 pounds pork stew meat, cut in 1½-inch chunks
1½ pounds leftover ham, cut in 1½-inch chunks (about 4 cups)
¼ cup instant minced onion
1 teaspoon salt
1 bay leaf
2 cups cubed potatoes
2 yellow straight-neck squash, cubed
⅓ cup chopped parsley
¼ cup lime juice
1 teaspoon coriander seed
½ teaspoon pepper
3 underripe bananas, cut in 1-inch chunks

About 1 hour and 45 minutes before dinner: In large Dutch oven or kettle, simmer pork and ham with onion, salt, bay leaf and 2 cups water, covered, for 1 hour. Add potatoes, squash, parsley, lime juice, coriander and pepper. Cook 20 minutes or until pork is fork-tender. Add bananas, heat 10 minutes more. Discard bay leaf.

Serve with: Lettuce wedges with mayonnaise and corn relish • Fresh fruit bowl • Coffee

LEMON-CABBAGE ROLLS
pictured on page 160

Time in Kitchen: ½ hour
Free Time: ½ hour
Servings: 4

1 medium cabbage
¾ cup elbow macaroni
2 tablespoons butter or margarine
½ cup minced onions
1 10-ounce can condensed cream-of-celery soup
1 tablespoon lemon peel
2 tablespoons lemon juice
1 cup minced, leftover cooked lamb
2 tablespoons minced parsley
⅛ teaspoon pepper

About 1 hour before dinner: Parboil cabbage in boiling salted water 20 minutes, then carefully remove 8 leaves. Cook macaroni as package label directs; drain. Preheat oven to 375°F.

In medium saucepan, in butter, sauté onion, until tender; add undiluted soup, lemon peel and juice; stir until boiling. Combine macaroni, lamb, parsley, pepper and ¼ cup lemon sauce. Pour remaining sauce into 1½-quart greased baking dish. Place ¼ cup meat mixture onto each cabbage leaf. Roll up and tuck in ends; place on top of sauce in baking dish; cover and bake ½ hour.

Serve with: Assorted rolls • Coconut custard pie • Tea

LAMB CURRY

Time in Kitchen: 20 minutes
Free Time: ½ hour
Servings: 4

2 tablespoons butter or margarine
¾ cup sliced onions
1 cup diced celery
1 garlic clove, minced
1½ cups cut-up, leftover cooked lamb
1 teaspoon curry powder
salt
2 cups lamb gravy, diluted with water;
　or 2 chicken- or beef-bouillon cubes,
　dissolved in 2 cups hot water
4 cups hot cooked rice (page 11)

About 50 minutes before dinner: In skillet, in hot butter, sauté onions, celery and garlic until lightly browned. Add lamb, curry powder, salt to taste, gravy. Simmer, covered, ½ hour.

To serve: Arrange hot rice in ring on platter. Turn lamb curry into center. Pass choice of Curry Accompaniments: chutney, salted nuts, raisins, flaked coconut.

Veal Curry: Make as above, substituting cut-up, cooked veal for lamb.

Serve with: Green salad • Pineapple chunks • Cookies

FRANKS RISOTTO
pictured on page 160

Time in Kitchen: 45 minutes
Servings: 6

2 tablespoons butter or margarine
1½ cups regular white rice
¾ cup minced onions
½ teaspoon salt
1½- to 2 teaspoons curry powder
3 chicken-bouillon cubes
1 10-ounce package frozen peas
1 cup chopped apple
1 cup chopped tomato
6 frankfurters

About 45 minutes before dinner: Preheat oven to 375°F. In medium saucepan, in butter, sauté rice, onions, salt and curry powder, until onions are tender. Dissolve bouillon cubes in 3 cups boiling water and add to rice; bring to boiling; cover and simmer 10 minutes, then add peas and cook 5 minutes. Combine apple, tomato and rice mixture and place in 2½-quart greased baking dish. Slice frankfurters into 1-inch pieces and arrange in baking dish with rice. Cover; bake 15 minutes.

TURKEY ALFREDO CASSEROLE

Time in Kitchen: 15 minutes
Free Time: ½ hour
Servings: 4

4 cups chopped cooked turkey
2 cups turkey gravy
1 cup chopped almonds
6 tablespoons heavy cream
2 tablespoons chopped parsley
2 tablespoons lemon juice
1 teaspoon salt
½ teaspoon curry powder
½ teaspoon onion salt
⅔ cup dry bread crumbs
¼ cup butter or margarine, melted

About 45 minutes before dinner: Preheat oven to 350°F. In medium bowl, mix turkey and next 8 ingredients; spoon into 4 greased 10-ounce ovenproof casseroles. Mix bread crumbs with butter; sprinkle on top of turkey. Bake, uncovered, ½ hour on middle rack of oven. (Place sheet of foil on rack below to catch drippings.)

BROCCOLI WITH SOUR CREAM ON TURKEY

Time in Kitchen: 25 minutes
Servings: 4

1 bunch broccoli
1½ cups sour cream
2 teaspoons prepared mustard
¼ teaspoon lime juice
salt
4 large slices, leftover cooked turkey
paprika

About 25 minutes before dinner: Cut large leaves and bit of lower stalks from broccoli; wash well. Lay broccoli in 10-inch skillet in 1 inch boiling salted water. Cook, uncovered, 10 minutes, then cover and boil 5 minutes more or until fork-tender; drain.

Meanwhile, combine sour cream, mustard, lime juice and 1 teaspoon salt. Arrange turkey on platter; top each slice with 3 pieces broccoli; spoon on sauce; sprinkle with paprika.

TURKEY WITH ASPARAGUS

Time in Kitchen: 25 minutes
Free Time: 20 minutes
Servings: 6

2 10-ounce packages frozen asparagus
½ cup butter or margarine
3½ cups cut-up cooked turkey
1½ teaspoons salt
¼ teaspoon pepper
¼ teaspoon thyme leaves
2 eggs, separated
½ cup sour cream
½ cup milk

About 45 minutes before dinner: Cook asparagus as label directs. Arrange in 12″ by 8″ baking dish. Preheat oven to 375°F.

In skillet, melt butter; add turkey; sauté until hot; add salt, pepper, thyme; arrange over asparagus.

Blend yolks with sour cream and milk; beat egg whites; fold into yolk-cream mixture; spoon over turkey. Bake 20 minutes or until golden.

TURKEY-DINNER RAREBIT

Time in Kitchen: ½ hour
Servings: 4

1 10-ounce package frozen carrots and peas
½ cup thinly sliced celery
2 tablespoons butter or margarine
2 tablespoons all-purpose flour
½ teaspoon salt
dash cayenne
¼ teaspoon dry mustard
½ teaspoon Worcestershire
1 cup milk
1 8-ounce package process sharp American cheese, cubed
1 tablespoon minced green pepper
1 cup fresh tomato wedges
toast or toasted, split English muffins
sliced roast turkey

1. *About ½ hour before dinner:* In double-boiler bottom, cook carrots and peas, celery in salted water until tender.
2. While vegetables cook, make sauce: Set double-boiler top in place; melt butter. Stir in flour, salt, cayenne, mustard and Worcestershire; stir in milk; cook until smooth and thickened. Add cheese; stir until melted.
3. With slotted spoon, lift vegetables

from bottom to sauce in top; add green pepper, tomato wedges. Cover; heat thoroughly.

4. *To serve:* Top toast with turkey slices; spoon on sauce.

FLORENTINE TURKEY

Do-Ahead Dish
Time in Kitchen: 20 minutes
Free Time: 25 minutes
Servings: 4

1 10-ounce package frozen chopped spinach
butter or margarine
3 tablespoons all-purpose flour
1 teaspoon monosodium glutamate
1 teaspoon salt
dash cayenne
1½ cups milk
¼ cup grated Parmesan cheese
½ cup light cream
2 cups cooked turkey, in chunks
¼ cup packaged dried bread crumbs
butter or margarine

Early in day: Cook spinach as label directs; arrange in 1½-quart casserole.

In saucepan, melt 2 tablespoons butter. Stir in flour, monosodium glutamate, salt and cayenne. Gradually stir in milk; cook, stirring constantly, until it thickens and comes to boiling. Add cheese, cream. Stir over low heat, until cheese melts. Add turkey; pour over spinach. Sprinkle with crumbs; chill.

About ½ hour before dinner: Preheat oven to 350°. Dot casserole with butter. Bake 25 minutes; brown under broiler.

DEEP-DISH TURKEY PIE
pictured on page 157

Time in Kitchen: ½ hour
Free Time: 45 minutes
Servings: 4

6 small potatoes, quartered
4 medium onions, quartered
4 carrots, cut in strips
3 cups cubed, cooked turkey
2 tablespoons chopped parsley
butter or margarine
2 tablespoons all-purpose flour
½ teaspoon salt
⅛ teaspoon pepper
1 13¾-ounce can chicken broth
1 8-ounce can refrigerated biscuits
2 small yellow onions, thinly sliced

About 1 hour and 15 minutes before dinner: In large, covered saucepan over medium-high heat, in 2 cups water, cook potatoes, onions and carrots for 15 minutes or until tender-crisp; drain well in colander. Mix vegetables, turkey and parsley in 3-quart baking dish. Preheat oven to 350°F.

In same saucepan, melt 2 tablespoons butter; blend in flour, salt and pepper. Gradually stir in chicken broth and cook, stirring constantly, until sauce thickens and comes to boiling. Pour over turkey-vegetable mixture.

With hands, flatten biscuits and pat an onion slice onto middle of each. Arrange biscuits over top of turkey mixture and brush with a little melted butter. Bake 45 minutes or until biscuits are golden.

Serve with: Tray of stuffed celery, radish roses, olives, cranberry-orange relish • Frozen baked pumpkin custard • Coffee

ADAM'S TURKEY CASSEROLE

Time in Kitchen: 15 minutes
Free Time: 45 minutes
Servings: 8

6 cups crumbled corn bread
½ teaspoon poultry seasoning
1 teaspoon celery seed
⅛ teaspoon pepper
salt
¼ cup minced onion
3 tablespoons chopped parsley
½ cup melted butter or margarine
5 cups leftover cooked turkey or chicken, in small or large pieces
¼ cup butter or margarine
¼ cup all-purpose flour
2 cups chicken broth
2 eggs, well beaten
1 quart milk

About 1 hour before dinner: Preheat oven to 375°F. In large bowl, combine corn bread, poultry seasoning, celery seed, pepper, ¾ teaspoon salt, onion, parsley, melted butter. With fork, toss together. In 13″ by 9″ baking dish, spread in layer. Arrange turkey evenly over top.

In large skillet, melt ¼ cup butter; stir in flour and 1½ teaspoons salt until smooth. Stir in broth; heat. Combine eggs and milk; add to sauce; cook until slightly thickened, stirring. Pour this sauce over turkey; bake 45 minutes.

Serve with: Molded fruit salad • Chocolate frosted cupcakes • Coffee

TURKEY OR CHICKEN À LA QUEEN

Time in Kitchen: 20 minutes
Servings 6

butter or margarine
¼ cup slivered, blanched almonds
2 tablespoons all-purpose flour
dash pepper
1½ teaspoons salt
dash paprika
2 cups light cream
1 egg yolk, beaten
2 cups cut-up, leftover cooked turkey or chicken
1 20-ounce can pineapple tidbits, drained
toast slices

1. *About 20 minutes before dinner:* In skillet, in 2 tablespoons butter, sauté almonds until light golden; set aside.
2. In double-boiler top, over hot, *not boiling,* water, melt ¼ cup butter; add flour, pepper, salt and paprika, stirring, until smooth and thickened.
3. Slowly stir in cream. Then stir small amount of sauce into beaten egg yolk; return yolk mixture to remaining sauce, continuing to stir until smooth and thickened.
4. Add turkey or chicken and pineapple. Pour over toast and top with sautéed almonds.

Ham-and-Turkey: Substitute cut-up, cooked ham for 1 cup turkey or chicken. If desired, substitute chopped walnuts or pecans for slivered almonds.

Serve with: Spinach, onion and celery salad with garlic-cheese dressing • Orange or raspberry sherbet • Vanilla wafers • Coffee

CRUNCHY CREAMED TURKEY

Time in Kitchen: ½ hour
Servings: 4

2 tablespoons butter or margarine
¼ cup chopped green pepper
1 onion, thinly sliced
1 10½-ounce can condensed cream-
   of-chicken soup
½ cup milk
½ teaspoon seasoned salt
¼ cup coarsely cut cashew nuts
2 cups cut-up, leftover cooked turkey
   or chicken
1 cup cooked carrot slices
Savory Noodles (below)
chopped parsley

About ½ hour before dinner: In sauce-pan or large skillet, in butter, sauté green pepper and onion until tender. Stir in undiluted soup, milk, seasoned salt; add nuts, turkey and carrots; heat thoroughly. Serve in ring of Savory Noodles; sprinkle with parsley.

Savory Noodles: Cook one 8-ounce package wide noodles as label directs; drain. Into large bowl, measure 1 teaspoon salt, ½ teaspoon nutmeg, ¼ teaspoon pepper, 2 tablespoons butter or margarine, 2 tablespoons grated Parmesan cheese; add noodles and toss gently with a fork.

Serve with: Chilled fruit cocktail • Brownies • Tea

CHICKEN-LIMA BAKE

Time in Kitchen: 20 minutes
Free Time: ½ hour
Servings: 4

1 10-ounce package frozen Fordhook
   limas
1 10½-ounce can condensed cream-
   of-mushroom soup
½ cup milk
1 cup cubed cooked chicken
1¼ cups crushed potato chips

About 50 minutes before dinner: Cook limas as label directs. Preheat oven to 350°F. In 1½-quart casserole, combine limas, undiluted soup, milk, chicken and 1 cup of the potato chips; top with remaining potato chips. Bake ½ hour.

CHICKEN-BISCUIT PIE

Time in Kitchen: 20 minutes
Free Time: 15 minutes
Servings: 4

2 tablespoons butter or margarine
4 onions, thinly sliced
1 tablespoon minced green pepper
1 10½-ounce can cream-of-mushroom
   soup
½ cup milk
1 cup cubed cooked chicken
½ cup cooked vegetables
1 8-ounce can refrigerated biscuits

About 35 minutes before dinner: Pre-heat oven to 425°F. In skillet, in butter, sauté onions and green pepper until tender. Add undiluted soup, milk, chicken and vegetables. Turn into 9-inch pie plate. Top with biscuits. Bake 15 minutes or until biscuits are brown.

OVEN-BAKED CHICKEN HASH

Time in Kitchen: 10 minutes
Free Time: 20 minutes
Servings: 4

2 cups diced, cooked potatoes
2 cups diced, leftover, cooked chicken
  or turkey
1 cup heavy or whipping cream (or ¼
  cup melted butter or margarine plus
  ¾ cup milk)
2½ teaspoons onion salt
¼ teaspoon pepper

About ½ hour before dinner: Preheat oven to 375°F. In 10″ by 6″ baking dish, combine potatoes and rest of ingredients. Bake 20 minutes or until bubbling hot.

Serve with: Molded cabbage-carrot salad • Orange cake

EASY CHICKEN PIE

Time in Kitchen: 15 minutes
Free Time: 15 minutes
Servings: 4

2 tablespoons salad oil
4 small onions, thinly sliced
1 tablespoon minced green pepper
1 10½-ounce can condensed cream-
  of-mushroom soup
dash salt
dash pepper
½ cup milk
1 cup cooked chicken, in large pieces
½ cup cooked mixed vegetables
Biscuit dough (made with 1 cup buttermilk-biscuit mix)

About ½ hour before dinner: Preheat oven to 450°F. In skillet, in oil, sauté onions and green pepper until tender; add soup and next 5 ingredients. Pour into 9-inch pie plate. Roll dough into 10-inch circle; place on top of chicken; flute edge; prick top. Bake 15 minutes.

Serve with: Grape, cabbage and carrot slaw • Blueberries with cream

SWEET-POTATO-CHICKEN PIE

Time in Kitchen: 20 minutes
Free Time: ½ hour
Servings: 4

2 17-ounce cans yams or sweet
  potatoes
½ teaspoon nutmeg
¼ teaspoon allspice
¼ teaspoon salt
2 tablespoons melted butter or margarine
1 tablespoon sherry
2 tablespoons butter or margarine
1 medium onion, minced
2 3- or 4-ounce cans sliced mushrooms, undrained
½ cup quartered large stuffed olives
1 10½-ounce can condensed cream-
  of-mushroom soup
dash pepper
2 cups cut-up, cooked chicken or
  turkey

About 50 minutes before dinner: In bowl, place drained yams and mash well. Beat in nutmeg, allspice, salt, melted butter and sherry.

Line 9-inch pie plate with potato mixture, building up the edges about ½ inch high. Preheat oven to 350°F.

In skillet, in butter, sauté minced

onion until tender. Add mushrooms with liquid, olives, undiluted soup, pepper, chicken; heat, stirring often. Pour mixture into prepared crust. Bake ½ hour.

Serve with: Tomato aspic rings and cucumber slices on chicory • Butter-brickle cake (from mix) • Tea

---

CHICKEN-AND-HAM PIE

Time in Kitchen: ½ hour
Free Time: ½ hour
Servings: 4

1 cup sifted all-purpose flour
1 teaspoon double-acting baking
　powder
½ teaspoon salt
1 cup unseasoned mashed sweet
　potatoes
⅓ cup melted shortening
1 egg, beaten
1 10½-ounce can condensed cream-
　of-chicken soup
¼ cup milk
1 cup diced, leftover cooked ham
1 cup diced, leftover cooked chicken
　or turkey
⅛ teaspoon pepper
⅛ teaspoon ground cloves
2 teaspoons parsley flakes
1 cup cooked or canned peas

Early in day: Into bowl, sift flour, baking powder, and salt. Add sweet potatoes, melted shortening and egg; blend well. Refrigerate.

About 45 minutes before dinner: Preheat oven to 425°F. Heat undiluted soup with milk; add ham, chicken, pepper, cloves and parsley. Into 9-inch pie plate, turn half of chicken mixture. Scatter peas on top; top with rest of

chicken mixture. On very well floured surface, gently roll out sweet-potato mixture into 10-inch circle. Lift onto pie plate over chicken mixture. Flute edge; make slits in top crust. Bake ½ hour.

Serve with: Marinated asparagus salad • Sponge cake

PINEAPPLE-CHICKEN CHOW MEIN

Time in Kitchen: 25 minutes
Servings: 4

¼ cup salad oil
1 cup sliced onions
3 cups diagonally sliced celery
1 16-ounce can bean sprouts,
　undrained
1 13¼-ounce can pineapple tidbits,
　drained
2 chicken-bouillon cubes
3 teaspoons salt
¼ teaspoon pepper
2 tablespoons brown sugar
2 tablespoons cornstarch
¼ cup soy sauce
2 cups slivered, cooked chicken
2 3-ounce, or 1 6-ounce can chow-
　mein noodles

About 25 minutes before dinner: In Dutch oven or large saucepan, heat salad oil. Add onions, celery, bean sprouts with liquid, pineapple, bouillon cubes dissolved in ½ cup hot water, salt, pepper and brown sugar. Cover; bring to boiling.

Mix cornstarch with soy sauce; stir into vegetable mixture. Add chicken; cook, stirring, 3 to 6 minutes or until smooth and thickened. Serve over hot crisp chow-mein noodles.

HOT CHICKEN SALAD

Time in Kitchen: 15 minutes
Free Time: 25 minutes
Servings: 4

2 cups cooked chicken chunks
1½ cups chopped celery
2 teaspoons minced onion
½ teaspoon grated lemon peel
¼ cup canned diced, roasted almonds
¼ teaspoon salt
⅛ teaspoon pepper
1 tablespoon lemon juice
⅔ cup cooked salad dressing
1 4-ounce package shredded Cheddar cheese (1 cup)
1 cup crushed potato chips

About 40 minutes before dinner: Preheat oven to 375°F. In bowl, mix chicken with next 8 ingredients. Divide salad among four 10-ounce casseroles; top each with cheese, potato chips. Place casseroles on cookie sheet; bake 25 minutes.

Serve with: Corn chips • Pickled peaches • Cheesecake

CHICKEN CRUNCH

Time in Kitchen: 20 minutes
Servings: 6

2 tablespoons butter or margarine
1 medium onion, sliced
1 medium green pepper, cut into strips
1¼ cups chicken broth
3 cups sliced celery
1 tablespoon soy sauce
1 3- or 4-ounce can mushrooms
2 cups cut-up, leftover cooked chicken
2 tablespoons cornstarch
½ cup coarsely broken walnuts

About 20 minutes before dinner: In skillet, in hot butter, sauté onion until tender; stir in green pepper, chicken broth, celery, soy sauce. Cover; simmer 10 minutes. Drain mushrooms; reserve liquid. Add chicken, mushrooms. Mix cornstarch with 3 tablespoons mushroom liquid; stir into chicken; bring to boiling. Add walnuts.

ASPARAGUS-CHICKEN CASSEROLE

Time in Kitchen: 20 minutes
Servings: 4

2 10-ounce packages frozen asparagus
butter or margarine
1 large onion, chopped
2 3-ounce cans sliced mushrooms, drained (reserve liquid)
4 tablespoons all-purpose flour
1½ teaspoons seasoned salt
1 teaspoon paprika
1 teaspoon basil
2 cups milk
2 tablespoons sherry
2 cups cut-up cooked chicken
4 slices toast

About 20 minutes before dinner: Cook asparagus as label directs. Meanwhile, in medium saucepan, in 3 tablespoons butter, lightly brown onions and mushrooms. Stir in flour, seasoned salt, paprika and basil, then gradually stir in milk and mushroom liquid; cook until smooth and thickened. Preheat oven to 400°F.

Lay toast in 10″ by 6″ baking dish; top with asparagus, dot with butter. Add sherry, chicken to sauce; spoon around asparagus. Bake 10 minutes.

CHICKEN WITH NOODLES

Time in Kitchen: ½ hour
Servings: 6

2 tablespoons butter or margarine
1 medium onion, thinly sliced
2 cups coarsely sliced cabbage
1 6-ounce can whole mushrooms, drained, quartered
1 tablespoon cornstarch
½ teaspoon salt
⅛ teaspoon pepper
2 tablespoons soy sauce
1 cup canned chicken broth
1 10-ounce package frozen, whole green beans
2 cups cut-up leftover cooked chicken
4 cups seasoned hot cooked noodles
4 radishes, sliced
1 green onion, cut up

About ½ hour before dinner: In large skillet, over medium heat, melt butter. In it, sauté onion until tender. Add cabbage and mushrooms and sauté for 3 or 4 minutes.

In small bowl, combine cornstarch, salt, pepper, soy sauce and chicken broth, stirring until smooth. Pour over vegetables in skillet. Add green beans and chicken; bring to boiling. Simmer, covered, 8 to 10 minutes, or until vegetables are tender-crisp.

Arrange seasoned hot cooked noodles around edge of large serving dish. Heap chicken-vegetable mixture in the center. Garnish with radishes and green onions. Pass additional soy sauce.

Serve with: Mixed green salad with French dressing • Frozen apple turnovers • Coffee

CHINESE-STYLE CHICKEN

Time in Kitchen: 20 minutes
Servings: 6

3 tablespoons cornstarch
2 cups milk
2 cups diced, leftover cooked chicken
1 10½-ounce can condensed cream-of-mushroom soup
1 4-ounce can chopped mushrooms, undrained
1 8-ounce can water chestnuts, drained, sliced
⅛ teaspoon each: salt, pepper, marjoram and monosodium glutamate
½ teaspoon paprika
1 tablespoon sherry
2 3-ounce cans chow-mein noodles

About 20 minutes before dinner: In saucepan, mix cornstarch with some of milk to form smooth paste; add chicken, undiluted soup, mushrooms, water chestnuts, salt, seasonings, sherry and remaining milk. Cook over low heat until hot.

To serve: Heat noodles; arrange on large platter; spoon on chicken.

Serve with: Romaine and cucumber salad • Sherbet • Tea

POTATO-EGG SURPRISE

Time in Kitchen: 1 hour
Servings: 4

4 baking potatoes
1 10½-ounce can condensed cream-of-celery soup
½ cup shredded process Cheddar cheese
4 hard-cooked eggs, sliced
1 cup diced leftover ham
milk
salt and pepper

About 1 hour before dinner: Preheat oven to 400°F. Scrub potatoes; bake 45 minutes or until tender when tested with fork.

Meanwhile, in double-boiler top, in undiluted celery soup, melt cheese. Gently stir in eggs and ham. If mixture is too thick, add a tablespoon or two of milk. Season to taste with salt and pepper. Cook, stirring, until heated through. Keep hot.

To serve: Using a sharp knife, cut an "X" through skin of each potato. Firmly squeeze potato until snowy interior bursts through opening. Spoon ham and egg mixture into and over each potato. Makes 4 servings.

SPANISH OMELETTE

Time in Kitchen: 15 minutes
Servings: 4

2 tablespoons butter or margarine
1 small onion, chopped
1 tomato, peeled and sliced
2 leftover cooked potatoes, diced
1 pimiento, diced
2 tablespoons cooked peas
4 eggs
1 teaspoon salt
¼ teaspoon pepper

About 15 minutes before dinner: In small skillet, in butter, fry onion lightly. Add tomato and rest of vegetables. Cook a few minutes, stirring. Beat eggs; add salt and pepper; pour into pan. Cook over low heat, shaking pan occasionally, until underside is lightly browned, top almost set; brown top under broiler, about 2 minutes. Quickly invert onto warm serving platter.

WONDERFUL HASH

Time in Kitchen: 50 minutes
Servings: 4

2 cups coarsely chopped leftover cooked beef, lamb or pork
3 cups coarsely chopped leftover cooked potatoes
½ cup minced onions
1 teaspoon salt
¼ teaspoon pepper
⅓ cup milk
2 tablespoons salad oil

About 50 minutes before dinner: In large bowl, combine meat, potatoes, onion, salt, pepper and milk; mix well.

In large skillet over low heat, heat salad oil. Spread hash evenly in bottom of skillet. Cook over low heat 30 to 40 minutes or until underside is browned and crusty. Do not stir; occasionally, using spatula, lift edge of hash to check browning. When browned, run spatula around edge of hash to loosen; fold one half onto other half; remove hash to platter. Nice served with chili sauce or piccalilli.

Lentils with Meat, page 188

Super Chef's Salad, page 186

Frankfurter-Potato Salad, page 188

Shimmering Chicken Mold, page 190

Macaroni-Tuna-Bean Salad, page 189
Blueberry Biscuits, page 217

Top: Marinated Vegetable Salad, page 197
Bottom: Honeydew Crescents, page 200

Top left, clockwise: Red Cabbage-Grape Slaw, Broccoli-Mimosa Salad, Apple Slaw, Blushing Green Salad, Petal Cheese Salad, Garden Cheese Salad, Grape-Poppy-Seed Slaw, Pineapple-Carrot Slaw, pages 196–199

SATISFYING
SALADS
Many of these are a meal in themselves, especially welcome on sultry days. Others serve well as side dishes

Main-Dish Salads

SUPER CHEF'S SALAD

pictured on page 179

2 8-ounce bottles Italian dressing
1 9½-ounce can whole artichoke hearts
12 pitted jumbo ripe olives
about ¼ pound Swiss cheese
1 very large head chicory
2 large heads Boston lettuce
2 Belgian endives
12 super-colossal stuffed olives
1 small green pepper, seeded
½ pound boiled ham slice
4 hard-cooked eggs
12 to 16 medium radishes
½ pound cooked turkey roll
1 bunch field salad or watercress, washed, drained
3 2-ounce cans rolled fillets of anchovies
1 pint cherry tomatoes
3 tablespoons chopped pimientos

1. *Several hours before dinner:* In bowl, pour ¼ cup Italian dressing over drained, halved artichoke hearts; cover. Cut each ripe olive crosswise into 3 slices; cut cheese into 24 strips, each about 2″ by ¼″ by ¼″. Slip a ring-like olive slice over each cheese strip; wrap them up; refrigerate all.
2. Separate chicory, lettuce, endives, leaf by leaf, discarding wilted outer leaves; wash and dry well. In 3½-cup fluted mold, against back rim, arrange about 6 large chicory leaves, slightly overlapping. Arrange 6 lettuce leaves in fan shape; tuck them in front of chicory leaves, filling mold. Tuck some endive leaves here and there in this bouquet, also between chicory and back rim of mold; wrap bouquet and refrigerate.

3. Into large salad bowl, tear rest of chicory, lettuce and endives into bite-size pieces. Quarter stuffed olives lengthwise; cut pepper and ham into julienne strips; slice eggs; score radishes as pictured; cut turkey into 1-inch chunks; cover; refrigerate all.
4. *About ½ hour before dinner:* Unwrap salad bouquet; place at back center of large 21″ by 14″ tray with lettuce leaves facing front. Arrange field salad around bouquet. Arrange anchovies, stuffed olives, pepper strips, artichokes, ham strips, egg slices, olive ends, olive-cheese strips, radishes, turkey and cherry tomatoes, as pictured. In large bowl, combine rest of dressing with pimientos.

Serve with salad greens and dressing. Makes 10 servings.

Serve with: French bread • Lemon sherbet

JET-AGE CHEF'S SALAD

4 Belgian endives, thinly sliced, crosswise
½ cup diced, pared cucumber
⅓ cup thinly sliced radishes
⅓ cup watercress leaves
1 cup raw green beans, thinly sliced, diagonally
1 cup peeled avocado chunks
½ pound boiled ham, slivered
½ teaspoon seasoned salt
⅛ teaspoon seasoned pepper
½ cup bottled herb dressing
1 tablespoon vinegar

About 15 minutes before dinner: Have vegetables well chilled, before preparing salad. In large salad bowl, toss endives, cucumber, radishes, watercress, green beans, avocado chunks and ham. Sprinkle with seasoned salt, pepper. Pour on dressing, vinegar; toss. Makes 4 servings.

Serve with: Jellied consommé • Blueberry tarts

OUR CHEF'S SALAD

1 10-ounce package frozen broccoli spears
1 10-ounce package frozen asparagus spears
1 9-ounce package frozen artichoke hearts
¼ pound fresh mushrooms, sliced
bottled oil and vinegar dressing
2 quarts salad greens
½ pound boiled ham, cut julienne style
¼ pound boiled tongue, cut into long strips, ¾ inch wide
½ pound Swiss cheese, cut into long strips, ⅜ inch wide
1 cup cooked chicken, cut into strips
1 cup cherry tomatoes
4 hard-cooked eggs, sliced
4 narrow pimiento strips
favorite dressing

1. *Several hours before dinner:* Cook broccoli, asparagus and artichoke hearts, as labels direct; chill each.
2. *One hour before dinner:* Start marinating mushrooms and artichoke hearts in oil and vinegar dressing to cover.
3. *Just before dinner:* In large salad bowl, arrange salad greens, then alternate broccoli spears, asparagus, ham, tongue, cheese and chicken strips.
4. Remove mushrooms, artichoke hearts from dressing; arrange on salad with cherry tomatoes, egg slices; garnish with pimiento. Pass dressing. Makes 8 servings.

SALAMI-BOLOGNA CHEF'S SALAD

2 quarts mixed salad greens
¼ pound salami, slivered
¼ pound bologna, slivered
4 ounces shredded process Cheddar cheese
½ cup cauliflowerets
1 garlic clove, minced
½ teaspoon salt
¼ teaspoon pepper
1 tablespoon vinegar
¼ cup salad oil

Early in day: Place greens in salad bowl; cover; refrigerate. Just before dinner, arrange salami, bologna, cheese and cauliflowerets on top of greens. Sprinkle with garlic, salt, pepper, vinegar and oil; toss well. Makes 4 servings.

FRUIT CHEF'S SALAD

1 medium head iceberg or romaine lettuce, in bite-size pieces
1 8-ounce container cottage cheese
1 cup canned pineapple chunks
¼ cup raisins
3 oranges, peeled, sectioned
¼ cup chopped walnuts
2 tablespoons French dressing

Just before dinner: Place greens in salad bowl. Arrange cheese in middle; surround with fruits and nuts. Toss well with dressing. Makes 4 servings.

AVOCADO-SPINACH SALAD
pictured on page 136

1 envelope garlic-cheese dressing mix
¾ pound fresh spinach, in bite-size pieces
½ head iceberg lettuce, in bite-size pieces
4 hard-cooked eggs, quartered
1 cup packaged croutons
¼ pound Swiss cheese, shredded
¼ pound Swiss cheese, cut into ¼-inch strips
2 ripe avocados, peeled, cut in half, then sliced crosswise
½ red onion, thinly sliced

About 20 minutes before dinner: Make garlic-cheese dressing as label directs. In large salad bowl, toss spinach with rest of ingredients. Serve with dressing. Makes 4 main-dish servings.

LENTILS WITH MEAT
pictured on page 177

1 16-ounce package lentils
salt
¼ cup vinegar
2 tablespoons salad oil
¼ teaspoon seasoned pepper
¼ cup minced red onion
1¼ teaspoons tarragon
8 to 10 round cooked turkey slices
8 to 10 round head-cheese slices
9 or 10 red onion rings
radishes, thinly sliced

About 2 hours before dinner: Place lentils in small kettle with 2 quarts water and 1 tablespoon salt. Cook, covered, over medium heat, for ½ hour or until barely tender; drain; rinse well with cold water. Toss with 2 teaspoons salt, vinegar, salad oil, seasoned pepper, minced onion and tarragon; refrigerate 1 hour or more.

To serve: Heap lentils on small platter. Fold slices of turkey and head-cheese in half; alternate around lentils. Scatter onion rings on top; tuck in radish slices. Makes 8 servings.

Serve with: Hot rolls • Strawberries with cream • Tea

FRANKFURTER-POTATO SALAD
pictured on page 180

16 frankfurters
12 large potatoes
1 cup heavy or whipping cream
2 cups mayonnaise
4 teaspoons prepared mustard
chopped green onions
bottled capers
2 teaspoons salt
¼ teaspoon pepper
24 to 32 hard salami slices
parsley sprigs

Day before: In saucepan, simmer franks in water to cover, 5 minutes; drain; cover; refrigerate. Cook; cool; dice potatoes (3 quarts) cover; refrigerate.

About 2 hours before dinner: Cut frankfurters into ¾-inch crosswise slices. In large bowl, whip cream; combine with mayonnaise, mustard, ⅔ cup onions, 3 tablespoons capers, salt and pepper. Fold in potatoes and all but 20 frankfurter slices. Mound salad in 2-quart salad bowl. Top with 20 frankfurter slices, sprinkle with 2 teaspoons onions, 1 teaspoon capers.

Around salad, tuck "salami roses," made by folding each salami slice in half then in half again; garnish centers with parsley sprigs. Refrigerate. Makes 16 servings.

Serve with: Bread sticks • Melon with lemon wedges • Iced coffee

CHICKEN-AND-HAM POTATO SALAD

4 large whole chicken breasts
8 medium carrots
2 pounds cooked potatoes
¼ pound sliced boiled ham
1 cup dill pickles, cut into ½-inch cubes
½ cup sweet pickled red peppers, cut into ½-inch cubes
1 10½-ounce can peas, drained
1½ to 2 teaspoons salt
¼ teaspoon pepper
¼ cup lemon juice
¾ cup mayonnaise
2 tablespoons prepared mustard
¼ cup chopped, pitted, ripe and green olives

Day before: Simmer chicken and carrots in boiling salted water to cover, until both are tender; refrigerate.

Early in day: Bone and skin breasts; cut into cubes. Cut carrots, potatoes and ham in ½-inch cubes. In bowl, combine chicken, carrots, potatoes, ham, pickles, red peppers, peas, salt, pepper, lemon juice. In bowl, mix mayonnaise, mustard; reserve ¼ cup; mix rest with chicken salad; cover; refrigerate.

Just before dinner: Heap salad in an attractive bowl; cover with reserved mayonnaise mixture, then sprinkle with olives. Makes 6 servings.

MACARONI-TUNA-BEAN SALAD
pictured on page 182

1 pound green beans
½ teaspoon salt
1 8-ounce package shell macaroni
¼ cup chopped parsley
2 7-ounce cans tuna, drained
Italian dressing
2 medium tomatoes
4 hard-cooked eggs, quartered

Early in day or 3 hours before dinner: Wash, stem green beans; diagonally cut into small pieces. In medium saucepan, in 1 inch boiling, salted water, cook beans tender-crisp, about 15 minutes.

Meanwhile, cook macaroni as label directs; drain. In large bowl, combine macaroni, beans, parsley and tuna. Toss with ½ cup dressing; cover; chill. Cut tomatoes into chunks; toss with 2 tablespoons dressing. Cover; chill.

Toss tomatoes with macaroni salad. Place eggs on top. Makes 6 servings.

Serve with: Tomato juice • Blueberry Biscuits, page 217 • Lemon-glazed poundcake

SHIMMERING CHICKEN MOLD
pictured on page 181

1 3½-pound broiler-fryer, quartered
¼ cup sherry
1 medium onion, sliced
2 tablespoons salt
½ teaspoon white pepper
3 envelopes unflavored gelatin
1¼ cups large cooked ham chunks
1 pound Ribier or Tokay grapes
8 to 10 watercress leaves
2 cups coarsely chopped watercress
bottled green-goddess salad dressing

1. *Day before:* In large saucepan, in 6 cups boiling water, simmer chicken quarters, sherry, onion, salt and pepper ½ hour or until chicken is fork-tender.
2. Remove chicken to bowl. Strain chicken broth; skim off fat; refrigerate. Skin and bone chicken; cut meat into large chunks; cover; refrigerate.
3. In medium saucepan, in ½ cup cold water, soften 2 envelopes gelatin. Stir in 3 cups cold chicken broth; heat, stirring constantly, until gelatin dissolves. Add chicken meat and ham; set aside.
4. With knife, split, seed enough grapes to lay, skin side out, as a rim around outer bottom edge of 7-cup mold. Spoon chicken-ham mixture into mold, about ½-inch deep, to hold grape halves in place. Refrigerate until firm.
5. Refrigerate rest of chicken-ham mixture until slightly thickened, then spoon enough into mold to cover grape halves. Press 1 watercress leaf against side of mold, just above chicken mixture, then piece of chicken and piece of ham on each side of cress leaf, to hold leaf in place. Repeat leaf pattern around mold. Spoon in rest of chicken-ham mixture and refrigerate mold until firm.

6. When firm, in small saucepan, place ¼ cup cold water; sprinkle on 1 envelope gelatin to soften. Stir in 1¾ cups chicken broth; cook, stirring, until gelatin dissolves and liquid boils. Remove from heat; stir in chopped watercress. Refrigerate until lukewarm. Pour into mold. Chill until set.
7. *About 15 minutes before dinner:* Set mold in warm water, just to rim, for 10 seconds. Lift from water; shake slightly to loosen gelatin. Unmold onto serving plate. Garnish with grapes.
8. Cut mold into 8 wedges. Serve each with grapes and dressing. Makes 8 servings.

Serve with: Bran muffins, page 215 • Raspberry sherbet

CHICKEN-MELON SALAD

3 cups cooked chicken chunks
2½ cups seedless grapes
2 cups diced celery
1½ cups mayonnaise
6 tablespoons milk
1½ tablespoons chutney
1½ teaspoons curry powder
¼ teaspoon salt
1½ large cantaloupes
lettuce leaves

Early in day: In medium bowl, combine chicken, grapes and diced celery.

In bowl, mix mayonnaise, milk, chutney, curry powder, salt; pour over chicken; toss. Cover; chill.

About 10 minutes before dinner: Cut melons into 6 wedges; remove seeds, cut off rind. Place wedges on lettuce leaves. Spoon salad on top. Makes 6 servings.

CRUNCHY CHICKEN SALAD

1 cup mayonnaise
¾ cup sour cream
1½ tablespoons lemon juice
2½ teaspoons salt
5 cups diced cooked chicken
2 cups diced celery
1 cup chopped cashew nuts
lettuce leaves

Just before dinner: In large bowl, combine mayonnaise, sour cream, lemon juice and salt. Add chicken, diced celery and cashews; toss lightly. Serve on lettuce leaves. Makes 8 servings.

Serve with: Spiced peaches • Parker-house rolls • Devil's food cake • Coffee

DELUXE CHICKEN SALAD
FOR A CROWD

3 quarts plus 1 to 3 cups large pieces cooked chicken or turkey
1 bunch green onions, chopped (1 cup), or 1 cup finely minced onions
about 2 bunches celery with tops, sliced (6 cups)
1 dozen eggs
1½ cups coarsely chopped walnuts
2 tablespoons butter or margarine
3 cups mayonnaise
½ cup wine vinegar
1½ cups milk or chicken broth
2 teaspoons salt
¼ teaspoon pepper
2 heads lettuce
½ bunch watercress

Day before: Cook chickens (see page 8); cut off meat in large pieces; refrigerate with broth. Prepare green onions, celery. Hard-cook, shell eggs. Refrigerate all.

At least 2½ hours before dinner: Sauté nuts in butter 5 minutes or until crisp and golden. Drain on paper towels; cool. Chop eggs. Combine mayonnaise, vinegar, milk, salt, pepper; toss with chicken, eggs, nuts, green onions and celery. Refrigerate.

To serve: Arrange salad on lettuce; garnish with watercress. Makes 25 servings.

CURRIED SEAFOOD SALAD

1 6½- or 7-ounce can tuna, broken up, chilled (1 cup)
1 cup cooked or canned cleaned shrimp, chilled
½ cup chopped celery
¼ cup cut-up ripe or stuffed olives
½ cup mayonnaise
2 tablespoons lemon juice
1 teaspoon (or more) curry powder
3 cups cold cooked rice
2 or 3 tablespoons French dressing
½ cup chopped parsley

Just before dinner: In large bowl, combine tuna, shrimp, celery and olives; add mayonnaise, blended with lemon juice and curry powder; toss. Toss rice with French dressing and parsley; spoon onto serving platter; heap salad on top. Makes 4 to 6 servings.

Chicken Curry: Substitute 2 cups cooked chicken for tuna and shrimp; add ¼ cup chutney to mayonnaise.

Serve with: Assorted breads • Vanilla ice cream with hot butterscotch sauce

CRAB-STUFFED AVOCADO

½ cup mayonnaise
½ cup minced celery
¼ cup minced pimiento
lemon juice
dash hot pepper sauce
⅛ teaspoon Worcestershire
2 ripe avocados
salt
crisp salad greens
1½ cups cooked crab or lobster meat

About ½ hour before dinner: Combine mayonnaise, celery, pimiento, 2 teaspoons lemon juice, hot pepper sauce, Worcestershire. Halve avocados lengthwise; remove pits; sprinkle with lemon juice, salt. Arrange each half on crisp greens; fill halves with crab; top each with some of dressing. Makes 4 servings.

Serve with: Corn chips • Peach shortcake • Iced tea or coffee

SCALLOPS VINAIGRETTE

1 pound or 3 medium white potatoes
1 pound fresh scallops (or frozen scallops, thawed)
1 cup thinly sliced green celery
2 tablespoons chopped pimiento
2 tablespoons minced onion
2 tablespoons chopped parsley
¼ cup vinegar
2 tablespoons salad oil
1 teaspoon salt
⅛ teaspoon pepper
4 lettuce cups

1. *Early in day:* Wash, pare, then halve potatoes; thinly slice into bite-size pieces. In medium saucepan, in boiling, salted water to cover, simmer potatoes 5 minutes or until almost tender.
2. Meanwhile, slice scallops, across the grain, into thin disks. When potatoes are almost tender, add scallops; bring water to boiling; cover; simmer for 5 minutes or until scallops are cooked, but still tender. Carefully drain away liquid. Let potatoes and scallops cool slightly; cover; refrigerate.
3. Meanwhile, in bowl, toss celery, pimiento, onion, parsley, vinegar, oil, salt, pepper. Cover; refrigerate.
4. *To serve:* Add scallops and potatoes to vinaigrette dressing; toss until evenly mixed. Arrange on lettuce cups. Makes 4 servings.

Serve with: Hot peas and mushrooms • Spongecake with lemon frosting • Coffee

SOUTH PACIFIC SALAD

6 8-ounce frozen rock-lobster tails
2 cups shredded iceberg lettuce
1 teaspoon salt
⅛ teaspoon pepper
1 10-ounce package frozen peas and carrots, cooked
mayonnaise
lemon juice
¼ cup bottled capers, drained
1 to 2 pimientos, cut in strips
1 cucumber, pared and sliced
1 cup ripe olives
3 medium tomatoes, quartered
carrot curls
1 avocado, peeled and sliced

Several hours before dinner: Cook lobster tails, following directions on page

8. Remove meat from shells; reserve shells. Slice some meat from each lobster tail; chop rest; toss it with shredded lettuce, salt, pepper, peas and carrots, 2 to 3 tablespoons mayonnaise and lemon juice to taste.

Stuff each shell with some of this mixture; lay lobster slices on top; spread lightly with mayonnaise; cover; refrigerate.

About 15 minutes before dinner: Arrange lobster tails on platter; garnish each with some capers, pimiento strips. Surround with cucumber, olives, tomatoes, carrot curls, avocado (brushed with lemon juice). Makes 6 servings.

Serve with: Strawberry sundae • Sugar cookies • Coffee

BOSTON FISH SALAD

1 16-ounce package frozen cod, perch or flounder, thawed, drained
1 cup mayonnaise
1 cup minced celery
½ cup grated carrot
1 tablespoon capers
2 teaspoons lemon juice
½ teaspoon salt
¼ teaspoon onion salt
1 small head Boston lettuce
2 hard-cooked eggs, sliced
1 cup sliced, cooked beets

About 1 hour before dinner: Bake fish as label directs; cool. In large bowl, flake fish and combine next 7 ingredients. Chill.

To serve: Arrange fish on bed of lettuce with egg slices on top, beets around sides. Makes 4 servings.

Serve with: Medley of fresh fruit salad topped with coconut • Coffee

TUNA-BEAN SALAD

2 15-ounce cans red kidney beans, drained
1 13-ounce can tuna, drained
1 teaspoon salt
¼ teaspoon pepper
1 teaspoon granulated sugar
5 red-onion slices
½ cup cider vinegar

About 3 hours before dinner: In salad bowl, mix beans, tuna, salt, pepper, sugar, some of onion slices, separated into rings, vinegar. Cover; chill 2 hours.

Garnish with rest of onion rings. Makes 6 servings.

PIQUANT TUNA SALAD

4 medium carrots, sliced diagonally
½ pound tiny white onions
1 cup white vinegar
¾ cup granulated sugar
1 tablespoon pickling spice
¾ teaspoon salt
2 medium tomatoes, sliced
1 13-ounce can tuna, drained
1 8-ounce can pitted, ripe olives
6 hard-cooked eggs, halved
salad greens

Day before: In saucepan, place carrots and onions with water to cover. Cover pan; boil 20 minutes. Meanwhile, in saucepan, stir vinegar, 1 cup water, sugar, pickling spice, salt; heat to boiling; cool.

Place tomatoes, tuna, drained olives, eggs in dish. Add drained carrots, onions. Pour on pickling liquid; cover; chill. Turn food often.

To serve: Drain; place on greens. Makes 8 servings.

SUMMER SALMON SALAD

2 envelopes unflavored gelatin
⅓ cup granulated sugar
salt
½ cup lemon juice
¼ cup quartered, thin cucumber slices
2 egg yolks
1 cup milk
dash cayenne
2 tablespoons butter or margarine
2 tablespoons all-purpose flour
2 7-ounce cans salmon, drained, flaked
½ cup minced celery
¼ cup diced ripe olives
2 tablespoons mayonnaise
2 teaspoons grated onion
chicory and cucumber slices for garnish

1. *Early in day:* In medium bowl, soften 1 envelope gelatin in ½ cup cold water. Stir in 1 cup boiling water, sugar and ¼ teaspoon salt until thoroughly dissolved; add ¼ cup of the lemon juice.
2. Pour small amount gelatin mixture into fish-shaped mold; chill until almost firm; arrange cucumber slices in overlapping row down center of mold. Carefully add more gelatin mixture to just cover cucumber slices; chill until almost firm. Carefully add remaining gelatin mixture; chill until firm.
3. Soften second envelope gelatin in ¼ cup cold water. In medium bowl, beat egg yolks slightly; beat in milk, ¾ teaspoon salt, cayenne. Set aside.
4. In medium pan, melt butter; stir in flour until well mixed. Gradually stir in egg mixture, stirring constantly until mixture is smooth and just boiling. Remove from heat; stir in softened gelatin. Fold in salmon, celery, olives, mayonnaise, grated onion and ¼ cup lemon juice; pour into mold. Chill until firm. Unmold on platter; garnish with chicory, cucumber slices. Makes 8 servings.

FIESTA HAM SALAD

3 cups cut-up cooked ham
1 12-ounce can whole-kernel corn, drained
1 cup chopped green pepper
2 medium tomatoes, chopped
2 tablespoons minced onion
2 tablespoons mayonnaise
1 teaspoon salt
⅛ teaspoon pepper
spinach leaves

About 15 minutes before dinner: In large bowl, combine ham, corn, green pepper, tomatoes and onion. Toss with mayonnaise, salt and pepper. Line salad bowl with spinach; mound salad in center. Makes 4 servings.

JEWEL-TONED HAM-SALAD MOLD

1 envelope unflavored gelatin
2 teaspoons minced onion
½ teaspoon salt
1 teaspoon horseradish
½ cup canned pineapple juice
2 tablespoons pickle relish
mayonnaise
2¼ cups shredded cabbage
1 tablespoon diced pimiento
1½ cups ground cooked ham
1 teaspoon prepared mustard
6 tablespoons cottage cheese
½ teaspoon lemon juice
salad greens

Early day before: In medium bowl, sprinkle gelatin on ¼ cup cold water to soften. Add ¾ cup boiling water; stir until dissolved; refrigerate. When gelatin is slightly thickened, add onion, salt, horseradish, pineapple juice, pickle relish, 2 tablespoons mayonnaise.

Divide gelatin mixture in half. To one half, add cabbage, pimiento; mix well; pour into 1-quart mold; refrigerate until set. To other half of gelatin, add ham; mix thoroughly; spoon over cabbage mixture in mold. Refrigerate until set.

Blend together ¼ cup mayonnaise, prepared mustard, cottage cheese, lemon juice. Refrigerate.

To serve: Unmold salad on greens; top each serving with 1½ tablespoons cheese dressing. Makes 6 servings.

Serve with: Brown bread • Peaches and blueberries • Cinnamon cookies • Tea

Side Salads

OLD-FASHIONED SALAD WITH CREAMY DRESSING

¾ cup mayonnaise
¼ cup milk
½ teaspoon salt
½ teaspoon lemon-pepper seasoning
1 head iceberg lettuce, shredded
1 large green pepper, diced
1 large tomato, cut in wedges

About ½ hour before dinner: In small bowl, combine mayonnaise, milk, salt and lemon-pepper seasoning. Cover; refrigerate.

Just before dinner: In large salad bowl, toss lettuce, green pepper and tomato with dressing. Makes 6 servings.

COTTAGE-CHEESE-AND-SPINACH SALAD

2 cups torn fresh spinach leaves
⅓ cup sliced green onions
1½ cups sliced pared cucumber
½ cup sliced radishes
salt and pepper
1 16-ounce container cottage cheese
1 cup sour cream
2 teaspoons lemon juice

About 10 minutes before dinner: Toss spinach with next 3 ingredients; sprinkle with salt and pepper; arrange on individual salad plates or in bowls. Place mounds of cottage cheese on top of vegetables; spoon sour cream mixed with lemon juice over cheese. Makes 4 servings.

PICKLED BEETS

½ teaspoon dry mustard
1 tablespoon granulated sugar
½ teaspoon salt
½ teaspoon ground cloves
½ garlic clove
6 tablespoons vinegar
2 cups drained, sliced cooked or canned beets
salad greens

Early in day: Combine mustard, sugar, salt, cloves, garlic; stir in vinegar, ¼ cup water. Place beets in bowl. Pour vinegar mixture over beets; refrigerate.

To serve: Remove garlic; drain beets; place on bed of greens. Makes 6 servings.

HEAD LETTUCE WITH FOAMY DRESSING
pictured on page 105

1 medium head iceberg lettuce
½ cup mayonnaise
½ teaspoon granulated sugar
1 tablespoon heavy cream
¼ teaspoon seasoned salt
dash chili powder
2 egg whites, stiffly beaten
ripe and stuffed green olives for garnish
grated cheese, chopped green onions
   for garnish

Early in day: Cut out core end, 2 inches down from head of lettuce; hold, cored end up, under running cold water to loosen leaves; invert; drain; refrigerate.

Just before dinner: Mix mayonnaise with next 4 ingredients; fold into beaten whites. Set lettuce head on large plate; fill with dressing. Garnish with olives, cheese, green onions. Serve in 6 wedges.

WILTED LETTUCE

1 head Boston lettuce, in bite-size
   pieces
¼ cup sliced green onions
1 tablespoon chopped parsley
5 bacon slices
¼ cup vinegar
dash garlic salt
1½ teaspoons granulated sugar
1 teaspoon dry mustard
¼ teaspoon each: salt and pepper
2 hard-cooked eggs, chopped

About 20 minutes before dinner: Toss lettuce with onions and parsley. In medium skillet, fry bacon until crisp; drain, crumble into salad bowl.

Pour off all but ¼ cup bacon fat in skillet; add vinegar and next 5 ingredients. Bring to boiling, stirring; pour over salad; toss. Garnish with eggs. Serve at once. Makes 4 servings.

BLUSHING GREEN SALAD
pictured on page 184

2 teaspoons lemon juice
1 tablespoon salad oil
⅓ cup plain yogurt
½ teaspoon paprika
dash hot pepper sauce
½ teaspoon salt
pinch garlic powder
2 cups seedless grapes
4 stalks celery, coarsely chopped
2 pears, diced
2 heads Bibb lettuce

Up to 1 hour before dinner: Blend lemon juice and next 6 ingredients; chill. Toss grapes, celery, pears. Arrange lettuce in 4 salad bowls; fill with mixture; chill. Pass dressing. Makes 4 servings.

SPINACH-CUCUMBER SALAD

1 10-ounce bag spinach, washed
1 large cucumber, sliced
1 11-ounce can mandarin-orange
   sections, drained
¾ cup French dressing

Just before dinner: Into salad bowl, tear spinach. Add cucumber and mandarin-orange sections. Toss with dressing. Makes 8 servings.

MARINATED VEGETABLE SALAD
pictured on page 183

1 10-ounce package frozen lima beans
1 10-ounce package frozen whole-kernel corn
1 4-ounce jar sliced pimientos, drained
¾ cup diced celery
2 tablespoons minced onion
½ cup herb-and-garlic French dressing
lettuce leaves

Day before: Cook lima beans and corn as labels direct. In bowl, toss beans, corn, pimientos, celery, onion, French dressing. Cover; refrigerate; stir often.

To serve: Line serving bowl with lettuce. Toss vegetables and pile on lettuce. Makes 6 servings.

CRISP VEGETABLE SALAD

1 medium green pepper, coarsely grated
1 8-ounce can water chestnuts, drained and sliced
2 cups finely sliced celery
6 radishes, finely sliced
2 teaspoons minced onion
1 teaspoon lemon juice
½ teaspoon salt
⅛ teaspoon pepper
about ⅓ cup bottled Italian dressing
6 lettuce leaves

Early in day: Refrigerate green pepper. In bowl, toss chestnuts and next 4 ingredients. Cover tightly; refrigerate.

About 15 minutes before dinner: Sprinkle vegetables with salt, pepper, green pepper; toss with dressing. Serve in lettuce cups. Makes 6 servings.

HARLEQUIN SALAD BOWL

1 20-ounce can white kidney beans, drained
1 15-ounce can red kidney beans, drained
½ cup chopped green onions
½ cup oil-and-vinegar dressing
¼ cup chopped parsley
1 teaspoon salt
¼ teaspoon pepper

Day before: In medium bowl, mix all ingredients. Refrigerate, covered, stirring occasionally.

Just before dinner: Lightly toss salad. Makes 6 servings.

BROCCOLI MIMOSA SALAD
pictured on page 184

½ cup apple juice
6 tablespoons cider vinegar
2 tablespoons salad oil
½ teaspoon seasoned salt
¼ teaspoon seasoned pepper
½ teaspoon basil
2 10-ounce packages frozen broccoli spears
2 hard-cooked eggs, chopped

1. *About 4 hours before dinner:* In jar, combine apple juice, cider vinegar, salad oil, ¼ cup water, seasoned salt, seasoned pepper, basil; shake well; chill.
2. Cook broccoli as label directs; cool. Pour some of dressing over broccoli; cover; refrigerate, tossing occasionally.
3. *Just before serving:* Arrange broccoli on individual salad plates; sprinkle each with some of chopped egg. Pass extra dressing. Makes 6 servings.

SOUR-CREAM SLAW

1 large head crisp green cabbage
minced onion
⅔ cup each: diced celery, slivered
   green pepper, grated carrots
½ cup sliced radishes
1 cup sour cream
½ teaspoon sugar
3 teaspoons salt
2 tablespoons tarragon vinegar
canned pineapple spears, large stuffed
   green olives, large ripe olives for
   garnish

Early in day: Remove several leaves from cabbage head; chill. Shred enough remaining cabbage to make 8 cups. In large bowl, combine cabbage, 2 tablespoons minced onion, celery, green pepper, carrots and radishes; chill.

In small bowl, combine sour cream, 2 teaspoons minced onion, sugar, salt and vinegar; cover; refrigerate.

Just before dinner: Toss sour-cream dressing with cabbage. Line salad bowl with reserved leaves. Heap slaw in center; garnish with pineapple spears and olives. Makes 8 to 10 servings.

GRAPE-POPPY-SEED SLAW

pictured on page 184

¼ cup bottled Italian salad dressing
¼ cup tomato juice
⅔ cup halved seedless grapes
1 quart finely shredded green cabbage
½ teaspoon poppy seed

Just before dinner: Combine salad dressing with tomato juice and grapes. Pour over cabbage; toss. Sprinkle with poppy seed. Makes 4 servings.

PINEAPPLE-CARROT SLAW

pictured on page 184

1 15¼-ounce can pineapple chunks
¼ cup juice drained from pineapple
¼ cup oil-and-vinegar salad dressing
¼ teaspoon tarragon
½ teaspoon salt
1 quart finely shredded green cabbage
1 small carrot, thinly sliced

Just before dinner: Drain juice from pineapple, reserving ¼ cup. In jar, combine juice with salad dressing, tarragon and salt; shake well. Add pineapple chunks to cabbage; pour on dressing; toss well. Makes 4 to 6 servings.

RED CABBAGE-
GRAPE SLAW

pictured on page 184

4 cups shredded red cabbage
few ice cubes
2 cups whole or halved seeded green
   grapes
dressing (step 1 of *Broccoli Mimosa
   salad,* page 197)
2 teaspoons salt

About 3 hours before dinner: Place shredded cabbage in large bowl; top with a few ice cubes; refrigerate. Also refrigerate grapes. Make dressing, omitting salad oil; refrigerate.

Just before dinner: Drain cabbage; remove any ice cubes, then sprinkle it with salt and toss thoroughly; add grapes and dressing; toss again. Makes 8 servings.

PETAL CHEESE SALAD
pictured on page 184

1 8-ounce container each: cream cottage cheese, large-curd cottage
cheese
½ cup coarsely grated carrot
2 tablespoons minced celery
½ teaspoon celery salt
chopped watercress
½ teaspoon salt
¼ teaspoon onion powder
dash seasoned pepper
1½ carrots, thinly sliced, crosswise
4 cherry tomatoes, thinly sliced

About ½ hour before dinner: Mix cottage cheeses with carrot, celery, celery
salt, 2 tablespoons chopped watercress, salt, onion powder and pepper.

Divide among 4 individual salad
bowls; lay carrot slices around outside
edge, just touching cottage cheese and
overlapping slightly.

Radiate watercress sprigs from
center of cottage cheese, with tomato
slices in center. Makes 4 servings.

GARDEN CHEESE SALAD
pictured on page 184

1 8-ounce container creamed cottage
cheese
½ to ¾ teaspoon salt
⅛ teaspoon white pepper
chopped chives
1 cucumber
2 or 3 medium tomatoes

About 1 hour before dinner: Combine
cheese with salt, pepper and ¼ cup
chives.

Run tines of fork lengthwise through
unpared cucumber; slice. Slice tomatoes thin; cut in half.

Mound cheese in 4 salad bowls; reserve some for garnish. Top with some
of cucumber and tomato. Around edge,
alternate rest of tomato and cucumber.
Top with cheese; sprinkle with chives.
Makes 4 servings.

APPLE SLAW
pictured on page 184

¼ cup bottled Italian salad dressing
¼ cup sweet pickle juice
¼ teaspoon salt
1 unpared apple, cubed
1 quart shredded green cabbage

Just before dinner: Combine salad
dressing and rest of ingredients; toss
to coat. Makes 4 servings.

LIMELIGHT
VEGETABLE MOLD

2 3-ounce packages lime-flavor gelatin
2 cups sour cream
2 cups shredded carrots
2 cups diced celery
¼ cup chopped pimiento
carrot curls and celery fans for garnish

Early in day: In bowl, dissolve gelatin
in 1½ cups boiling water. Chill until
consistency of unbeaten egg whites.
With electric mixer on low speed, beat
gelatin a minute until smooth; beat in
sour cream; fold in carrots, celery, pimiento. Pour into 1-quart mold. Chill
until firm.

Unmold onto platter. Garnish with carrot curls, celery fans. Makes 8 servings.

ORANGE GELATIN MOLD
pictured on page 86

2 3-ounce packages orange-flavor gelatin
2 cups orange juice
4 large oranges, peeled

Early in day: Dissolve gelatin in 1½ cups boiling water. Stir in orange juice; chill until consistency of unbeaten egg whites.

Chop two oranges; cut other two into ⅛-inch slices. Pour ½ cup gelatin into 1½-quart ring mold; arrange ½ cup chopped oranges on top; chill until barely set. Fold remaining chopped oranges into remaining gelatin; pour into mold. Chill. Just before gelatin sets, slide orange slices inside outer edge of mold. Chill until firm. Unmold on salad greens. Makes 6 to 8 servings.

CRANBERRY-SALAD MOLD

1 3-ounce package strawberry-flavor gelatin
1 14-ounce jar cranberry-orange relish
1 3-ounce package lime-flavor gelatin
4 drops green food color
1 3-ounce package cream cheese
½ cup mayonnaise
½ cup heavy or whipping cream, whipped
2 cups miniature marshmallows

Early in day: In medium bowl, dissolve strawberry gelatin as label directs but use 1 cup water; add cranberry relish. Pour into 1½-quart mold; chill until firm. Meanwhile, prepare lime gelatin as label directs; add food color; chill until mixture is partially set.

In small bowl, beat cream cheese until fluffy. Stir in mayonnaise. Fold into lime gelatin. Stir in cream, marshmallows. Pour over strawberry-cranberry layer. Chill until firm. Unmold onto serving platter. Makes 8 servings.

HONEYDEW CRESCENTS
pictured on page 183

1 3-ounce package lime-flavor gelatin
1 medium honeydew melon
½ cup seedless green grapes, halved
½ cup purple grapes, halved, seeded
1 small pear, cut in bite-size pieces
2 tablespoons frozen orange-juice concentrate

Early in day: In small bowl, dissolve gelatin in 1 cup boiling water. Chill until slightly thickened. Meanwhile, cut rind from honeydew melon. Cut thin slice from bottom so it will stand upright. Cut large slice from top. Remove seeds and pulp. Stand melon in deep bowl.

In medium bowl, toss grapes and pear with orange-juice concentrate.

Brush melon with 3 tablespoons of the thickened gelatin. Add remaining gelatin to fruit mixture. Fill melon. Chill 4 hours or until firm.

To serve: Cut melon crosswise into 3 slices; halve each. Makes 6 servings.

Supper Sandwich, page 210

Sandwich-by-the-Mile, page 213

Top: Striped Loaf, page 212
Bottom: Sandwich Torte, page 211

French-Toast Sandwiches, page 213

Cheese Pumpernickel, page 214

Onion-Sesame Bread with Hamburger, page 216

Hearthside Loaf, page 212

SANDWICHES AND BREADS

The sandwiches given here need only a beverage and dessert to round out the meal. The breads are all meant as go-alongs

Sandwiches

BIG BOY

Time in Kitchen: ½ hour
Free Time: 1 hour
Servings: 8

¾ pound beef chuck, ground
½ cup packaged dried bread crumbs
¾ teaspoon cornstarch
1 egg, beaten
½ cup light cream
½ teaspoon salt
½ teaspoon garlic salt
4 tablespoons salad oil
2 onions, thinly sliced
1 green pepper, thinly sliced
1 oval loaf Italian bread
1 11-ounce can spaghetti sauce with meat
½ pound sliced mozzarella cheese
6 packaged process cheese slices
¼ cup butter or margarine, softened

1. *About 1½ hours before dinner:* For meatballs: In bowl, combine beef with bread crumbs and next 5 ingredients. Shape into 40 small meatballs.
2. In skillet, in 2 tablespoons hot oil, brown meatballs; remove; set aside.
3. In same skillet, in rest of oil, sauté onions and green pepper, about 5 minutes. Preheat oven to 375°F.
4. Slice bread lengthwise, horizontally, into 3 even slices. Spread bottom slice with half of spaghetti sauce. On top, arrange meatballs then mozzarella and process cheese. Spread second slice with some of butter; cover with onion and green pepper. Top with buttered crust slice, gashed for easier slicing. Place on greased cookie sheet. Wrap all in aluminum foil. Bake 1 hour or until hot. Unwrap. Cut through gashes.

SUPPER SANDWICH
pictured on page 201

Time in Kitchen: ½ hour
Servings: 6

1 14-inch loaf Italian whole wheat bread
butter or margarine, softened
1 16-ounce can sauerkraut
1 tablespoon horseradish
1 tablespoon brown sugar
½ teaspoon onion salt
dash pepper
½ cup chopped green pepper
½ cup chopped pimiento
2 12-ounce cans chilled corned beef
pasteurized process cheese spread
dill pickles

About ½ hour before dinner: With sharp knife, trim bottom and top crusts from bread; split loaf lengthwise; spread cut surfaces with butter. Preheat broiler 10 minutes if manufacturer directs.

In bowl, combine drained sauerkraut, horseradish, brown sugar, onion salt, pepper, green pepper and pimiento.

Spoon sauerkraut over bread halves. Cut corned beef from each can into 3 lengthwise slices; lay 3 slices, diagonally, on each bread half. Spoon some cheese spread over tops; place on broiling pan; broil until cheese bubbles. Serve with dill pickles.

Serve with: Mugs of icy cold birch beer • Melon wedges

SANDWICH TORTE
pictured on page 204

Do-Ahead Dish
Time in Kitchen: ½ hour
Servings: 6

4 ounces blue cheese
butter or margarine
green food color
1 4½-ounce can deviled ham
red food color
fresh dill
1 7-inch round loaf rye bread
1 8-ounce package cream cheese
1 teaspoon horseradish
pimiento-stuffed olives, sliced
¼ cup sliced blanched almonds, toasted
9 to 10 cooked shelled, deveined shrimp
6 slices smoked salmon

1. *Day before:* Cream blue cheese with 3 tablespoons butter and 1 drop green food color; cover; set aside.
2. Blend deviled ham with 1 drop red food color; cover; set aside.
3. Cream ½ cup butter with ¼ cup chopped dill; cover; set aside.
4. Cut bread into 4 crosswise slices, ½-inch thick; trim crusts; make even rounds 6 inches in diameter.
5. Spread bread round with blue-cheese filling, top with bread round; spread with deviled-ham filling; top with bread round; spread with dill-butter filling; top with bread round. Wrap in waxed paper; refrigerate.
6. *About 1 hour before dinner:* Blend cream cheese with horseradish; frost torte. Garnish with olive slices, almond slices, sprig of dill and shrimp. Cut salmon slices into 12 long strips; roll each up; put a dill sprig in each; garnish torte. Chill.

HOT CHICKEN SANDWICHES

Time in Kitchen: 20 minutes
Free Time: 1 hour 10 minutes
Servings: 6

2 teaspoons prepared mustard
¼ cup butter or margarine, softened
12 slices white bread
1 cup grated Parmesan cheese
2 cups coarsely chopped cooked chicken
½ teaspoon salt
¼ teaspoon pepper
1 10-ounce package frozen peas, cooked
½ cup chopped green onions
1 10½-ounce can condensed cream-of-mushroom soup
4 eggs, slightly beaten
1½ cups milk
10 bacon slices

1. *About 1½ hours before dinner:* Preheat oven to 325°F. Grease 12″ by 8″ baking dish. Combine mustard and butter; spread on one side of each bread slice; fit 6 slices, buttered side up, in dish.
2. Reserve 1 tablespoon cheese. Combine rest of cheese, chicken, salt, pepper, 1 cup of peas and green onions; spread over bread; cover with rest of bread, buttered side up.
3. Beat together undiluted soup, eggs and milk. Pour over bread. Sprinkle with reserved cheese. Bake 1 hour and 10 minutes.
4. Meanwhile, in skillet, fry bacon until light brown, but still limp. Insert tip of fork in end of each slice; turn fork to wrap bacon around it; slip bacon curl off fork; fasten with toothpick; finish cooking. Drain on paper towels; use as garnish. Sprinkle with more peas.

STRIPED LOAF
pictured on page 204

Do-Ahead Dish
Time in Kitchen: 40 minutes
Servings: 12

1 29-ounce loaf unsliced white bread
3¼ cups butter or margarine, softened
¾ cup grated radishes
¾ teaspoon salt
¾ cup crumbled blue cheese
½ cup finely chopped parsley
1½ teaspoons curry powder
1 teaspoon caraway seed
12 slices packaged thinly sliced pumpernickel bread
4 thin slices boiled ham
lettuce
cherry tomatoes

1. *Day before:* Cut top, bottom and end crusts from bread; slice lengthwise into 7 even slices; wrap in plastic wrap.
2. For radish-butter: Combine ¾ cup butter, radishes and salt.
3. For cheese-butter: With pastry blender, mix ¾ cup butter, cheese and parsley until smooth.
4. For curry-butter: Combine ¾ cup butter with curry powder.
5. For caraway-butter: Combine 1 cup butter with caraway seed; cover; chill.
6. Place 1 slice white bread on large piece of waxed paper; spread with ⅓ radish-butter; cover with about 4 slices pumpernickel bread (laid side by side with crusts trimmed to fit edges of white bread). Spread pumpernickel with ⅓ cheese-butter; cover with 1 slice white bread; spread with ⅓ of curry-butter; cover with another slice of white bread. Repeat layering twice more, starting with radish-butter.
7. Wrap loaf in waxed paper; chill.

8. *About 1 hour before dinner:* Soften caraway-butter. Unwrap sandwich loaf; with sharp knife, trim off side crusts; place on serving tray. Spread top and sides with caraway-butter; lay ham slices, side by side, across top. Garnish with lettuce and tomatoes, held in place with picks; refrigerate 45 minutes. Slice with sharp knife.

Serve with: Chilled pineapple juice • Ice-cream sundae

HEARTHSIDE LOAF
pictured on page 208

Time in Kitchen: 15 minutes
Free Time: ½ hour
Servings: 6

1 18-ounce loaf unsliced white bread
½ cup butter or margarine, softened
⅓ cup minced onions
3 tablespoons prepared mustard
1 tablespoon poppy seed
2 teaspoons lemon juice
few drops hot pepper sauce
12 slices process Swiss cheese
6 bacon slices

1. *About 45 minutes before dinner:* With bread knife, gently slice layer from top crust of bread. Then make six slightly diagonal cuts, at equal intervals, from top almost through to bottom of loaf. Lightly grease cookie sheet. Preheat oven to 350°F.
2. In small bowl, combine butter, onions, mustard, poppy seed, lemon juice and hot pepper sauce. Reserve 3 tablespoons. With small spatula, spread remaining mixture on cut surfaces of bread.
3. Place two cheese slices in each bread slit, cut so they poke out slightly.

Place loaf on cookie sheet. Spread reserved butter mixture over top and sides of loaf. Bake ½ hour or until loaf is lightly browned.

4. Meanwhile, cook bacon slices until crisp, about 10 minutes. Drain on paper towels; keep warm. When loaf is done, lay bacon slices across top.

5. *To serve:* With wide spatulas, remove loaf to serving dish; cut through slices.

FRENCH-TOAST SANDWICHES

pictured on page 205

Time in Kitchen: 20 minutes
Servings: 6

4 eggs, slightly beaten
½ teaspoon salt
2 tablespoons granulated sugar
½ cup milk
½ pound sliced bacon
butter or margarine
12 slices bread

About 20 minutes before dinner: Preheat oven to 400°F. In medium bowl, combine eggs, salt, sugar, milk. Place bacon slices on rack in shallow baking pan. Bake 10 minutes. Turn off oven; let bacon remain there.

Meanwhile, in skillet, melt a little butter. Dip each bread slice into egg mixture; sauté on both sides. Place on papertowel-lined cookie sheet; keep warm in oven; sauté rest of slices.

Place 2 bacon slices between every 2 slices of toast; cut in half diagonally; place on serving plate. Crumble rest of bacon on top.

Serve with: Jug of pancake syrup • Orange-Gelatin Mold, page 200 • Milk

---

SANDWICH BY THE MILE

pictured on pages 202–203

Time in Kitchen: 1 hour
Servings: 6

1 long loaf French bread
shrimp, cooked, shelled, deveined
cucumber, scored, thinly sliced
cocktail frankfurters, heated
sautéed bacon slices
hard-cooked egg slices
thin green-pepper strips
small tomato, thinly sliced
leafy celery tops
natural Swiss cheese, thinly sliced
radishes, thinly sliced
bologna, thinly sliced
hard salami, thinly sliced
green onions, thinly sliced
ripe and stuffed green olives

1. *About 1 hour before dinner:* Cut 3 even horizontal slices from one end of loaf to other, not quite through to bottom. Cut away ⅛ inch from each slice to make room for fillings.

2. Using picture as guide, in the first lengthwise slit, tuck some of the shrimp and cucumber slices; alternate with some of the cocktail frankfurters and sautéed bacon slices. Repeat these two combinations, to the end.

3. Starting at the middle slit, tuck in some of egg slices and green-pepper strips; alternate with some of tomato slices and celery tops. Repeat these two combinations to the end of the loaf.

4. Fill the remaining slit with some of the Swiss cheese and radish slices, alternating with some of the bologna, salami and green-onion slices. Repeat, as before filling loaf to end. Skewer ripe and stuffed green olives on party picks; stick them into loaf. Refrigerate until needed. Cut into crosswise slices.

Breads

CHEESE PUMPERNICKEL

pictured on page 206

½ cup butter or margarine, softened
½ cup shredded Cheddar cheese
¼ cup chopped chives
2 tablespoons prepared mustard
1 16-ounce loaf round pumpernickel
    bread

About ½ hour before dinner: Cream butter with cheese, chives and mustard. Preheat oven to 425°F.

Cut bread into 12 crosswise slices, about ¾-inch thick, not quite through bottom crust. Spread cheese mixture into every other slice; wrap in foil. Heat 20 minutes. Unwrap; cut through bottom crust. Makes 6 servings.

CHEESE BREAD

2 cups sifted all-purpose flour
2 teaspoons double-acting baking
    powder
1 teaspoon dry mustard
1 teaspoon salt
dash pepper
2 eggs, beaten
¼ cup melted butter or margarine
⅔ cup milk
1 cup shredded Cheddar cheese

Early in day: Preheat oven to 375°F. Into large bowl, sift flour, baking powder, mustard, salt, pepper.

Combine eggs, butter, milk; add all at once to flour mixture; with wooden spoon, beat just until dry ingredients are moistened; stir in cheese. Pour into greased 9″ by 5″ loaf pan. Bake 1 hour or until cake tester inserted in center comes out clean. Cool on rack 10 minutes; remove from pan. Makes 1 loaf.

PEANUT-BUTTER BREAD

¾ cup chunk-style peanut butter
¼ cup butter or margarine
2 cups sifted all-purpose flour
½ cup granulated sugar
1½ teaspoons double-acting baking
    powder
1 teaspoon salt
½ teaspoon baking soda
1 tablespoon grated orange peel
1 egg, beaten
1 cup milk

Early in day: Preheat oven to 350°F. In large bowl, with electric mixer at medium speed, cream peanut butter and butter until fluffy. Sift flour, sugar, baking powder, salt, baking soda together over mixture; work with fork until crumbs form. Stir in peel, egg, milk, just until moistened. Pour into greased 9″ by 5″ loaf pan. Bake 55 minutes or until cake tester comes out clean. Remove from pan; cool on rack. Makes 1 loaf.

BIG BREAD ROUNDS

1 8-ounce can refrigerated crescent
    rolls
1 egg yolk, slightly beaten
1 teaspoon sesame seed

About 20 minutes before dinner: Preheat oven to 375°F. Unroll crescent rolls on cookie sheet. Cut two 1-inch strips from short side. Place one strip along each lengthwise side. With rolling pin, roll out into 10-inch circle. Brush with egg; sprinkle with sesame seed. Bake about 10 minutes. Makes one 10-inch round.

BRAN MUFFINS
pictured on page 37

1 cup all-purpose flour
½ teaspoon salt
3 teaspoons double-acting baking powder
1 cup bran flakes
1 cup milk
2 tablespoons shortening
¼ cup granulated sugar
1 egg, beaten

About 45 minutes before dinner: Preheat oven to 400°F. Grease well about twelve 2½-inch muffin-pan cups. Sift flour, salt, baking powder. In medium bowl, soak bran in milk 5 minutes.

Meanwhile, in small bowl, with spoon, beat shortening with sugar until light; add egg; stir smooth; stir into bran. Add flour mixture; stir until just mixed, no longer. Fill muffin-pan cups two thirds full. Bake 25 minutes or until done. Makes 12 muffins.

Raisin-Nut: To flour mixture, add ½ cup chopped walnuts and ½ cup raisins.

Orange Glazed: Just before baking, sprinkle muffins with 2½ teaspoons grated orange peel and ¼ cup granulated sugar, combined.

POPPY-SEED ROLLS
pictured on page 35

2¾- to 3¼ cups all-purpose flour
¼ cup granulated sugar
½ teaspoon salt
1 package active dry yeast
5 tablespoons margarine, softened
⅔ cup very hot tap water
2 eggs (at room temperature)
poppy seed

Several hours before dinner: In large mixing bowl, mix ¾ cup of flour, sugar, salt and undissolved yeast. Add margarine. Gradually add very hot tap water to dry ingredients; beat 2 minutes at medium speed on electric mixer, scraping bowl occasionally. Add 1 of the eggs and ½ cup flour, or enough flour to make a thick batter. Beat at high speed 2 minutes, scraping bowl occasionally. Stir in additional flour to make a soft dough. Turn out onto lightly floured surface; knead until smooth and elastic, 8 to 10 minutes. Place in greased bowl, turning to grease top. Cover; let rise in warm place (80° to 85°F.) until doubled in bulk, about 1 hour.

Punch dough down; turn out onto lightly floured surface. Divide dough into 2 equal pieces. Then divide each into 6 pieces. Shape each into smooth ball. Place on greased cookie sheets, about 2 inches apart. Cover; let rise in warm place, until doubled in bulk, about 1 hour.

Preheat oven to 400°F. Carefully brush rolls with remaining egg, beaten, then sprinkle with poppy seed. Bake about 10 to 15 minutes or until done. Remove from cookie sheets and cool on racks. Makes 12 rolls.

PUMPERNICKEL-RYE BREAD

1 13¾-ounce package hot-roll mix
⅔ cup unsifted rye flour
1 egg yolk
3 tablespoons light molasses
1½ teaspoons caraway seed
2 tablespoons melted shortening

Early in day: Prepare hot-roll mix as label directs, adding rye flour, egg yolk, molasses, caraway seed and shortening. Let rise in warm place (80°F. to 85°F.) about 1½ hours or until double in bulk.

Punch down, then shape dough into loaf; place in greased 10″ by 5″ loaf pan; let rise again about 1 hour or until double in bulk. Preheat oven to 375°F.

Bake bread 40 minutes, or until loaf sounds hollow when tapped with finger. Cool in pan 5 minutes, then remove to rack to completely cool. Makes 1 loaf.

TUXEDO SUPPER BRAIDS

1 13¾-ounce package hot-roll mix
1 egg yolk
sesame seed
poppy seed

1. *Early in day:* Make up hot-roll mix and let rise as label directs. When raised, knead dough several times on floured surface; cut into 24 equal pieces.
2. For each braid, shape each of 3 pieces of dough into rope 10 inches long, then braid the 3 ropes together, pinching ends securely. Repeat 7 times more, making 8 braids in all.

3. Place braids 1½ inches apart on large greased cookie sheet; let rise until doubled. Ten minutes before baking, preheat oven to 375°F. Beat egg yolk with 1 teaspoon water. Brush braids with egg mixture. Sprinkle half with sesame seed, half with poppy seed.
4. Bake 20 minutes or until golden brown. Makes 8 braids.

ONION-SESAME BREAD WITH HAMBURGER
pictured on page 207

2 packages active dry yeast
5 cups buttermilk-biscuit mix
1 10-ounce can condensed onion soup
¼ cup melted butter or margarine
2 teaspoons sesame seed
¼ cup natural shredded Cheddar cheese

About 1½ hours before dinner: In large bowl, mix yeast and 1½ cups biscuit mix. In medium saucepan, heat undiluted soup and ⅓ cup water until very warm (120° to 130°F.). With electric mixer at medium speed, gradually add liquid to dry ingredients. Beat 2 minutes, scraping bowl occasionally. Add ½ cup more biscuit mix to make thick batter; beat 2 minutes at high speed. With spoon, stir in remaining 3 cups mix to make soft dough.

Turn dough onto lightly floured surface and knead until smooth and elastic, about 10 minutes. Pour butter into 13″ by 9″ baking dish. Sprinkle with 1 teaspoon of the sesame seed; cool. Roll dough to fit baking dish. Place on top of sesame seed; sprinkle with cheese and remaining sesame seed. Cover with towel; let rise in warm place (80° to 85°F.) away from draft, until doubled, about 1 hour. (Dough is doubled when two fingers pressed lightly into dough leave a dent.)

Preheat oven to 400°F. Bake 25 minutes or until done. Turn out on rack. Serve hot, cut into squares and split, with hamburgers.

HOT BISCUITS

2 cups sifted all-purpose flour
3 teaspoons double-acting baking powder
1 teaspoon salt
6 to 7 tablespoons shortening
⅔ to ¾ cup milk

1. *About ½ hour before dinner:* Preheat oven to 450°F. Into bowl, sift flour, baking powder, salt. With pastry blender or 2 knives used scissor-fashion, cut in shortening until mixture is like coarse cornmeal.
2. Make well in center; pour in ½ cup milk. With fork, mix lightly, quickly. Add enough more milk to form dough, just moist enough to leave sides of bowl and cling to fork as ball. Turn onto lightly floured surface.
3. Knead 6 or 7 times, working gently.
4. Roll dough ½ inch to ¾ inch thick for high fluffy biscuits, ¼ inch thick for thin crusty ones.
5. With floured 2-inch biscuit cutter, cut out biscuits.
6. With spatula, lift biscuits to ungreased cookie sheet. Place 1 inch apart for crusty biscuits, nearly touching for soft-sided ones.
7. Lightly press dough trimmings together; roll and cut as before. With pastry brush, brush biscuit tops with milk, melted butter or light cream. Bake 12 minutes or until a delicate brown. Makes 19 biscuits.

BLUEBERRY BISCUITS
pictured on page 182

1 8-ounce can refrigerated biscuits
½ cup blueberries
granulated sugar
1 tablespoon grated lemon peel
melted butter or margarine

About ½ hour before dinner: Preheat oven to 400°F. Separate biscuits. With kitchen shears or sharp knife, split each biscuit in half *horizontally*.

In small bowl, combine blueberries, 2 tablespoons granulated sugar and grated lemon peel. Spoon a little blueberry mixture in center of one half of each biscuit; top with the other half. With fingers, pinch edges together to seal. Repeat with remaining biscuits.

Place biscuits in well-greased 2½-inch muffin-pan cups. Brush with melted butter; sprinkle with sugar. Bake 12 minutes or until golden. Makes 10.

MAGIC FRENCH BREAD

2 8-ounce cans refrigerated buttermilk biscuits
1 egg white, slightly beaten
sesame seed

About 45 minutes before dinner: Preheat oven to 350°F. Open up cans of biscuits, but *do not* separate. On lightly greased cookie sheet, place rolls of biscuit dough, end to end, to form loaf.

Brush with egg white, then sprinkle with sesame seed. Bake ½ hour or until a rich golden brown. Makes 1 loaf.

BRIOCHE À LA MAXIM
pictured on page 110

¼ cup butter or margarine
1 4-ounce can chopped mushrooms, drained
2 packages frozen brioches, thawed

About 20 minutes before dinner: In bowl, combine soft butter with mushrooms. Preheat oven to 350°F.

Twist out "cap" on top of each brioche; spread heaping teaspoon of mushroom butter in each; replace caps. Bake 10 minutes. Makes 12 brioches.

TOASTED POPPY-SEED BREAD
pictured on page 39

8 ½-inch-thick French bread slices
3 tablespoons butter or margarine, softened
poppy seed

About 10 minutes before dinner: Preheat broiler if manufacturer directs. Spread bread with butter; sprinkle with poppy seed. Place on broiling pan; broil 1 or 2 minutes. Makes 4 servings.

BISCUIT BREAD STICKS

1 8-ounce can refrigerated biscuits
1 egg white, slightly beaten
poppy seed

About ½ hour before dinner: Preheat oven to 400°F. Cut each biscuit in half crosswise; then, between palms of hands, roll each half into pencil-like strip, 6 to 8 inches long. Brush with beaten egg white.

Place on lightly greased cookie sheet; sprinkle lightly with poppy seed. Bake bread sticks 5 minutes on each side. Makes 20 bread sticks.

CRANBERRY-BANANA BREAD

¼ cup butter or margarine, softened
1¼ cups granulated sugar
1 egg, beaten
2 cups sifted all-purpose flour
1½ teaspoons double-acting baking powder
1 teaspoon salt
½ teaspoon baking soda
⅔ cup mashed ripe bananas
1¼ cups cranberries, coarsely chopped
½ cup chopped walnuts

1. *Day before:* Preheat oven to 350°F. In medium bowl, with spoon, blend butter with sugar; add beaten egg and beat smooth.
2. Sift together flour, baking powder, salt and baking soda; add to creamed mixture all at once, mixing with spoon just until all flour is moistened.
3. Fold in mashed bananas, cranberries and walnuts.
4. Pour into greased 9" by 5" loaf pan. Bake 65 minutes, or until cake tester inserted in center comes out clean. Cool in pan 10 minutes; remove from pan and cool on wire rack. Serve, sliced, next day. Makes 1 loaf.

INDEX

M—O